Leaders ...
the
Timely Mandate of This Message

"I am convinced we are in that season known as the last days of the end times. One of the most serious issues confronting the Church is the warning by both Jesus and His apostles of mounting persecution. This "epistle" by Charles Crismier desperately needs to be read and received so that Christians—parents, grandparents and leaders—can be prepared from the heart."

–Dr. Robert Jeffress, Senior Pastor,
First Baptist Church, Dallas

"Even though Jesus assured mankind, 'Blessed are they which are persecuted for righteousness' sake, for theirs is the kingdom of heaven,' almost everyone would still rather avoid it. Yet for sincere followers of Christ, not only is persecution unavoidable in today's world, explains Charles Crismier, it is not even something to dread, but to faithfully, and even joyfully, embrace. *When Persecution Comes:Preparing Hearts for Perilous Times* is a much-needed, comprehensive and ultimately hope-filled handbook for Christians who recognize they're indeed living through increasingly 'perilous times.'"

–David Kupelian, award -winning journalist,
Managing Editor of World Net Daily and
bestselling author of *The Marketing of Evil*

"Without a doubt, our Lord warned His disciples, both then and future, to prepare for serious opposition because of our trust in Him and our allegiance to His name. Opposition, in these End Times, intensifies to outright Persecution as we approach Christ's return, and that promised persecution is now sweeping the world, including the West and America. But from my view as a serious-minded Christian journalist, the professing followers of Christ are seriously unprepared. Chuck Crismier's new book, *When Persecution Comes*, is not only a serious and much-needed wake up call, but provides both strength and hope for all who claim Christ's name. Truly a book touching the deepest recesses of our hearts for "Such a Time as This."

–Joseph Farah , Founder of World Net Daily (WND)

"*When Persecution Comes* is a must read for those living in these Last Days before the return of Christ."

–Phil Hotsenpiller, Pastor, Influence Church and
author of *It's Midnight in America*

"Chuck Crismier's new book, *When Persecution Comes*, is insightful, impacting, and hard hitting! I highly recommend this great work that will prepare you for the days ahead. Buy it, read it, and apply it!"

~David J. Giammona, US Army Colonel, Retired,
Author/Speaker/Commentator

"For more than 30 years, Chuck Crismier has been a watchman on the wall, sounding the alarm. Now, in these urgent days, he brings one more urgent warning. Church of America, are you ready?"

~Dr. Michael Brown, Founder and President, The Line of Fire, Radio Host, Foremost Messianic Jewish Apologist

"*When Persecution Comes* provides a crucial warning to the Church that today's persecution and marginalization of Christianity is only the beginning of a full attack on Faith in America and the West and by the government and society of the New World Order. It is as thorough as it is convincing and provides Biblical strategies pastors and families must use to stand strong in America's emerging post-Christian society. *When Persecution Comes* is a must-read for every believer who understands the challenge of our day."

~Chuck Mason, Battleground Ideas
Podcast, battlegroundideas.com, Author

"Although we know that Christians face persecution in other countries, we cannot neglect the fact it is happening here in America. In this book, Chuck Crismier prepares us for what lies ahead: he shows that secularism is never neutral, but always seeks to stamp out Christian influence. Read this book and share it with others, so that all of us might have our minds ready to act courageously, and hearts that count it a privilege to suffer for Christ."

~Erwin W. Lutzer, Pastor Emeritus,
Moody Church, Chicago, Author

"*When Persecution Comes* is a compelling wake-up call for Christians and the Church as a whole. Its timely message urges us to break free from the complacency of cultural Christianity and to stand firm in our faith. This book will remind you of the hope you have in Jesus, even in the face of trials. I pray its message spreads across churches in our nation."

~Kenza Haddock, LPCS,
author of *The Ex-Muslim's Guide to Christianity*

"Chuck Crismier has provided a sobering yet hopeful treatment of persecution. He not only addresses biblical and prophetic texts to clarify the Bible's teachings on persecution, but offers contemporary examples that remind Christians that many members of Christ's body in America are experiencing persecution of various sorts. An important work for Christians seeking to remain faithful to Christ in troubling times.

~James Spencer, PhD, Author,
www.thejamesspencer.com

"The brilliance and excellence in scholarship of Chuck Crismier has never been more on display than in this new book, *When Persecution Comes*. It is not only an outstanding presentation of his amazing knowledge of God's word and contemporary issues, but this book helps prepare us as believers for the End Times. Not only is Pastor Chuck a modern-day prophet and spiritual watchman, but he has taken the best parts of his daily radio program and compiled them into this magnificent work. *When Persecution Comes* is trying to awaken believers to how our Lord desires us to deal with the persecution setting its venomous fangs into each of our families and churches. Chuck awakens us to the reality that evilness in many forms is on a pathway of persecution to anyone who is a follower of Christ Jesus and a believer in the Judeo-Christian Foundation that shaped our great nation. Pastor Crismier digs…like a great attorney prosecuting a mystifying case he provides the best explanations on eschatology I've ever seen. His systematic unpacking of scripture helps give us hope and assurance that God is in control of our lives and the circumstances impacting our culture and churches. Like the Apostle Paul, Chuck encourages us to 'Wake up and rise from our slumber.' This is a must read for anyone truly concerned about the current direction of our nation."

~Dr. Jim Grassi,
Founder and President, Men's Ministry Catalyst,
Best-selling Author and International Speaker

Charles Crismier's new book, *When Persecution Comes: Preparing Hearts For Perilous Times* is, apart from Sacred Scripture, one of the most important books you could possibly read. It is a good antidote to a very common evangelical malady, the "It-Can't- Happen-Here Syndrome." Too many American Christians turn a blind eye to the growing tsunami of persecution that is occurring right now.

You must do more than just read this book. You need to read it devotionally and with the stated intent that the Lord wold search your heart and prepare you for the perilous times that are already upon us.

I applaud Charles Crismier for his timely book.

~ Pastor Larry Spargimino, Ph.D.
Host, Watchman on the Wall Broadcast
of Southwest Radio Church

WHEN
PERSECUTION
COMES

PREPARING HEARTS FOR PERILOUS TIMES

WHEN
PERSECUTION
COMES

PREPARING HEARTS FOR PERILOUS TIMES

CHARLES CRISMIER

All Scripture quotations are taken from the King James Version of the Bible.

The choice of the King James Version was based upon its continued prominence as the most quoted, read, remembered and published version in the historical life of the Western world. Emphasis is indicated by bold-faced type to highlight portions of the text for particular focus throughout.

When Persecution Comes — *Preparing Hearts for Perilous Times*
Copyright © 2024 by Charles Crismier

Published by
Carpenter's Son Publishing
Franklin, TN
and
Elijah Books
P.O. Box 70879
Richmond, VA 23255

ISBN 978-1-956370-55-3

Interior Design by Pine Hill Graphics
Cover Design by Dave Eaton

Printed in the United States of America

Table of Contents

Dedicated With Enduring Love

TO MY FAITHFUL WIFE and helpmate, Kathie, with whom, through many dangers, toils and snares, we have together already come, and now with patience press on with increasing gratitude for the hope that lies ahead with the soon return of our Lord and Savior, Jesus Christ.

Your Grateful Husband,
Chuck

THE HERALD OF HISTORY

"The Sound of the Trumpet is Drawing Near"

THE MARCH OF HISTORY is not over until the "mystery of the woman, and of the beast that carrieth her" is made manifest, "drunken with the blood of the martyrs of Jesus" (Rev. 17:6-7) to establish the Deceiver's global government over humankind, seeking to deprive all of the hope of eternal salvation. The battle lines are being clearly drawn and the final calculated processes are nearing culmination. As Jacques Delos, former head of the resurrecting "Rome" said, "We must hurry. History is waiting." The question hovering over Christ's heralding of the persecution looming ahead is…

Am I Prepared to Stand?

What does it truly mean to follow Jesus in perilous times characterized by global persecution soon to ravage the western world? The sound of the trumpet is drawing near. How are you preparing your family, those in your sphere of influence… yes even those in your congregation or fellowship groups? Time will tell. So let us, together, prepare our hearts to stand in this increasingly evil day!

Yours in Kingdom Hope,

Founder and President,
SAVE AMERICA Ministries

PREPARE YOUR HEART

WHAT YOU ARE ABOUT TO READ is neither scaremongering nor sensationalism. Rather, it is a sincere, yet sobering, translation of biblical truth regarding the most tyrannical and terrifying leader ever and soon to rule the world, whose coming will be preceded by and culminate in unprecedented persecution of true believers in Jesus Christ as Messiah.

Because this treacherous man will gain his global authority by flattery, he will present the greatest test of your trust through masterful deception such that if it were possible, he will, as Jesus warned, seduce even the small remnant of true believers in Christ to damnation. Those who resist the seduction will be preserved through persecution.

As you read, it is not fear of man but rather the "fear of the Lord" that will be restored, leading every sincere believer to a strengthened faith prepared to endure the unprecedented challenges that lie ahead.

The IMPOSTER, the counterfeit christ, indeed—the ANTICHRIST, will soon be presented gloriously and globally with a false salvation calculated to "steal, kill and destroy" as Satan's final representative on earth. Painful persecution will enforce his diabolical deception. To be forewarned is to be forearmed. Let true faith rise in your soul, for as Jesus soberly warned, only "He that endureth to the end shall be saved" (Matt. 10:22, 24:13; Mk 13:13).

Yet how shall we endure? Are we, are you, truly prepared to endure the "trial by fire" which the apostle Peter and Christ himself warned was coming upon the earth (I Pet. 1:6-7, 4:12-13; Matt. 24:9-10)?

To be forewarned is to be forearmed! As you read the pages that follow, your mind and heart will be quickened, realizing perhaps as never before that you are called to the Kingdom "for such a time as this." You will be prepared to courageously stand in the evil day and to emerge victorious as unparalleled persecution sweeps not only the world at large but also the western world, including American life, seemingly untouchable by such ravages.

Join with us as we prepare to boldly live out our faith amid the seemingly unfathomable persecution of which Jesus and His disciples sought passionately to prepare us. Take courage! Your chariot is ready for the journey.

PART 1

THE PROMISE OF PERILOUS TIMES

"The diabolical deception designed by the Deceiver will appear to most people on the planet as reality…. Those who resist or fail to embrace this false 'reality' will be persecuted."

ARE THESE THE "LATTER DAYS" of human history? Some may say "absolutely!" Many others would reply, "It certainly seems so." Then again there are those more skeptical asking, "How can we really know?" And finally, we find the mockers, even among professing Christians, who disdainfully deny any biblically-defining characteristics of our times.

Yet the more profound and destiny-defining question is not so much the precise day or hour of our time. Rather, it is "How should we then live?" given what we do know and the growing body of biblical evidence literally screaming at us in the stormy winds swirling in the gathering global tempest that is enveloping our world?

Prophetic Time

Prophetic time frames the present. The framing of our times, our thoughts, our priorities and our decisions is one of the primary purposes of biblical prophecy. Prophecy gives perspective to the present and future. It serves as does a frame around a photograph or painting, drawing our gaze in greater focus to the primary object to be viewed and appreciated. Prophecy also serves to authenticate biblical authority. When God, by and through His prophets, have spoken with specificity in the past of things to come at a later time, the eventual fulfillment brings concurring credibility to other messages or warnings given so that we are more prone to take heed.

Prophetic time *frames* must be appreciated to be understood. For purposes of this book, we look primarily to those prophecies related to the Second Coming of Christ which is unfolding in three increasingly narrowing periods—

1. The end times or last days,
2. The latter days, and
3. The end of the age.

THE LAST DAYS—The "last days," or as frequently called "the end times" began with the death and resurrection of Jesus the Messiah "Christ" and the outpouring of His spirit at Pentecost or "The Feast of Weeks." The apostle Peter confirmed the beginning of this *last days* season in Acts 2:16-21 declaring:

> This is that which was spoken of by the prophet Joel;
> And it shall come to pass in the **last days**, saith God, I
> will pour out my spirit upon all flesh… (Joel 2:28-30).

This *last days* period is believed by most to encompass a period of approximately 2000 years until the "end of the age" and the Second Coming. Obviously, we are still living in that broad period of biblical prophecy.

THE LATTER DAYS—The "Latter days" would seem to be a much narrower period of time in the latter part of the *last days*. The length of these latter days is not disclosed or defined with specificity in Scripture. They are the latter part of the last days.

There are a number of references to these *latter days* in the Bible. The prophet Ezekiel spoke poignantly of that period in his description of the purpose and time of the terrifying battle of Gog and Magog against a re-born, re-gathered Israel to "take a spoil" (Ezek. 38-39). He warned this horrendous and calamitous secret confederation of nations would take place "in the latter days." Since Israel has now celebrated over 75 years since her rebirth, and since Israel (by the testimony of her own leaders) only now lives in unwalled villages in relative peace—a condition described by Ezekiel—we might reasonably conclude that we are in the season of the *latter days*, a limited period commonly referred to as the *end times*.

THE END OF THE AGE (WORLD)—Jesus spoke of yet another seemingly much narrower period of time at the very conclusion of these *last days*. Just two days before His crucifixion, His disciples gathered with Him on the Mount of Olives overlooking the eastern gate of Jerusalem. They inquired of Jesus privately asking, "What will be the sign of your coming, and of the end of the world?" (Note: The KJV uses "end of the world" while some translations state "end of the age").

It is important, for prophetic understanding, to be consciously aware of these three ever-narrowing time frames, the last of which is "the end of the world" or "the end of the age." It is in this final period, the exact length of which is not biblically defined yet the season of which can be clearly discerned, in which we find the prophesied emergence of the Anti-Christ, a counterfeit of the savior Messiah—the IMPOSTER.

A Time of Diabolical Deception

It is also interesting that both Jesus and His apostles warn of the massive deception that will be (and now is) enveloping the earth. Of perhaps greater import is that all biblical warnings, especially in the New Testament gospels and epistles, are to the church—to professing

Christians. It is we who are admonished to flee from the false, to love that which is true and holy and to beware of seducers who "wax worse and worse, deceiving and being deceived" (II Tim. 3:13).

The pagans or unbelievers are already deceived and are under condemnation: unless committed to Christ in confession of genuine faith as displayed in repentance and obedience, they face eternal damnation and judgment (Jn. 3:18). They will embrace the beast system governing the world at the end of the age and will gladly receive the infamous "mark of the beast" imposed by THE IMPOSTER—the counterfeit "prince of peace."

The looming question, however, lies not in the determined destiny of unbelievers and dis-believers, but rather with professing followers of Jesus Christ who, through spiritual weakness, either wittingly or unwittingly, embrace the prophesied counterfeit "prince of peace"— the false messiah. As Jesus clearly warned, we cannot serve two masters. Our genuine love of Christ and trust in our heavenly Father will be seriously tested by whether or not we submit to His counterfeit, thus irrevocably determining a terrifying eternal destiny (Rev. 14:9-11).

Unfortunately, the diabolical deception designed by the Deceiver (Satan), will appear to most people on the planet as reality—as truth— as ultimate hope and long-awaited peace. Those who resist or fail to embrace this false "reality" will be persecuted.

Hope Amid Looming Horror

As Christians we are people of hope. Christ's second appearing has been embraced throughout history as "that blessed hope" of the Church (Titus 2:13). Our Lord himself warned, however, of the earthly horrors to come with Satan's final efforts to steal, kill and destroy, taking as many as possible with him to eternal perdition. Yet Jesus encouraged us saying, "in the world you will have tribulation, but be of good cheer. I have overcome the world" (Jn. 16:33). He gave final warning to His disciples, "Take heed that no man deceive you" (Matt. 24:4), warning also of painful persecution (Matt. 24:9-10).

The message of this book is not for the sensation seeker. Rather it is to lovingly equip those who take their faith in Christ seriously, both to understand the times and to identify the biblically-revealed truths and characteristics of the coming IMPOSTER. Knowing those things, how should we then live, realizing serious persecution has been promised both by our Lord and by His apostles?

The LORD is my light and my salvation; whom shall I fear? the LORD is the strength of my life; of whom shall I be afraid? (Ps. 27:1).

Part 1
PROBING THOUGHTS for PROPHETIC TIMES

1. What are the "last days?"
2. What biblical term is used to describe the "end times"?
3. Do you think we may now be living in the period described as "the end of the world" or "end of the age"?
4. What characteristic did both Jesus and the apostle Paul use to describe these times? Consider the ways in which deception is enveloping the world and yes, even the church.
5. How would you know if you have strong faith if there is no strong test?
6. Will increasing persecution be the final test of your trust?

Chapter 1

THE PREMISE OF PERSECUTION

"…these things will they do unto you
For my name's sake… (Jn. 15:21).

PERSECUTION WAS PROMISED. Jesus, the Messiah and Lord of His Church, made it clear for all of His followers. "If the world hate you, ye know that it hated me before it hated you" (Jn. 15:18).

Yeshua wanted His disciples—the twelve—and all who would follow in their footsteps to be consciously aware of the cost of discipleship, of which cost He had continuously reminded them. He called them to "remember." "Remember the word that I said unto you," He said.

> The servant is not greater than his lord. If they have
> persecuted me, they will persecute you; if they have
> kept my saying, they will keep yours also (Jn. 15:20).

So…Why Does Persecution Come?

Persecution is promised to all genuine followers of Yeshua, the Savior, because of His name. As Jesus declared:

> But all these things will they do unto you for my
> name's sake, because they know not him that sent me
> (Jn. 15:21).

There is something about that name! Names are important. God actually decreed certain names because of their important and even prophetic significance. He changed the name of Abram to *Abraham* to declare forever Abram's fatherhood of many nations beginning with Israel (Gen. 17:4-7). Sarai, Abram's wife, also received a divine name change to *Sarah*, meaning "mother of nations" (Gen. 17:15-16).

Of Abraham's seed was to come a blessing upon the Gentiles—the entire world—through Jesus Christ that you and I might "receive the promise of the Spirit through faith" (Gal. 3:14). Writing of the antipathy between Hagar who birthed Ishmael and Sarah who birthed Isaac (the son of promise), the apostle Paul noted: "But as then he that was born after the flesh [Ishmael] persecuted him that was born after the Spirit [Isaac], even so it is now" (Gal. 4:29).

Persecution is endemic to the walk of faith through the name of Yeshua, Jesus, whose very name *Yeshua* was commanded by God the Father, that "he shall save his people from, their sins" (Matt. 1:21). His name also was declared *Emmanuel* by the Father to represent the Father's ongoing presence among the people as "God with us" (Matt. 1:23).

A Name Above Every Name

Persecution arises because of the name God the Father ascribed to His Son as "the Word made flesh" (Jn. 1:14), because from the beginning "the" Word was with God, and the Word was God (Jn. 1:1).

The Jewish people take the name of God seriously. They call His self-revealed name Jehovah or Yehovah "the ineffable or unspeakable name" as being holy beyond the lips of humankind, commonly spelled as YHVH יהוה known as the tetragrammaton. When Moses was drafted by God to deliver the descendants of Abraham, Isaac and Jacob from Egypt, he asked God to reveal His name, to which God replied "I AM THAT I AM," telling Moses to declare to Israel "I AM hath sent me unto you" …" Yehovah God of your fathers…this is my name for ever" (Ex. 3:13-15).

Yeshua, as the only-begotten Son of God, declared that He was Yehovah in the flesh because He identified himself with the Father in authority. "Therefore did the Jews persecute Jesus, …and sought the more to kill him," "because he not only had broken the sabbath, but also said that God was his Father, making himself equal with God" (Jn. 5:16-18). Again, Yeshua declared "I and my Father are one. Then the Jews took up stones again to stone him" (Jn. 10:30-31).

Why is this historical and spiritual understanding necessary to comprehend Jesus' declaration that "If they persecuted me, they will also persecute you" (Jn. 15:20)? It is because of the spiritual and prophetic import of His name. The apostle Paul revealed the implication of the name Yeshua most clearly in writing to the Philippian church, declaring Jesus was Messiah because "he humbled himself, and became obedient unto death, even the death of the cross" (Phil. 2:8).

> Wherefore God also hath highly exalted him, and given him **a name which is above every name:**
>
> That at the name of Jesus [Yeshua] every knee should bow…and that every tongue should confess that Jesus Christ [Yeshua the Messiah] is Lord, to the glory of God the Father (Phil. 2:9-11).

The Jews could not and do not receive the "name above every name," deeming it blasphemy, claiming it is belief in more than one God in defiance of the Torah which affirms "Yehovah our God is one" (Deut. 6:4). They look for a man like Moses as their Messiah—not someone purporting to be divine. And for this reason, they crucified the "Lord of Glory," the "King of the Jews," calling his blood upon their heads (Matt. 27:25).

The elders of Israel envied the name and authority it represented. Even a crusty Roman governor, the ruthless Pontius Pilate, saw through the charade, "for he knew that the chief priests had delivered him for envy" (Mk 15:10; Matt. 27:18). Their envy drove them to a frenzy of persecution, choosing rather Barabbas and Caesar over one called Christ or Messiah (Matt. 27:20; Jn. 19:14-16). Thus, they rejected the "chief cornerstone" of Israel and the world's hope because of envy over the name that would be "above every name."

Envy Over the Name

Should it then come as a surprise that the apostles also were persecuted, driven by raging envy over the name of Yeshua as Messiah? As was his custom, Paul and Silas reasoned with the Jews in the synagogue at Thessalonica, showing from the Torah that Messiah (Christ) was to suffer and rise again as Messiah.

> But the Jews which believe not, **moved with envy,** … set all the city on an uproar…crying, These that have turned the world upside down are come hither also (Acts 17:5-6, see also vs 1-4).

It is not Jews only but the entire non-believing Gentile world that will ultimately rise up in furious envy over the name that is declared to be "above every name." Both Jew and Gentile will vehemently declare, "We will not have this man to reign over us" (Lk. 19:14). As did the Jewish priests, so will Gentile presidents, primes ministers, politicians and even pastors and popes declare, "Give us Caesar." And so, a counterfeit Christ will be empowered to rule and reign over planet earth for a "time, times, and the dividing of time" (Dan. 7:25).

War Against the Name

The counterfeit "prince of peace," in the purported pursuit of peace to eradicate the influence, power and authority of the Messiah's name, "shall destroy many: he shall also stand up against the Prince of princes" (Dan. 8:25). "And his power shall be mighty, but not by his own power: and he shall destroy wonderfully, and shall prosper…and shall destroy the mighty and the holy people" (Dan. 8:24).

Yet the one with the name shall stand and shall reign. "And out of his mouth goeth a sharp sword, that with it he should smite the nations: and he shall rule them with a rod of iron."

> And I saw heaven opened, and behold a white horse;
> and he that sat upon him was called Faithful and true,
> and in righteousness he doth judge and make war.
>
> And he was clothed with a vesture dipped in blood:
> and his name is called The Word of God.
>
> And he hath on his vesture and on his thigh a name
> written, KING OF KINGS, AND LORD OF
> LORDS (Rev. 19:11-16).
>
> The name of Yeshua HaMashiach shall prevail against
> his persecutors.
>
> And the kingdom and dominion, and the greatness of
> the kingdom under the whole heaven, shall be given
> to the people of the saints of the most High, whose
> kingdom is an everlasting kingdom, and **all domin-
> ions shall serve and obey him** (Dan. 7:27).

But Persecution Lies Ahead

The apostle Paul endured immeasurable persecution. He counted it all worth the eternal reward, boldly stating: "For me to live is Christ, and to die is gain" (Phil. 1:21). Before reminding the church of the name that would ultimately rule and reign, he gave us clear warning.

> For unto you it is given in the behalf of Christ, not
> only to believe on him, but also to suffer for his sake
> (Phil. 1:29).

Therefore, my brethren, we must prepare for persecution. This, together with spiritual repentance and obedience to the Word, Will and Ways of the Father, is the ultimate and true "Prepping" for the trying times ahead.

How then do we prepare? Does God give us guidance in this regard? How are we to endure, since Jesus warned:

> But he that shall endure unto the end, the same shall
> be saved (Matt. 24:13).

Ponder this point prayerfully. If true followers of Jesus as Messiah were to be somehow removed from this planet before a promised season of ever-mounting persecution, all the warnings of Jesus and His apostles to prepare for such sufferings would be either false or, at best, moot…meaningless. What we might deeply desire in our flesh and what we must prepare for in the spirit are deeply and provocatively contrary to each other. In other words, this great battle of our feelings as opposed to our true faith now confronts each of us with the ultimate endtime battle of our flesh or carnal nature versus our reborn spiritual nature. Will you be victorious in this winner-take-all battle most likely setting the stage for your eternal destiny?

Preserve me, O God: for in thee do I put my trust
(Psa. 16:1).

Chapter 1
PROBING THOUGHTS for PROPHETIC TIMES

1. Why does God consider names important? Do you?
2. In what ways does the name of Jesus or Yeshua become the powerful motivator for persecution, locally, nationally and globally?
3. The Bible asks "Who is able to stand before envy" (Prov 27:4)? Why might *envy* be the vicious, yet hidden, driver of growing global persecution?
4. Do you actually believe God has promised persecution?
5. Why might it matter deeply...even eternally...what you think about persecution?
6. Why is the very idea of suffering for Christ almost insufferable to most Americans who profess Christ's name?

Chapter 2

THE PROMISE OF PERSECUTION

*"Our perception of persecution reveals what
We think it means to be a disciple."*

PERSECUTION IS PROMISED! But why? When we normally consider the very concept of God's promises, we conjure up what we think to be "good" things, "encouraging" words and expectations of "comfort" and "hope." So, how then are we to receive and process a clear promise of persecution for our faith when we persistently and rightly quote the Lord's words through the mouth of Jeremiah?

> For I know the thoughts that I think toward you…
> thoughts of peace, and not of evil, to give you an
> expected end (Jer. 29:11).

Viewpoint Determines Destiny

Perhaps our confusion in the contrary thoughts conveyed by these seemingly opposite promises is rooted in our lack of understanding of God's greater purposes and processes in order to actually reach the desired "expected end." As God told us through the prophet Isaiah:

> For my thoughts are not your thoughts, neither are
> your ways my ways, saith the LORD (Isa 5:8).

Our viewpoint as it relates to God's Word, His promises and His purposes, is critically important. When God has spoken, how do you respond? Does my response depend upon whether or not I like or agree with what the Lord has said, or do I set my mind and heart in immediate agreement? As it is written: "Can two walk together, except they be agreed (Amos 3:3)?

Our tendency "in the flesh" is to actively or passively reject or ignore that which the Scriptures say if what is said does not align with my personal feelings, desires or expectations. This attitude of the heart is dangerous, because it sets our own will against God's will, setting the course of a destiny, the consequences of which we do not currently perceive…but God does. Viewpoint always sets the course of destiny.

God's View of Persecution

Apparently our Creator sees persecution very differently than do we. He seemingly deems persecution needful—even essential—to accomplish His eternal purpose, whether for individual persons, His Church or the world. Christ made this plain when He, even in concluding the Beatitudes in His Sermon on the Mount, conferred blessing upon those persecuted.

> Blessed are they which are persecuted for righteousness' sake: for theirs is the kingdom of heaven.

> Blessed are ye, when men shall revile you, and persecute you, and shall say all manner of evil against you falsely, for my sake.

> Rejoice, and be exceeding glad: for great is your reward in heaven: for so persecuted they the prophets which were before you (Matt. 5:10-12).

Persecution is clearly not only promised but is part of God's plan and purpose to prepare us for blessing in His eternal Kingdom as fellow laborers with Yeshua, Jesus our Messiah. Jesus calls us to "remember" what He has said.

> The servant is not greater than his lord. If they have persecuted me, they will also persecute you; if they have kept my saying, they will keep yours also (Jn. 15:20).

Our View of Persecution

In order to come to grips with greater understanding of God's view of persecution; perhaps we should take a closer look at our own view as western Christians. Please understand! This epistle is written precisely to the professing believers in Yeshua as Messiah in the broader western world. That "world" is, in reality, the resurrected Roman empire that governed in the time of Christ and will again govern at our Lord's Second Coming under the guise of a New World Order led by a Great Reset into a global and godless government.

What geographical areas encompass that "western world?" These are the nations of Europe (the EU), of the Americas, of the remnant nations of the British Empire, i.e., Canada, New Zealand, Australia, Scotland, Ireland, Wales, etc., and that comprise NATO (the North Atlantic Treaty Organization), including the Vatican with its globalistic, New World Order intentions. All other geographical regions of the world, whether Asia, China, India or the Mid-East have significantly different experiences and therefore viewpoints regarding persecution, its meaning, purposes and prophetic implications as well as on-the-ground life responses.

One might say, *Well, isn't persecution the same everywhere? Isn't persecution always persecution wherever and whenever it is encountered or endured?* The answer is both Yes and No. The level of cultural response to professing Christians in one area of the world as to persecution is often very different from other areas. Also, what is perceived as significant persecution varies by region, often related to historic events, cultural orthodoxies and expectations as to what it really means to follow Yeshua as Lord and Savior. Perhaps shocking to American Christians, what is implicit to becoming a Christian in China, Iran or in Saudia Arabia, is very much different and sobering than the light-weight, touchy-feely gospel promoted and marketed in North America and increasingly in the whole of the western world.

Counting the Cost

Our perception of persecution and its degree is directly related to our understanding of what it means to be a disciple of our Lord. The historic understanding of what it means to be a *disciple*, whether from the viewpoint of Jesus' original disciples or of the entire early church, both Jew and Gentile, was that outside rejection, resistance and persecution were part of the package of embracing Yeshua as Messiah and Savior. The problem this poses for the American and western church is that such an understanding does not sell or market well.

Since the Church Growth movement beginning in the early 1970s, the gospel message was redefined for church-growth and marketing purposes to promise only blessings of following Jesus but ignoring the burden implicit in discipleship. Jesus had said He would build His church and we are to make disciples, "Teaching them to observe [obey] all things whatsoever I have commanded you" (Matt. 28:19-20). In the chutzpah of American exceptionalism, our spiritual leaders decided it was easier and more demonstrably expedient to build churches rather than to make genuine disciples. The devastating consequences of that prideful distortion of Jesus' command are demonstrable not only on American shores but across the seas where we have marketed the same deceptive message.

But it did not end there. As has been said, "What the parents practice in moderation, the children will take to excess." Thus, the baby-boomer generation that conceived and promulgated the Church Growth movement passed the baton to their younger ministry cohorts who, in even greater impudence, decided the Church

Growth movement was not sufficiently successful in marketing the gospel. The "gospel" as presented to date, they concluded, was not sufficiently attractive (or—the good news was not good enough) for the times. Thus was born the Seeker Sensitive movement in the late 1980s that surgically removed all remaining vestiges of the cost of discipleship so as to seduce supposed "seekers" to embrace Christ without conviction of sin and a corresponding walk of obedience. The very word obey thus became the most hated word among "Christians," a fact that has been incontrovertibly confirmed by dozens of pastors and parachurch ministers on our daily radio broadcast *VIEWPOINT*, Confronting the Deepest of America's Heart and Home from God's Eternal Perspective (saveus.org).

This radical change of alleged "Christian" viewpoint concerning what it truly means to follow Jesus has also dramatically affected our ability to accurately assess persecution and our response to it. Rather than seeing persecution and testing as a genuine part of God's plan and purpose, the strong tendency now has been to justify almost any conceivable way to avoid it. That means pandering increasingly to the ways of the culture in order to hopefully endear ourselves by accommodating increasingly to cultural mandates.

The heart of the gospel of salvation from sin to a walk of righteousness is thus eviscerated. We have, in effect, forfeited or sacrificed our alleged faith on the altar of a man-pleasing expediency. And if that is significantly true, what then is persecution? And do we now possess any dependable foundation of true faith in order to stand in this evil day? The apostle Peter has something to say to each of us in this regard.

Peter's Perspective on Persecution

As you well know, the apostle Peter was one of our Lord's closest disciples. Peter, James and John were the only ones privileged to join their Master at the Mount of Transfiguration (Matt. 17:1-12). It was Peter also who sought to protect Jesus from the persecution of crucifixion and was sternly rebuked by the Lord, declaring to Peter's face: "…thou savourest not the things that be of God, but those that be of men" (Matt. 16:21-23). In further response Jesus made abundantly clear His expectation of a true disciple and follower. Here are His words that seem not to compute, except in theory, to our generation.

> If any man will come after me, let him deny himself, and take up his cross, and follow me.
>
> For whosoever will save his life shall lose it: and whosoever will lose his life for my sake shall find it (Matt. 16:24-25).

Jesus reinforced that message in Luke 14:27, stating: "And whosoever doth not bear his cross, and come after me, **cannot** be my disciple" (emphasis added). And again, the Lord confronted His Jewish brethren who purported to follow Him, saying that they must be willing to be participants in both His life and suffering. The unfortunate response of nearly all, except the chosen disciples, is characteristic of human fleshly nature and prescient of the likely response of most professing Christians in the increasing difficult times ahead. As it is written:

> From that time many of his disciples [other than the twelve] went back, and walked no more with him (Jn. 6:30-68).

So how then did Peter perceive persecution after having walked with the Lord intimately for over three years, after receiving rebuke for his fleshly outlook, after witnessing the crucifixion and resurrection; and after receiving and preaching at the outpouring of the Holy Spirit at Pentecost? He declared, "But the end of all things is at hand: be ye therefore sober [serious minded], and watch unto prayer (I Pet. 4:7). He had already informed the world and the Jewish people that the last days began at the wrap-up of Jesus' earthly ministry with the crucifixion, resurrection and outpouring of the promise of the Holy Spirit (Acts 2:14-21).

Peter minces no words in reinforcing the call to suffering if one is to truly embrace Jesus as Messiah, Savior and Lord. It should be sobering to American pastors and parishioners as well as to all western professing believers. Believers throughout other regions of the world already deeply understand and have embraced this call to absolute discipleship. Consider with requisite solemnity Peter's admonition to us all.

> Forasmuch then as Christ hath suffered for us in the flesh, arm yourselves likewise with the same mind: for he that hath suffered in the flesh hath ceased from sin;

> That he no longer should live the rest of his time in the flesh to the lusts of men, but to the will of God (I Pet. 4:1-2).

Peter encourages us to understand and accept the reality of persecution and suffering in our time and however it comes. He does not want you or I to be taken unawares. We must, of necessity, take his words as warning but also as supreme calling to the cause of Christ in our time. Let these words sink into your spirit so that we may walk in the true Spirit of Christ.

> Beloved, think it not strange concerning the fiery trial which is to try you, as though some strange thing happened unto you:

> But rejoice, inasmuch as ye are partakers of Christ's sufferings; that, when his glory shall be revealed, ye may be glad also with exceeding joy.

If ye be reproached for the name of Christ, happy are
ye; for the spirit of glory and of God resteth upon
you: on their part he is evil spoken of, but on your
part he is glorified (I Pet 4:12-14).

The Will of God Revealed

Lamentably to our human, fleshly minds and carnal thinking, persecution and suffering are promised as a premier characteristic of the
life of a genuine disciple of Christ. Such thinking has so far escaped
the teaching of western Christians for nearly 70 years that it under-
standably comes as a jolt to our sensibilities. That comes as no mystery. But the true message of the gospel demands that the doctrine of
suffering for the name of Christ be reborn in our minds and hearts or
we will be unprepared for the trials to come. If we were to have somehow escaped those trials, neither Jesus nor his apostles would have
warned us to prepare.

From God's perspective, suffering and persecution are necessary
to fulfill His plan and purpose for a people called by the name of His
persecuted Son. Those who cannot or will not embrace this truth will
be part of the great falling away and will likely become persecutors
of those who are faithful, thus increasing the thrust of persecution
through betrayal, just as Jesus warned (Lk 12:51-53; Mk 10:28-31; Jn
16:1-2). Even so, Lord Jesus come.

Wherefore let them that suffer according to the will of
God commit the keeping of their souls to him in well
doing, as unto a faithful Creator (I Pet. 4:19).

*Be of good courage, and he shall strengthen your
heart, all ye that hope in the LORD (Ps. 31:24).*

Chapter 2
PROBING THOUGHTS for PROPHETIC TIMES

1. Why, or in what ways, might our viewpoint regarding persecution actually define the course of our destiny?
2. Why do western Christians seem to have a very different view of persecution as compared with others throughout the world? Why might it matter?
3. In what way or ways does our perception of persecution reflect our understanding of what it means to be a disciple of our Lord?
4. In what ways did the Church Growth and then Seeker Sensitive movements change professing believers' views regarding persecution as a significant factor in the life of a Christian?
5. How do you understand and apply Jesus' words: "If any man will come after me, let him deny himself, and take up his cross, and follow me" (Matt. 16:24)?
6. Can you envision how those who refuse to identify with Christ and His apostles regarding persecution will most likely be part of "the great falling away" or apostasy of which both Jesus and the apostle Paul warned (II Thess. 2:3; Matt. 24:13; Mk 13:13; Matt. 10:22)?

Chapter 3

THE PRESENTATION OF PERSECUTION

"Persecution serves as a sign of authentication
Of our relationship with Jesus Christ."

PERSECUTION COMES DRESSED in many differing forms of attire. It also manifests in a variety of patterns and degrees. For this reason, many find it difficult to either identify or acknowledge the existence of persecution. Does real persecution only exist, by definition, in its most violent and virile expressions, or is persecution a pattern of attitudes and behaviors that reveal open rejection of, or antipathy for, genuine belief in Jesus as Messiah, Savior, Lord and King?

The "Clothes" of Persecution

Persecution, from a biblical perspective, is always clothed in unrighteous attitudes and behaviors toward Jesus and therefore His true disciples or followers. As Yeshua expressly declared:

Remember… The servant is not greater than his lord. If they have persecuted me, they will also persecute you; if they have kept my saying, they will keep yours also.

But all these things will they do unto you **for my name's sake,** because they know not him that sent me [Emphasis added].

He that hateth me hateth my Father also (Jn. 5:20-21, 23).

But what is the manner of "these things" they will do unto you? What outward "clothes" do "these things" wear? And are true followers of Yeshua to become persecution "clothing inspectors" or are we to realize that "these things" are merely that which was promised and prophesied so that we might not be intimidated and drawn away from our intimacy with and our trust in Christ?

Some will differ, and even argue, that many of the items identified here are not real persecution, saying things like…

- Well, that's just the way things are.
- Well, everyone has a different point of view in a democracy.
- Well, that isn't a sufficiently serious attitude or behavior to be labelled as persecution.
- Well, what we experience in the West doesn't rise to the level of violence seen in the Islamic world.

But in a very real sense, just as we commonly say that "Beauty is in the eye of the beholder," so persecution is likewise identified or felt by the recipient, regardless of the untouched persons or groups who would prefer not to admit to a growing, ever metastasizing, pattern of persecution in America. Surely, we would not be willing to "go to war" with our fellow believers as to whether or not they now are facing persecution.

Of greater importance—yes, the gravity of this entire epistle—is not so much to identify and earmark anyone's perception as true persecution, but rather our purpose is how to prepare our minds and hearts so as not to be overwhelmed by the "fiery trials" that are coming

(I Pet. 4:12), and what is now and will continue to motivate them as we approach the soon return of Christ—Yeshua HaMashiach.

What Lies Behind Persecution?

Persecutors wear a variety of "clothes." Some appear by outward appearance as common citizens with no apparent persecutorial presence, open animosity, or obnoxious antagonism. Many carefully hide their indignant ideas and intentions. Others are overt and leave nothing to the imagination as to their vituperative belligerence or hatred. The forms of persecution arising from each will vary depending on the depth of the motivations that persuade them to action. Yet each carries the mantel of persecutorial motivation that increasingly grips our world with particular focus on Jews (antisemitism) and on genuine Christians (persecution).

As we see the increasingly unnerving signs of such persecution worldwide, and now particularly in the Western world (the resurrecting Roman Empire), our natural tendency is to put primary focus on outward behavior as opposed to the inward attitudes that drive and design the visual evidence of persecution. This is much like the parents who want their children to behave well for public display but who focus little on the heart.

Jesus made clear that outward behavior is the product or symptom of a defiled or corrupted inward being, declaring, "…for out of the abundance of the heart the mouth speaketh" (Matt. 12:34). For that reason, Jesus' Sermon on the Mount focused exclusively on the attitudes of our being, hence "Beatitudes," only then concluding with His warning and blessing concerning persecution.

How, then, are we to discern the underlying motivations driving the many manifestations and degrees of that which we perceive as persecution? As the levels of animosity toward both Christians and Jews increase, what outward forms of persecution might we expect and need to understand, thus enabling a godly or Christ-like response rather than fleshly reaction?

Discerning the Driving Forces Behind Sources of Persecution

It might aptly be said that "Persecution is persecution, so why the importance of discerning the underlying driving forces or motivations precipitating various expressions and levels of persecutions?" The reason is that there are times and occasions where the continuance or severity of the animosity might be mitigated without compromise of principle if we truly perceived with wisdom and understanding from an eternal and Christ-like attitude and viewpoint. Yet to be clear, most forms and levels of persecution cannot be mitigated without a dramatic change of attitude on the part of the persecutor. As we briefly explore most of these underlying forces defining both the form and extent of perceived persecution; we must return to the word ***ATTITUDE*** as the starting point.

1. How Attitude Fosters Persecution

Attitude underlies and pervades all persecution, both for the persecutor and the persecuted. Those attitudes and viewpoints determine both the driving force of the persecutor and the defining response of the one or group persecuted. Since we have no real control over the mind, heart and attitude of the persecutor, we can only deal with our own minds, hearts and attitudes as the object of various forms and levels of persecution.

Unfortunately, however, our reactionary tendence is to focus, **not** on our *attitudes* but rather on their *actions*. We thus tend to dismiss as irrelevant our attitudes while accentuating the undeserved painful action perpetrated upon us. We find ourselves most often responding not in *faith* but in the *flesh,* and as we well know (at least in theory), that which is of the flesh reaps corruption (Gal. 6:8).

In other words, by our fleshly response we can actually frustrate what purpose God may have in our life to be accomplished through persecution by poisoning the waters of God's will through our unredeemed fleshly attitude. That is never a pretty picture, either to our Lord or to those onlooking, thereby also destroying our witness.

To assist all of us sincere followers of Christ in better preparing for the promised avalanche of persecution to come, we might want to prayerfully consider and probe the inner recesses of our own hearts in response to the following questions.

1. Do I tend to react rather than respond to others?
2. Am I highly sensitive to what others say about me or appear to do to me?
3. Am I patient or impatient in my response to others?
4. Is my level of or propensity to judgment tempered with mercy?
5. Am I prone to see myself as a victim?
6. Do I tend to murmur and complain a lot?
7. Would many consider me a hyper-sensitive person?
8. Have I actually accepted the promise of both Jesus and his apostles that persecution is to be expected if I am a true Christian, and that such persecution will accelerate as we approach the Lord's return?
9. Do I somehow believe that I am, or should be, the exception to the "rule"?
10. Am I infected with an entitlement attitude?
11. Do I consider myself "crucified with Christ" (Gal. 2:20)?
12. Does my carnal nature seem usually to supersede my spirit when they come into conflict?
13. Do I tend to be combative rather than Christ-like?
14. Do I think that I am entitled to be treated differently than Jesus was treated (Jn. 15:20)?
15. Am I driven more by the defensive (my rights) attitude of the culture than by the (my responsibilities) attitude of Christ (Jn. 5:30)?

Truly we are all human, and as such we wage this eternal spiritual war of our flesh against the spirit. But living IN the flesh is no spiritual excuse for not living according to the Spirit. The supreme tests of our alleged faith lie before us, just as they did for our Master who, in the flesh, "was in all points tempted like as we are, yet without sin." That, brethren, is why Yeshua, as our high priest, is "touched with the feelings of our infirmities" (Heb. 4:15).

Therefore, "let us hold fast our profession" of faith, realizing that "all things are naked and opened unto the eyes of him with whom we have to do" (Heb. 4:13-14). What then will we do, what will you do, when persecution comes in its many forms driven by its multitude of motivations? What might they be? And how might such persecution be expressed? Does it always come with the label of "PERSECUTION"?

2. Forms and Expressions of Persecution

"Many Christians in the West either deny or are ignorant of it," declared Voice of the Martyrs to Christian History Magazine, "but persecution is part of present reality. It has many forms—political oppression, ethnic hatred, religious prejudice, and outright hatred of Christians."[1]

The Christian History Institute reports:

> "Many value the fight to combat social persecution,
> such as human rights issues and human trafficking.
> Fighting for human rights is very significant work,
> but religious persecution (by contrast) is not a popular
> subject. Since Western churches seem to be experiencing
> little if any persecution, people see the issue as too nega-
> tive to fit with the 'good news' of the gospel. People fear
> that if Christians expose and combat persecution too
> vigorously, it might jeopardize interreligious dialogue."[2]

In defining persecution, the "Statement of the International Institute for Religious Freedom" declares:

> Persecution is any unjust hostile action which causes
> damage from the perspective of the victim. It can

come from multiple motivations and take multiple
forms and degrees.

We call an unjust action against a believer or a group
of believers motivated by religious reasons "religious
persecution." Other motivations such as ethnic hatred,
gender bias, or political ideologies may contribute.[3]

According to the Barnabas Fund, an international body formed to
support persecuted Christians, the following are ten forms of oppression against Christians, in ascending order of ferocity.

(1) Social discrimination;
(2) Institutional discrimination;
(3) Employment discrimination;
(4) Legal discrimination;
(5) Suppression of missionary activity;
(6) Suppression of conversion to Christ;
(7) Forced conversion from Christ;
(8) Suppression of corporate worship;
(9) Violence against individuals; and
(10) Community oppression—entire churches or faith groups
       attacked.[4]

From the Catholic perspective of Msgr. Charles Pope via his blog,
he identifies "Five Stages of Religious Persecution:

(1) Stereotyping the target group;
(2) Vilifying the target group for alleged crimes or misconduct;
(3) Marginalizing the target group's role in society;
(4) Criminalizing the target group or its works; and
(5) Persecuting the target group outright.[5]

This pattern seems to match the renowned *Rules for Radicals* which has become a virtual "bible" for political and religious liberal practitioners in America.[6]

3. Biblical Expressions of Persecution

From the Scriptures we discern God's focused concern regarding identifying persecution, expectation of persecution, and the variety of forms persecution takes when challenging a person's faith in Jesus as Messiah.

The most serious and respected focus of persecution was driven, and is still driven, by…

> Attacks against the Message
> Attacks against the Messenger
> Attacks against the Master as Messiah.

It should become obvious to an observant reader that the trajectory of the Church in the West, particularly in America, ever since the launch of the Church Growth Movement in the early 1970s followed by the Seeker Sensitive Movement in the late 1980s and early 1990s has been to diminish the Message, popularize the Messenger, and turn the Master into a virtual "mascot," all to avoid unpleasant cultural reaction, i.e., persecution. In our progressive effort to win the world by avoiding the world's disapproval, we have shockingly become a Christianized version of the world in order to avert the world's condemnation. Yet all who truly live godly in Christ Jesus will suffer persecution, even if it be an otherwise rejected remnant. Where, in your honest estimation, do you truly fit?

The Bible clearly portrays religious persecution against genuine Christians who refuse to shrink from their faith, without being cultural/ Christian chameleons, in at least nine ways or expressions of overt persecution.

(1) Beatings—Jesus, Paul, Peter and John.

(2) Stoning—Paul, and they tried to stone Jesus.

(3) Mocking—Jesus and Paul.

(4) Insults—Jesus at the cross, Paul accused of being "mad."

(5) Slander—Jesus, Paul, Silas.

(6) Ostracism—The blind man healed, and his parents thrown out of the synagogue.

(7) Intimidation—Peter and John.

(8) Imprisonment—John the Baptist, Peter, John and Paul.

(9) Death—Jesus, Paul, Peter, and all the apostles, with the possible exception of John. Also, many of the prophets, including Isaiah who was placed in a log and sawn asunder.

Because of Our Relationship

Because of our relationship to Jesus, Yeshua HaMashiach, persecution becomes our lot. In a sense, it actually affirms and confirms our genuine relationship to our Master. For that reason, true disciples can count on persecution at some… or all… levels.

Persecution serves as a sign of authentication of our relationship with Jesus Christ. Jesus made clear that our response to persecution is a veritable litmus test to determine the authenticity of our alleged faith. Consider prayerfully Jesus' words of warning.

> Whosoever therefore shall confess me before men, him will I confess before my Father which is in heaven.

> But whosoever shall deny me before men, [because of persecution or threats] him will I also deny before my Father which is in heaven.

> And he that taketh not his cross, and followeth after me, is not worthy of me.

He that findeth his life shall lose it: and he that loseth his life for my sake shall find it (Matt. 10:32-39)

Judge me, O God, and plead my cause against an ungodly nation: O deliver me from the deceitful and unjust man (Ps. 43:1).

Chapter 3
PROBING THOUGHTS for PROPHETIC TIMES

1. From your perspective, what "clothes" does persecution or the persecutor wear, enabling you to discern persecution?
2. Persecution is ALWAYS clothed in what distinguishing characteristics?
3. Which do you believe is most important to God:
   A. The attitudes of the persecutor?
   B. The attitudes of the one being persecuted?
   And what is the persuasive basis for your opinion?
4. How can a professing Christian's attitude actually foster, facilitate, even foment persecution?
5. What are the 3 things that, in one way or another, almost invariably precipitate persecution?
6. Have you ever experienced some form or level of persecution? How did you respond… or did you REACT? What might be the difference, either for you or the persecutor?

Chapter 4

PORTRAITS OF PERSECUTION

*"Over 360 million Christians are suffering per-
secution in the world as of 2023."*

"THE ENORMITY OF THE ISSUE, the gruesomeness of some
persecution events, and our natural inclination to turn away from difficult situations all keep Christians in the West from fully embracing
the reality of persecution and fully seeing how they themselves might
be experiencing it. According to the Bible, persecution will not cease
in this life, but will continue until Christ's return (Matt. 24:9-14)."[7]

Seeing the "Unseeable"

Persecution to many is an "unseeable" reality. It is "unseeable" particularly (perhaps exclusively) among Christians in the West, because
we do not want to see it or admit its reality even in our midst. A recent
article published by *Christian History Magazine* and christianhistory-
institute.org presents the problem we face with the title "Start seeing
persecution."[8] The following are a series of excerpts revealing our not-
so-righteous rejection of the reality of real persecution in our very
midst.

Many Christians in the West either deny or are ignorant of it, but persecution is part of present reality. It

has many forms—political oppression, ethnic hatred, religious prejudice, and outright hatred of Christians.

Generally speaking, persecution happens where Christians are seen as a threat to…
- Prevailing religious beliefs (especially where religious belief equals cultural, political or ethnic identity);
- Social stability (…family or community unity);
- Political allegiances.

Governments become persecutors when allegiance to the government clashes with Christians' ultimate allegiance to Christ—especially when the state seeks to be the ultimate authority and demands total allegiance.

The attempt to keep Christianity from being fully Christian—as when the name of Christ cannot be mentioned in public prayer—functions as a subtle form of harassment and discrimination. This harassment relegates Christianity to private life and keeps Christian influence from the public forum, in hope that it will merely fade away.

Many governments apply pressure hoping to stamp our Christianity altogether. Some Western countries allow religious freedom but impose laws that render religion ineffective in influencing public life, morals, or policy.

"One cannot desire freedom *from* the Cross when one is especially chosen *for* the Cross." [Emphasis added]

It seems that suffering for righteousness' sake is the method God uses to reach, redeem, and transform the world.[9]

In order to bring the reality of present persecution to our responsive consciousness, resurrecting it from our passive resistance, it becomes necessary to display it in "portrait" form lest we persist in perpetual denial until it is too late to prepare our minds and hearts to "stand in the evil day." Our purpose here is not to saturate our minds and hearts with which some have labelled a "persecution complex," but to make clear the biblical reality of our times if indeed we are living on the near edge of the Second Coming of our Lord. The apostle Peter well understood and experienced the reality of suffering for the name of Jesus as Messiah and so exhorted each of us…

> Forasmuch then as Christ hath suffered for us in the flesh, arm yourselves likewise with the same mind (I Pet. 4:1).

Sources of Persecution

Persecution is an "equal opportunity" threat and reality and therefore comes from many differing sources and for differing reasons that purport to justify the persecutorial attitudes and actions. The most common persecution source considered to be actual "persecution" is government itself, whether local or national. Overt religiously driven persecution also and usually is deemed real persecution. Family members are also serious sources of persecution, whether in the form of so-called honor killings or by shunning, or even through betrayal of which Jesus warned. Various forms of discrimination in employment and educational realms are increasingly driven by religious persecution… and yes increasingly also in the military.

But perhaps the most challenging areas for identifying persecution are presented in the form of growing cultural practices, attitudes and actions that contravene biblical standards of morality. While these are often labeled as "political," they are in truth "spiritual," revealing why the level of animosity toward Christians who seek to maintain biblically moral standards for themselves, their families and their nations or communities are increasingly met with vitriolic response including efforts to force compliance, even under malignant use of the legal system.

Then, perhaps shockingly, various professing Christians, purported Christian groups and denominations find themselves under attack by so-called "friendly fire." The manner and spirit of these "attacks" reveal whether they are mere corrective concerns within the Body of Christ or whether they become actual persecution for righteousness' sake.

Identifying Methods of Persecution

Just as there are many and varied sources of persecution, there are many and multiplied methods by which people are persecuted for their faith in Christ, whether overtly or covertly. Many—perhaps most—of these are listed here for our prayerful consideration and Christ-like response, but a preliminary warning is needed.

In a world and culture in which victimhood is rewarded and even idolized, our flesh or carnal nature is predisposed to see or label every difference of opinion as "persecution" much like anticipating a "monster under every bed" when acknowledging demonic forces at work in our world. When we yield to such a knee-jerk reaction, we demean the very danger that genuine persecution presents, thus nullifying the legitimacy of our representations of concern over very real persecution. For this reason we have, as Christians, been labelled as having a "Christian persecution complex"[10] or being told that Christian persecution in the West is "a myth."[11]

That warning concern having been made clear, we take a quick overview of the many methods and means by which persecution is implemented.

- ATTACKING CHRISTIAN PRACTICES—prayer, Bible studies, worship times and places under color of law or as "separation of church and state," or as zoning ordinances.
- CENSORSHIP

- CRIMINALIZATION of CHRISTIANITY
- CLAIMING THREATS TO DEMOCRACY
- CULTURAL MANDATES TO CONFORM OR BE OSTRACIZED
- COMPELLING USE OF FALSE OR DECEPTIVE WORDS/LANGUAGE
- COERCION FOR CONTROL via POLITICAL CORRECTNESS, MULTICULTRALISM or RELIGIOUS PLURALISM coupled with special issues, i.e., parenting, medical care (shots/vaccines, abortion, sex changes), environmentalism.
- DISCRIMINTAION
- DIVERSITY—INCLUSIVITY—TOLERANCE
- FINANCIAL CONTROL
- GENOCIDAL THREATS
- GOVERNMENT SANCTIONS—BRIBERY—THREATS
- GLOBALISM COMPELLING CONFORMITY
- INQUISITION and INTIMIDATION
- INTOLERANCE of OTHER FAITHS
- LABELLING WITH FALSE CHARACERIZATIONS
- PERVERSION OF LEGAL SYSTEM—PROCESS—PRINCIPLES
- PROTESTS OUTLAWED, REJECTED, RESPONDED by FINE or IMPRISONMENT
- REDEFINING GOD, JESUS and FAITH FUNDAMENTALS
- REMOVAL OF CHRISTIAN SYMBOLS
- SECULAR CULTURAL INTOLERANCE
- SUPPRESSION OF RELIGIOUS FREEDOM
- TYRANICALLY EXCEPTING CHRISTIANS and CONSERVATIVES from CLAIMING THE BILL of RIGHTS under the US CONSTITUTION
- THREATS FOR REVEALING or SPEAKING TRUTH

CONTRARY TO PREVAILING PROGRESSIVE POLITICAL MANDATES

We now look more explicitly at a sampling of various expressions of persecution both in the West and worldwide. It is necessary for us to not only read the words that attempt to convey the gravity of these circumstances but to also, in a meaningful way, experience the pain, the agony, in our own minds and hearts, otherwise leading us to passively conclude: *This could not happen to me, my family or even my country.*

THE WORLDWIDE SCOPE

1. "Over 360 million Christians suffering persecution in the world."[12]
2. From the Open Doors 2023 World Watch List:[13]
   a. "Over the 30 years of the Open Doors World Watch List reporting, the global phenomenon of Christian persecution has grown alarmingly" from 40 countries with high to extreme levels of persecution in 1993, to 76 countries in 2023.
   b. "In the top 50 alone, 312 million Christians now face very high or extreme levels of persecution."
   c. "Worldwide, 1 in 7 Christians now experience at least 'high' levels of persecution or discrimination; with 1 in 5 in Africa, 2 out of 5 in Asia, and 1 in 15 in Latin America." Rankings of the top 50 are set forth in the Appendix.
3. From the Religious Freedom in the World, Report 2023; published by Aid to the Church in Need:[14]
   a. In 2022, "Religious freedom was violated in countries where more than 4.9 billion people live, in 61 countries."
   b. Of the 71 countries with the highest persecution, the perpetrators are:

      i. 49 by authoritarian governments;

      ii. 21 by Islamist Extremism; and

      iii. 4 by Ethnoreligious Nationalism.

  c. "According to Pope Francis, conditions for Christians are worse now than they were in the days of the early Church."

4. "UN Scheme to Make Christians Criminals"[15]

  a. "Dozens of nations dominated by Islam are pressing the United Nations to adopt an anti-'defamation' plan that would make Christians criminals under international law."

  b. "The discrimination is 'wrapped in the guise of a U.N. resolution called "Combating Defamation of Religions,"' …that attempts to criminalize Christianity."

  c. The plan "is being pushed by the 57-member Organization of Islamic Conference nations, which has adopted the Cairo Declaration of Human Rights in Islam, 'which states that all rights are subject to sharia law, and makes sharia law the only source of reference for human rights.'"

  d. Published reports state that "the U.N. Commission on Human Rights' 53 members voted to adopt the resolution earlier this year, with opposition from the United States and the European Union."

  e. The ACLJ (American Center for Law and Justice) stated: "This radical proposal would outlaw Christianity… it would make the proclamation of your faith an international crime."

5. "Modern-day inquisition"—The "Bible Trial"

  a. A Christian member of parliament in Finland since 1995, acquitted earlier in 2023 after being accused of a "hate" crime for sharing her faith, is again prosecuted by her nation's legal system for the same "offense." What is the offense? It is a social media post in 2019 expressing concern over her church's holding a "Pride" event by posting a photo of a Bible verse in Finnish.

The prosecutors' 26-page appeal openly attacks the core doctrines of Christianity as "defamatory" and "hate speech." Päivi Räsänen, the accused, responded: "The contents of my writings and speeches represent the classical conception of marriage and sexuality, which is the same that Christian churches have taught for two thousand years." Päivi had also published a pamphlet in which she discussed what the Bible has to say about homosexuality, pointing out that homosexuality doesn't comply with the Christian concept of humanity.[16]

6. "Christian church crackdown in Ukraine"

The Russian Foreign Ministry released a scathing report on what it says is a "years-long campaign by Kiev to dismantle the Ukrainian Orthodox Church (OUC)." The report identifies 2018 as the year when a "full-scale, system-wide pressure" campaign against the OUC started. Since 2022, it has escalated further, backed by the Ukrainian government at all levels.

Dozens of churches have been seized by force and arson attacks winked at. The report declared the situation to be a "systemic crisis in world Orthodoxy."

Through this campaign of persecution, "The Kiev authorities and the West are trying to drive a wedge between the Russian and Ukrainian peoples, to destroy the spiritual affinity of Orthodox believers in the two countries." Meanwhile the U.S., which touts itself as a global champion of religious freedoms, "has been silencing information about the crimes perpetrated by Kiev," concluding that Washington tacitly approves the aggressive policies that appear to have involved "forced disappearances, torture and murders of UOC bishops and priests" based on "fake political pretenses."[17]

A further report by Moscow's envoy to the U.N. condemned Britain for blocking a persecuted Ukrainian bishop from addressing the Security Council because "they were afraid of the facts that he could cite… of persecution by Ukrainian authorities."[18]

7. "Biden Targets Hungary with New Visa Requirements"

   a. Hungary and her Prime Minister Viktor Orbán, have declared and are seeking to hold the line for the country as a Christian nation, refusing to kowtow to demands of the antichristian western world.

   b. In 2021, Budapest, under Orbán's government, "banned 'the display and promotion of homosexuality' in books and films accessible by youth."

   c. In early August 2023, the Biden administration, in retaliation to Hungarian resistance to welcome homosexuality, announced "a massive change to the American Visa Waiver Program that only affects certain Hungarian passport holders."

   d. Matt Schlapp, chairman of CPAC, stated: "Joe Biden and his administration seek to punish Hungary by using every diplomatic tool to persecute them for defending their borders, their families and their God given rights." He further stated: "Hungary is being singled out by the Biden administration because 'it stands out as a courageous country of less than 10 million people whose Prime Minister is willing to tell the globalists that Hungarians will decide what happens in Hungary.'"[19]

   e. A further report makes clear the persecutorial challenge from the anti-Christian Biden administration. Miklos Szantho, president of Hungary's Conservative Political Action Conference, also director of the Center for Fundamental Rights in Hungary, said: "…the nation will continue to stand for 'the three values of God, homeland and family.'" He stated that "more than 90% of Hungarians refused gender propaganda in schools..." "And this annoys, this frustrates the liberal mainstream, not only in Europe but globally," referencing the Biden administration attempting, through pressure, i.e., (persecution under color of policy) to "refuse our Jewish-Christian heritage."[20]

Muslims Leading Global Persecution

1. "The Islamic 'Reformation' is Here"
   "Muslim notions of 'improving' society include purging of 'infidels' and their corrupt ways... executing apostates and blasphemers" all required under and by strict interpretation of sharia law. "Islamic scriptural literalism is at odds with religious freedom, tolerance...." The West is hoping for an "Islam without Islam," secularization rather than reformation; "enlightenment that would slowly see the religion of Muhammad go into the dustbin of history." But the Islamic Reformation is producing massive and perhaps unprecedented persecution.[21]

2. "Muslim Hate for the Cross is Muslim Hate for the Gospel"
   "Christian ecumenists take note: Muslim hatred for the cross is a reflection of Muslim hatred for the Gospel—specifically, that Christ was crucified, killed, and resurrected, three doctrines absolutely central to Christianity that Islam categorically rejects." Sharia calls on Muslims to "break the cross"—the "very phrase...first uttered by none other than Muhammad, the prophet of Allah."[22]

3. "An Evil from the Pits of Hell"[23]
   In the month of June 2023, appalling atrocities were committed by Muslims slaughtering Christians indiscriminately. Here is but a sampling in order to grasp the gravity of persecution now being labelled "genocide."

a. Uganda—On June 16, "Islamic terrorists crying "Allahu akbar" (Allah is greater) stormed a private high school, where students were closing the night by singing Christian hymns." In 90 minutes, "the Muslim invaders committed unspeakable horrors against the Christians—murdering, in the end, at least 42 people, 37 of them teenage boys and girls. Most of the boys were burned alive."

b. Nigeria—"Muslim 'Fulani jihadists' slaughtered 2,500 Christians in just the first six months of 2023." In the years prior, 31,700 were slaughtered, 18,200 churches were burned down or destroyed and 50 million were forced out of their ancestral homes.

c. Democratic Republic of Congo—On June 8, an Islamic terror group hacked and beheaded 12 people—4 children, 4 women and 4 men.

d. Pakistan—"On June 7, the mutilated body of Shazia Imran Masih, a 40-year-old Christian widow was found… four Muslims had 'abducted, gang-raped and killed' her for refusing to convert to Islam and marry" a Muslim man. They slashed her neck and poured acid on her. But the authorities refused to do justice, claiming it as an accident.

4. "Killing Christians Takes Us to Paradise"[24]

a. Nigeria—Between July 4 and July 11, 2023, 35 Christians were butchered by Fulani herdsmen.

b. Mozambique—On July 9, 2023, jihadists beheaded a Christian fisherman.

c. Iran—More than 50 converts to Christianity were arrested in a rash of new incidents across 5 Iranian cities in July 2023.

d. Egypt—On a Sunday morning, two Christian women on their way to church were "disappeared" and have not been seen again.

   e. Uganda—On July 9, a Muslim man murdered his 31-year-old wife, a mother of three, hours after she became a Christian.

   f. Afghanistan—A July 13, 2023 report states that the Taliban are working to completely erase Christianity from the country. Christians captured face brutal torture and even death. Those remaining are fleeing for their lives.

   g. Austria—Two boys, aged 15 and 16, were put on trial July 16, 2023, because they were caught making plans to massacre as many as possible at a middle school. They admitted, "We wanted to shoot all the Christians in the class!" They added, "Killing Christians takes us to paradise."[25]

Persecution of Christians Becoming Genocide

A new report from the secular news magazine *NEWSWEEK* has announced that "the persecution of Christians across the world is fast becoming genocide and that the faith will soon disappear in some areas of the world, even in locations where its presence dates back to antiquity."

1. "The level and nature of persecution is arguably close to meeting the international definition of genocide according to that adopted by the UN."[26]

   a. Eradicating Christians through violence was the explicit objective of extremist groups in Syria, Iraq, Egypt, northeast Nigeria and the Philippines.

   b. The main impact of genocidal acts against Christians is **exodus**.

      i. "Christianity is at risk of disappearing" in the Middle East.

      ii. The Christian population in Palestine is now below 1.5 percent.

      iii. In Syria, where the word "Christian" was first used, the Christian population has dropped from 1.7 million in 2011 to below 450,000 in 2023.

    iv. In Iraq, the number of Christians has fallen from 1.5 million in 2003, to below 120,000 today.

    v. "Given the scale of persecution…its impact involves the decimation of some of the faith's oldest and most enduring communities."

2. The eradication of all professing Christians who will not declare allegiance to the rising global government are destined to be "selected out" from worldwide society.

What About the "Land of the Free?"

If the scope and vitriol of persecution has spread so vastly and pervasively throughout the world in just two decades, has the West— and particularly the United States— experienced a similar phenomenon? And if so, in what manners does persecution manifest itself in what Abraham Lincoln called, "The Last Best Hope of Earth?" Have we been willing to use alternative labels to describe what is, in reality, persecution driven by growing rejection of the Christian faith, of Biblical authority, and therefore a seething undercurrent of metastasizing hatred for those who sincerely bear the name of Christ? We must pull back the curtain so as to embrace the reality we now face.

O LORD my God, in thee do I put my trust: save
me from all them that persecute me, and deliver
me (Ps. 7:1).

Chapter 4
PROBING THOUGHTS for PROPHETIC TIMES

1. Why is persecution among Christians in the West "unseeable"?
2. Why does allegiance to Christ often produce persecution by secular government?
3. Can true Christians expect freedom *from* the Cross when the very confession of allegiance to Christ entails being chosen *for* the Cross?
4. Why must the very concept of global government imply virtual genocide of true followers of Christ? Try to think this through very carefully.
5. How could the "Land of the Free" become only the "Home of the Brave" if the foundation of faith in Christ is not substantially restored, beginning with "the fear of the Lord"? If "We the people" do not truly fear God and act accordingly, will we not be consigned to fearing man… and inevitable persecution?

Chapter 5

PATTERNS OF AMERICAN PERSECUTION

*"All Bible-believing Christians are 'the declared enemies
of godless progressivism and must ultimately be despised, derided,
demeaned and dethroned by whatev-
er means deemed remotely possible...."'*

PERSECUTION IS PROMOTED BY "PROGRESSIVE" POLITICS throughout the West. This is true throughout Europe and all western nations comprising the resurrected ancient Roman Empire foretold by the prophet Daniel to be in power at Christ's return just as it was at His first coming (Dan. 2:31-44).

America, as the putative leader in the West, is no exception and has become the apparent leader of western persecution by means of progressive politics. It is precisely because this godless "progressive" movement is the engine driving and motivating almost all things anti-Christian in America that it is sheltered from being labeled "persecution," because the contention is that it is only "political" and social, or cultural, and therefore not religious persecution. But it is what underlies as foundational to this viewpoint that, in practical application, becomes functional persecution?

Political Correctness, Multiculturalism and Religious Pluralism

The functional foundation of so-called progressive politics is the unholy trinity of what is commonly known as Political Correctness,

Multiculturalism and Religious Pluralism. A simple (but not simplistic) description of this unholy belief system is that all thinking, ideas and behaviors that serve to purportedly UNITE peoples and groups are by definition "good" and to be pursued to save the world from divisiveness, friction and war. Therefore, whatever seems to be at odds with this utopian concept is, by definition, evil and to be resisted and ultimately either destroyed or severely marginalized so as to have no effect in preventing progressivism from prevailing in every culture and nation.

It should not be difficult, then, to discern that the Christian faith as presented clearly in the Bible must be rejected as fundamentally contrary to the utopia salvation "gospel" of progressivism that humankind will ultimately "save" ourselves. Put differently, if as Jesus Christ declared himself: "I am **the** way, **the** truth, and **the** life: no man cometh unto the Father but by me," the Christian faith—and all who promote it and claim to be such Christians—are necessarily the declared enemies of godless progressivism and must ultimately be despised, derided, demeaned and dethroned by whatever means deemed remotely possible within the broader concepts of democratic life as the enemies of global unity.

For this reason, the majority of persecution in the West comes clothed in political jargon, social issues, multiplied court proceedings and media mockery, all calculated to compel Christians to conform to godless progressivism as the ultimate salvation message for world peace and prosperity. We now look behind the curtain to see what this looks like, even under the names of justice and democracy… yes, and even in the name of Christ himself.

Pressure to Persuade Breeds Persecution

Seldom does a day or week pass without a report—or numerous reports—of American citizens being pressured to submit and conform to the prevailing progressive values of an increasingly God-rejecting culture. This pressure is brought to bear through many common sources and builds incrementally in order to achieve the requisite level of pressure to compel or enforce compliance or conformity. Here we explore a representative sampling.

1. PARENTAL PRESSURE
   a. "Rejected foster parents fight state discrimination over Christian beliefs on sexuality."[27]
      In Massachusetts, the most profound early seedbed of Christianity in America via the Pilgrims and Puritans, the state's foster care system is categorically refusing to allow any professing Christian couple, however well qualified, to become foster parents if they refuse to embrace anti-biblical beliefs about marriage, sexuality and gender. While this may be construed as simply a Constitutional First Amendment issue, at root it is open rejection of foundational Christian faith under color of law. Yet Massachusetts and many states are struggling to find foster parents due to a deluge of parentless kids dumped into the system by an explosively godless culture.
   b. "'Shocked': Christian mom fights to adopt after refusing to affirm kids' gender transitions."[28]
      Jessica Bates filed a lawsuit against the state of Oregon when the state's Department of Human Services demanded that she agree to "support any adopted child's desire to have a gender transition."
   c. "Warning to California parents: You could lose your child under new gender affirmation bill AB 957."[29]
      i. The California Senate and Assembly approved a bill, AB 957, which would strip a parent of custody of a child if the parent resists the child's gender transition.
      ii. California resident Elon Musk who owns X, the former Twitter social media app, said: "This bill is a

wolf in sheep's clothing." "…if you disagree with the other parent about sterilizing your child, you lose custody. Utter madness!"

    iii. The California Assembly approved this bill by a vote of 57-16. The Senate approved by a vote of 30-9. Therefore, state senator Scott Wilk warned: "If you love your children, you need to flee California."

2. ATHLETIC PRESSURE

    a. "'Burned at the stake': Coach breaks silence of fallout from sharing post critical of trans athletes."[30]

        i. Kim Russell, head women's lacrosse team coach at Oberlin College in Ohio, spoke out against the ostensibly, yet historically, "Christian" college for retaliating against her after she shared on social media a post critical of male athletes participating in women's sports. The athletic director brought Russell in for several meetings before administrators and students where she was chastised for her Christian views that did not conform to new woke culture mandates.

        ii. Kim said, "I felt like I was burned at the stake. I felt like I was stoned and hanged at the same time." She said, "Every time I've spoken up, I've been silenced." "Right now," she lamented, "I feel like women are afraid to speak up…afraid to be cancelled."

    b. "Pro athlete shares her Christian beliefs with sports reporter, left totally shocked by what happened…."[31]

        i. Golfer Amy Olson competed at the Women's Open at Pebble Beach while she was seven months pregnant. A Global Golf Post interview was refused to be published because of Amy's pro-life, avowedly Christian beliefs. A writer at USA Today's Golfweek picked up the story of "the interview that never ran," but also never ran in Golfweek because the editors killed it.

  ii. The original reporter stated that he quit after 12 years with the publication because it would only run the piece "if we take out the abortion and the Christian stuff."

  iii. Amy stated the rising persecutorial reality of our times in clear terms. "But over the last decade, it's become extremely difficult because a lot of the things that Christianity stands for have become political battlegrounds. Christ hasn't changed His view on any of those things, but the culture has changed. So, it's a lot less acceptable to be an open Christian and to believe what Christianity has stood for the last 2,000 years."

3. MEDICAL PRESSURE

  a. "Medical center claims 'religious oppression' is just a Christian thing."[32]

    i. Vanderbilt University Medical Center in Nashville, Tennessee, in America's *Bible Belt,* claims Christianity oppresses minority faiths and must be "dismantled" or "fixed" by the Center's Diversity Equity and Inclusion (DEI) toolkit.

    ii. The toolkit also declares "Whiteness" to be a substitute for the terms "Christian and Englishmen," concluding that Christianity is, in reality, a premier engine of racism that must either be dismantled or somehow fixed.

4. LEGAL PRESSURE

  a. "God despisers target faith 'release time' for students."[33]

    i. The Freedom From Religion Foundation, in a full-court-press to oppose the presence of Christianity in America through lawsuits, is now going after an

Ohio program that allows students "release time" for private religious instruction through a LifeWise Academy program.

ii. Notwithstanding a 1952 Supreme Court decision approving such "release time" programs so long as privately funded and off campus, the Freedom From Religion Foundation continues its unrelenting legal efforts to eradicate Christianity from American society.

b. "Senators to FBI: Quit hiding details about anti-Catholic ideology."[34]

i. The FBI created an anti-Catholic memo accusing true Catholics of being domestic terrorists.

i. *The Federalist*, noted that the "Washington Regime" has no tolerance for those opposing its "pagan morality."

i. Senator Chuck Grassley of Iowa called out the FBI and its director for failing to reveal the truth of the pervasiveness of this anti-Catholic ideology from coast to coast and was joined by letter from six other senators accusing director Wray of "misleading testimony."

5. EDUCATIONAL PRESSURE

a. "State demands professors teach government-approved wokeness."[35]

i. California has enacted regulations requiring the more than 54,000 professors who teach in the California Community Colleges to teach the state-adopted ideology of "diversity, equity and inclusion."

ii. The Foundation for Individual Rights and Expression (FIRE) reports that "The regulations explicitly require professors to pledge allegiance to contested ideological viewpoints."

      iii. A lawyer for the FIRE foundation made it clear that "These regulations are a totalitarian triple-whammy. The government is forcing professors to teach and preach a politicized viewpoint they do not share, imposing incomprehensible guidelines, and threatening to punish professors when they cross an arbitrary, indiscernible line."

   b. "Christian student group must be treated like other campus organizations."[36]

      i. The 9th U.S. Circuit Court of Appeals ruled that a school district "can't selectively enforce discriminatory policies against Christian groups, while exempting secular ones."

      ii. A San Jose, California teacher complained about Fellowship of Christian Athletes members discussing issues concerning their faith on campus—particularly the millennia-old belief that marriage is between a man and a woman. The group was then prevented from operating as and under the "Associated Student Body."

6. MILITARY PRESSURE

   a. "Activist Seeks Removal of Christian Bookstore from Military Mini-Mall."[37]

      i. The founder of the Military Religious Freedom Foundation claims the Faith2Soar bookstore constitutes a government establishment of religion in violation of the U.S. Constitution and is pushing the Army and Air Force to remove it.

      ii. The bookstore legal response: "It would be unconstitutional and illegal for the government to exclude a bookstore or any other type of private business… simply because they are a Christian or other faith-based business."

7. BUSINESS PRESSURE
   a. "Best Buy fires whistleblower after leaks of manager saying Christian displays not OK, but LGBT training is."[38]
      i. A Best Buy Geek Squad employee was fired after speaking out against a mandatory LGBT training video.
      ii. The former employee said, "My ability to help and serve customers with electronic repairs and the sexual orientation of colleagues have nothing in common." He wrote: "In fact, sexuality has no place in the workplace, and forcing me to subject myself to conduct that I believe constitutes a sin…is simply unacceptable—in fact, it's unlawful."
   b. "Bank's attack…includes closing accounts."[39]
      i. JP Morgan Chase closed the business accounts of a doctor whose best-selling book *The Truth About COVID-19* exposed the virus was likely engineered in a lab and the vaccines would neither prevent infection nor transmission. Because COVID-19 presented serious political and religious concerns, Chase was seen as discriminating both politically and religiously.
      ii. JP Morgan Chase was already under suspicion for using its power to discriminate, i.e. persecute based on political and religious beliefs.
      iii. A shareholder resolution by the Bahnsen Group urged review of the bank's policies against religious and political beliefs. That resolution followed media reports that the bank cancelled customer accounts because they are "Christian or Conservative."
   c. "Famed attorney Lin Wood retires after being targeted…."[40]
      i. CBS News pictured the attorney holding up a Bible while speaking during a press conference on 2020

electoral results in Georgia. CNBC then reported that Wood retired "to avoid his potential disbarment in Georgia."

    ii. Wood, who had been a renowned and highly successful lawyer for 45 years as a member of the Georgia Bar Association and won a number of high-stake cases embarrassing to the media and liberal politics, had decided to gradually wind down his practice and retire long before the 2020 election. But the media sought to get back at Wood, making the public believe that his reputation as both a Conservative and evangelical Christian was besmirched by inevitable disbarment.

    iii. Wood thereafter said, "After 45 years of practicing law, I wanted out of the legal profession. I had had enough of its games." He then stated: "I am pleased CNBC used a photo of me holding up my favorite book, the Holy Bible. I am pleased that the article correctly quoted me as saying that 'God is sovereign over everything.'"

8. POLITICAL PRESSURE

  a. "An 'imposter Christianity' is threatening American democracy."[41]

    i. Philip Gorski, Yale University sociologist, says what he calls "White Christian nationalism represents a grave threat to democracy because it defines 'we the people' in a way that excludes many Americans."

    ii. In fact, he claims the Christian focus to be "perhaps the most serious threat [democracy] now faces."

  b. "The Growing Anti-Democratic Threat of Christian Nationalism in the U.S."[42]

    i. Declaring that "Our democracy is at stake," those who, through progressive politics seek to remove true, biblical Christianity from the public space now link the adjective "Nationalism" to the word *Christian* so as to make the word *Christian* itself to be rendered alien and offensive to the nation unless limited to the four walls of a church. Such is the viewpoint of the progressively liberal *TIME* Magazine.

ii. Political progressives, desiring desperately to eliminate God and influence of the Christian faith from all things deemed political now resort to labelling the morality of the Christian that does not align with their political objectives to be stunning anti-democratic attitudes, such as wanting to insure all who vote are eligible and identifiable so as to protect against voter fraud. They despise all references to the Christian foundations of the country as "Christian nationalism."

9. CHURCH PRESSURE

a. "Seminary leader under fire for exposing woke critical race theory in churches."[43]

i. Owen Strachan, provost and theology professor at Grace Bible Theological Seminary, came under fire as an *extremist* "for criticizing woke politics in Christian churches and organizations."

ii. Suddenly, Strachan found himself on the outs in the evangelical world. He lamented: "I don't mean wild folks way out on the left attacking me." "It was frankly…people I trusted. That was the hardest part."

iii. Strachan noted: "In our post-truth culture, the worst thing you call someone is an extremist." "That's what I began to hear."

iv. Monique Duson, writing for the Center for Biblical Unity, urged congregations to "be on guard for pastors using CRT terms." She criticized Max Lucado for repenting of his "white privilege." Without reservations, she warned: "If you hear your pastor suddenly start using terms [reflecting political wokeness and Critical Race Theory], then your church is probably going woke." But why? Because of the persecutorial pressure to conform to perceived progressive cultural norms to gain acceptance.

b. "What The Bleep Is Happening To Christian Music?"[44]

    i. "A few years back," wrote Kevin McNeese, the founder of *NRT*—newsreleasetoday.com —"I wrote the most visited editorial in our site's history titled, 'No More Bleeping Christian Music.' It went viral overnight." That was in 2002. Kevin wrote in that piece, "Swearing in Christian music is something previous generations of fans never had to deal with"—"honest songwriting." Anyone criticizing such "honesty" was rabidly accused of being "out of touch, snobby, churchy, goody-two-shoes, or as simply not welcome in this little swear club cool clique." "I took a brave, deep dive into the dark and dank corners of the Christian industry. Corners where artists dropped f-bombs in their worship without warning…."

    ii. Leaping forward 21 years to 2023, the founder of New Release Today declared "… recent developments have ignited new alarms" invading "what was once sacred space." Referencing Capitol Christian Music Group owned by Universal Music, the largest producer and publisher of Christian music, McNeese writes of new releases from Jesus Culture, We The Kingdom, The Belonging Co. and Dante Bowe, whose new video for his "vibey, summer

'Gospel' jam, 'Wind Me Up' features dozens of scantily clad women partying it up in sexual pose after pose," with "lyrics about desire, companionship, and arguably lust." From one moment of worship about Jesus' nail-scarred hands, we're "giving in to sexual desires while dropping [f-] bombs multiple times on the bridge in the next." And this is not alone among so-called Christian artists.

iii. "This is new and something I haven't seen," lamented McNeese. "We have a major Christian label pushing sexual and explicit lyrics and videos alongside legacy church worship albums and contemporary Christian artists."

iv. Here is persecution in religious clothing, bearing the name of Christ as a moniker but demanding the church submit to the larger culture as Master, or be mocked and derided for not being "honest." As NRT concluded too aptly: "The defense for inclusion of this content is simple. If you don't like it, you're the problem. You're a bigot. You're old fashioned. You're a transphobe. You're holier-than-thou. You're judgmental. You're out of touch. You're what's wrong with every single church in existence."

A further note...

And this same pattern has now found its way into the mouths of pastors and their messages from the pulpits of America, coast to coast, not to mention their podcasts, blogs and various media postings.

The entire American church is increasingly "persecuted" for failure to accept and celebrate the culture demands of purported Christian leaders seeking worldly acceptance and popularity in the name of Christ under the alleged ministry of evangelism. What wonderful deception!

c. "Radical Leftist Candidate Spits on Christianity."[45]

    i. Jessica Anderson, "attempting to sic the IRS" on the Christian based Family Foundation of Virginia, recorded herself on a podcast bashing Christianity.

    ii. "… I was an active member of my Southern Baptist Church," she said. "I was really engrossed in it because I found it at age 21." She then declared: "It's almost indoctrination…." "Yeah, it's very cultish."

    iii. Then, in an attempt to justify abortion in her new found radical political persuasion, she revealed her persecutorial purpose. "Hey like, that's all it is, that's all the Bible has become. It's become a faucet to spew hate by people who want to claim it as their crutch to be ugly." Then claiming God as asexual and transgender, she boldly declared: "The Old Testament should really just be dissolved."

10. GOVERNMENTAL PRESSURE

a. "A nation of snitches" DHS is grooming Americans to report on each other."[46]

    i. The American government is grooming the people to spy on each other as part of its Center for Prevention Programs and Partnership. Based on so-called "community policing," these programs insidiously turn us into an intolerant squealing bystander nation under the rubric of "See Something, Say Something."

    ii. As Attorney John Whitehead stated: "We are now the unwitting victims of an interconnected, tightly woven, technologically evolving web of real-time, warrantless, widening, mass surveillance," including snitch tip lines expanding policing to individuals throughout communities under the guise of fighting violent extremism in all its forms.

iii. "What this program is really all about is community policing on a global scale… to prevent violent extremism by targeting… racism, bigotry, hatred, intolerance, etc… to identify… individuals who could be construed as potential extremist 'threats.'"

iv. Anyone seen as opposing some government position or proclamation is then, by implication, an extremist. Since the FBI has already labelled sincere Christians as "extremists" for a variety of stances ranging from abortion, homosexuality, transgenderism, vaccination, etc, and since businesses and governmental agencies have already labelled and fired many who have refused to kow-tow to the raging woke culture, the handwriting is truly "on the wall" as to how the "community policing" will soon take the role of pervasive religious persecution.

"Yes, America is Persecuting Christians"[47]

The more and faster Americans flee from and repudiate the God of our fathers, the greater and more rapidly persecution grows against an increasingly smaller remnant who maintain and seek faithfully to keep "the faith which was once delivered to the saints" (Jude vs 3).

What's making life hard for Christians in America is the secular progressives. It's the liberals leading the revolution—sexual, woke, what have you—who are committed to their own religious system, and who brook no dissent to their orthodoxy and tolerate no disrespect to their idols." It is no longer enough for Christians to tolerate their degenerate "freedoms." Now "we must celebrate them too, or we will suffer."

Indeed, "the scales are tipping closer to 'Say Caesar is God' than most people realize." How then can or should we respond? And how is it possible to stand faithfully and courageously when, as the *Epoch Times* noted of Americans: "The Fear of Suffering is Driving Us

Crazy."[48] The answers to these piercing questions will be provided, in significant part, just ahead. Fear not, fret not, and let us move forward boldly toward our Lord's return.

The LORD is my strength and shield; my heart trusted in him, and I am helped: therefore my heart greatly rejoiceth; and with my song will I praise him (Ps. 28:7).

Chapter 5
PROBING THOUGHTS for PROPHETIC TIMES

1. What do you consider as "persecution currently taking place in America?

2. Why do you think many people mock the idea that persecution of Christians is truly taking place in America?

3. How would you define or describe the sources of persecution of Christians in America?

4. Do you feel or have you experienced any of the persecutorial "pressures" described?

5. In what ways do you see the word *democracy* itself being used to deride or destroy genuine Christian belief?

6. Can you see how the seemingly good phrase "See Something, Say Something" is gradually being embraced by government to use citizens to report alleged "hate" or refusal to obey the high priests of wokeness so that their neighbors, relatives, business colleagues and even friends might be labelled "extremists," thus requiring surveillance and potential persecution?

PART 2

PRESCRIPTION for PERILOUS TIMES

"That period became known as THE GREAT TERROR."
"No one was safe who did not fully embrace the new godless order...."

WILL YOU BE ABLE TO STAND amid the tsunami of persecution that is sweeping the earth as the spiritual foundations of the earth are broken up?

Our world has periodically faced difficult spiritual resistance and times of terrifying persecution of the saints. The French Revolution was a classic example. It began with political tensions and through God-defying leadership devolved into what was known as *The Terror*. A doctor invented the guillotine, named after himself, so as to provide the perceived most painless and humane method of severing one's head from his heart to dispense with any opposition he or she might present to the sweeping new world order of France.

Unfortunately for thousands, those perceived as threatening or posing even remote opposition to the new, lawless regime, were deemed to be insufferable and must also suffer the guillotine's blade. That period became known as *The GREAT TERROR!* No one was safe who did not fully embrace the new godless order that so rebelled against all things biblical as to literally change the days of the week from 7 to 10, install the 10-based decimal system and install the worshipful image of the Goddess of Reason in the Cathedral de Notre Dame.

Charles Dickens, in his *Tale of Two Cities*, said it "was the best of times, it was the worst of times." What will you call those times when they reappear, as they now are, on steroids?

Is there a prescription given by a loving God to enable us to endure such terrifying times when, as Jesus said, "Men's hearts [will] fail them for fear, and for looking after those things which are coming on the earth" (Lk. 21:26)? Please encourage yourself and those you love with God's simple "Prescription for Victory."

Chapter 6

PRESCRIPTION FOR VICTORY

"God's divine prescription makes clear how
He will enable us to press on through the storm to victory."

VICTORY REQUIRES A BATTLE! The very word *victory* implies a period of some level of warfare. Many speak of "spiritual warfare" but have little clue as to the real-life extent and implications of the battle ahead. Unfortunately, the statistical and spiritual facts on the ground reveal that most western Christians only imagine, in a largely theoretical way, the need for spiritual warfare, but have not yet even entered spiritual "boot camp."

The Need to Prepare

A nation or people group dare not enter a battle without serious and adequate preparation. Boot camp is just a preliminary "get ready" stage. But the majority of professing Christians in America and the western world have not truly experienced anything akin to spiritual boot camp.

Boot camp is designed to toughen up those who are conscripted or signed up. It is also calculated to bring individuals into a kind of mission-directed comradery such that the platoon does not fight the battle alone but is extraordinarily committed to one another. When one is wounded, all who are able come, without further command, to his or her aid. Victory demands a body committed to the battle.

Boot camp also prepares the unprepared but promised soldier to understand and properly handle the weapons of warfare. This is necessary to avert the casualties of so-called "friendly fire" which not only reduces the fighting force but also brings anguish to the force, undermining the precious esprit de corps needed to maintain a unified team.

Unfortunately, all of the established goals of boot camp have largely escaped the mind and ministry of professing western Christians, especially Americans, over the years since the mid-1950s, but in profound ways since the late 1960s. With the dramatic shift of Christian teaching in the early 1970s through the "God is Love" movement, and away from the scriptural balance of teaching the God of truth and judgment, the public and private persona of the church devolved into the lordship of feelings, thus in spiritual affect superseding the toughness and balance of both grace and truth once delivered to the saints. The results have been devastating, both in failure to disciple and in radically diminishing the authority of the scriptures called "the Sword of the Spirit" (Eph 6:17), the premier weapon of the follower of Christ.

In effect, the church has rendered itself virtually weaponless for the fifty years last passed—a half century of progressive unpreparedness. The spirit of unpreparedness metastasized throughout America, and by influence throughout the West, first by the Church Growth Movement that began in the early 1970s out of Southern California. The discipleship purpose of the church-gathered was purposefully diminished in order to grow churches by reducing scriptural demands of believers in order to woo unbelievers. Believers' preparation for spiritual warfare and to endure suffering for Christ was seriously weakened.

But evangelical church leaders persisted in their weakening of Christians' spiritual defenses by catapulting the Church Growth Movement into the Seeker Sensitive Movement of the 1990s. The collective effect was catastrophic! Unbelievers were seduced by those intent on developing mega churches by diminishing even further the discipleship and preparation of the saints in the pews.

Feelings became the ultimate arbiter of truth. The "Sword of the Spirit" was so dulled as to be a mere pretense of a weapon, useful more to be hung on a wall as a souvenir of battles long passed than to be employed as a genuine weapon against Satan's hordes preparing to launch vicious persecution. Pastors, parachurch leaders and publishers have been complicit in the ensuing carnage largely in pursuit of power, perks and position. How are we to recover so as to victoriously face the onslaught of persecution increasingly thrust upon us?

How To Prepare for Victory

The apostle Paul gave us both warning and direction in II Cor. 10:3-5. This passage is often somewhat spuriously quoted but is seldom truly applied and taken to heart, allowing the Sword of the Spirit to pierce our hearts to prepare us for the serious battles ahead. Prayerfully consider and meditate on his words.

> For the weapons of our warfare are not carnal [of the flesh], but mighty through God to the pulling down of strong holds;
>
> Casting down imaginations [our own reasonings and thoughts], and every high thing [non-biblical ideas we think are important or prefer to embrace] that exalteth itself against the knowledge of God, and bringing into captivity every thought to the obedience of Christ.

Here we find the foundation for victory for the battles of our minds and hearts as persecution mounts. We must necessarily return to this foundation daily amid the assaults that will increasingly surge against our natural or fleshly thoughts, ideas and emotions. Therefore, memorize and meditate on this passage as the default position from which you will combat the deceptive whiles of satanic pressures mounting almost daily.

Setting Victory's Stage in Hope

The apostle Peter well understood suffering. As with the apostle Paul, he was warned that great suffering would accompany his allegiance to Christ and the gospel of salvation and hope. As Jesus had so specifically warned and Paul had reiterated: "Yea, and all that live godly in Christ Jesus shall suffer persecution" (II Tim. 3:12). This persecution arises because of "the offense of the cross" (Gal. 5:11). And it then becomes clear why Jesus warned those who would truly and faithfully follow Him must "...deny himself, and take up his cross, and follow me."

> For whosoever will save his life shall lose it: and whosoever will lose his life for my sake shall find it.
>
> For what is a man profited, if he shall gain the whole world, and lose his own soul? (Matt. 16:24-26).

"Where is the hope," you ask? Peter makes it plain. Jesus had warned him of his tendency not to savour "the things that be of God, but those that be of men" (Matt. 16:23). Peter rose up in the flesh and rebuked Jesus in response to Jesus' advance warning to His disciples how He would "suffer many things... and be killed..." (Matt. 16:21). Perhaps shockingly, this great apostle wasn't as spiritual as we tend to think, for he, like us, had to come to grips with the issue of suffering and persecution which he ultimately resolved to our encouragement and hope. Let his faith-filled passion sweep through the membranes of your own mind and heart.

Peter declared that we are begotten "unto a lively hope," "reserved in heaven for you,"

> Who are kept by the power of God through faith unto salvation ready to be **revealed in the last time** [emphasis added].

Wherein ye greatly rejoice, though now for a season, if
need be, ye are in heaviness through manifold temptations [testing and trials]:

That the trial of your faith, being much more precious
than of gold that perisheth, though it be tried with
fire, might be found unto praise and honour and glory
at the appearing of Jesus Christ (I Pet. 1:3-7).

The stage of anticipated (but not sought) growing persecution and
accompanying suffering having been set, how then are those who "live
godly in Christ Jesus" to walk in victory amid such trials and tribulations,

Looking for that blessed hope, and the glorious
appearing of the great God and our Saviour Jesus
Christ (Titus 2:13)?

The Psalms, specifically Psalm 37, provide God's simple (but not
simplistic) prescription for victorious living for each of us, regardless
of troubling circumstances. Hope and peace lie straight ahead as we
daily embrace the Great Physician's prescription.

God's Prescription for Perilous Times

We must not play pretend that persecution and suffering will not,
in some measure, be our lot as we make our way to and through the
latter days of these end times. Remember Jesus' words of exhortation
amid His warning of these times, declaring:

But he that shall endure unto the end, the same shall
be saved (Matt. 24:13; Mk. 13:13).

Jesus was exhorting us to persevere even in the face of exceedingly
trying times and not give up. The apostle Paul also made this plain to
his ministry trainee Timothy, warning…

This know also, that in the last days perilous times shall come (II Tim. 3:1).

God's divine prescription makes clear how we can, and He by His grace, will enable us to press on through the storm to victory. Here, then, is this heart-strengthening, mind-confronting end-time R_x delivered to each of us in Psalm 37:1-7.

1. **FRET NOT!**

    "Fret not thyself because of evildoers…" (Ps. 37:1). Fretting is faith-less. It accomplishes nothing but allows us to become ever more dependent in our hearts upon favorable external circumstances. Fretting is borne of anxiety which devolves into fear, and as it is written, "Fear hath torment" (I Jn. 4:18). When we allow ourselves to fret over circumstances, whether small or great, we self-induce torment into our lives, rendering us incapable to live by faith. And "the just shall live by faith." Such faith must be coupled with belief and trust bound together by obedience (Hab. 2:4; Heb. 10:38).

    Fretting and fear are spiritual cousins. We are to fear God, not man or fleshly circumstances. Fear of man and his devices brings a snare to our souls (Prov. 29:25). It also reveals a foundational, fleshly spiritual disease of our beings, giving unwitting sway to the enemy of our souls. For this reason, the beloved apostle, John, forewarned:

    > There is no fear in love; but perfect love casteth out fear: because fear hath torment. He that feareth is not made perfect in love (1Jn 4:18).

    Fretting and worry are kinsmen. It is often said that "worry is a mild form of atheism." No wonder we are warned to "fret not."

Likewise, we, as with Israel before us, are perpetually warned by the Holy Spirit to "Fear Not." It breeds spiritual paralysis and prevents us from persevering in faith and trust.

2. **TRUST IN THE LORD**

"Trust in the LORD, and do good." In this and through this trust you shall live and be provided for daily (Ps. 37:3).

Many contend that they *love* the Lord, but few actually *trust* Him. If we truly trusted Him, we would *obey* Him, doing what He has commanded and refusing to engage in that which He has prohibited. Yet the very word *obey* has become increasingly the most hated, despised word among western Christians—especially American Christians, as proven both by decades of statistics and by a host of pastors and parachurch leaders who have appeared on the author's national radio broadcast *VIEWPOINT* over the past decade (accessible through saveus. org worldwide).

Why would we be so prone to reject the very word *obey* when it is the key to reveal to God our alleged love and trust? There are several reasons.

A. A spirit of rebellion has gripped the minds and hearts of professing believers increasingly as we see the day of our Lord's return approaching, just as prophesied.

B. The love of many is "waxing cold" as Jesus prophesied (Matt. 24:12).

C. The church has left her "first love" (Rev. 2:4), has become religiously proud but spiritually lukewarm and unacceptable to God (Rev. 3:15-16).

D. We have lost our spiritual hearing and discernment, turning our hearts and minds to the voices of the flesh, the culture, and the spirit of scientific man rather than that of the omnipotent Creator. Indeed, our hearing has become dull and our eyes are closing to the Lord's Kingdom call, seeking like the builders of Babel to build our own kingdoms, even in the name of Christ. And so, we are warned…

    (1) Take heed what you hear (Mk. 4:24);

    (2) Take heed how you hear (Lk. 8:18);

    (3) Make sure you do hear and heed what Jesus has said to the church (Rev. 2:7, 11, 17, 29; 3:6, 13, 22);

    (4) Be a doer of the Word and not merely a hearer (Jam. 1:22), which leads to self-deception.

E. We have drifted from the spirit of Christ and increasingly embraced the spirit of antichrist of which the apostle John warned. The very spirit and ways of the world have been embraced by the church and her leaders over the six decades last passed, revealed in…

    (1) The behavior of Christians deemed acceptable;

    (2) The messages proclaimed by pastors;

    (3) The methodologies embraced to ostensibly win the world by increasingly adopting the world's ways.

It is our absolute TRUST that God desires and will bless in these times that will increasingly trouble our souls. Ultimately, we will either trust God or the spirit of the Antichrist, a false trust that will lead not to the Promised Land but to perdition. And the trust that pleases God, revealing our true love, is revealed through and by our faith-filled obedience to His Word, His Will and His Ways. For "there is a way which seemeth right unto a man, but the end thereof are the ways of death" (Prov. 14:12; 16:25).

When all is said, the prescription for victory remains simply this:

Trust in the LORD with all thine heart; and lean not unto thine own understanding.

In all thy ways acknowledge him, and he shall direct thy paths.

Be not wise in thine own eyes: fear the LORD, and depart from evil (Prov. 3:5-7).

3. **DELIGHT IN THE LORD**

Here is a probing, motivational test of the reality of our relationship with the Lord. Do I truly delight in the Lord? Do I trust Him and obey Him because I truly *want* to, or do I purport to obey, love and trust Him primarily because I *ought* to? Motivations reveal our hearts and can also determine whether we will walk in victory or defeat. Motivations reflect attitudes, and contrary to much popular opinion, God is every bit as concerned about our attitudes as He is about our actions.

God's prescription for victory amid troubled times is activated by our attitude toward Him and His kingdom, driven by delight. As it is written: "I delight to do thy will, O my God: yea, thy law is within my heart" (Ps. 40:8).

The Psalmist David, second king of Israel upon whose throne Jesus the Messiah will ultimately reign, was called by God, "a man after mine own heart" (I Sam. 13:14; Acts 13:22). But why? What was it about David that set him apart for such divine approval? It was his absolute trust in the Lord amid unending trials as a result of his love for God's Word. Yet how was that trust and love manifested from the depths of his soul? It was his genuine *delight* in the Lord and His Word, Will and Ways. Consider the very first of the Psalms.

Blessed is the man that walketh not in the counsel of the ungodly…

But **his delight** is in the law of the LORD; and in his law doth he meditate day and night (Ps. 1:1-2; emphasis added).

That same spirit of delight is woven throughout Psalm 119, which should propel every believer to meditate therein regularly. The theme is unmistakable, reflecting the depths of the Psalmist's heart.

I will *meditate* in thy precepts…I will *delight* myself in thy statutes: I will not forget thy word (vs. 15-16).

…thy servant did meditate in thy statutes. Thy testimonies also are my *delight* and my counsellors (vs. 23-24).

I will *delight* myself in thy commandments, which I have loved.

My hands also will I lift unto thy commandments, which I have loved; and I will meditate in thy statutes (vs. 47-48).

Let thy tender mercies come unto me, that I may live: for thy law is my *delight*.

…they dealt perversely with me without a cause: but I will meditate in thy precepts (vs. 77-78).

If I truly delight in the Lord and in His Word, I will meditate in His Word day and night, which reveals my delight. In this way, God's Word becomes the unwavering anchor for my soul when trials, testings and persecutions arise. God's prescription for victory is both tried and true, but only for those who apply it!

4. **COMMIT YOUR WAY TO THE LORD**

Commitment is a choice… a daily choice. It requires not only a theoretical commitment such as a mere cognitive statement akin to "I am committed to Christ" but an actual and full trust in the Lord in functional reality. One often hears the words "He or she is a committed Christian," but you might have serious cause to wonder as to the meaning of the word *commitment* when observing such a person's true trust in the Lord when things get tough or in the person's day-to-day choices, behaviors and persistent fears and observable anxiety.

For this reason, the Psalmist's exhortation in Psalm 37:5 declares a link between the word *commit* and the word *trust*.

> Commit thy way unto the LORD; **trust** also in him;
> and he shall bring it to pass [Emphasis added].

This is a serious distinction for western professing Christians who consider *belief* to mean giving cognitive assent to certain religious facts but whose lives consistently fail to conform to what they say they believe. From God's perspective, such persons do not truly *believe* because they do not truly *trust*, revealing also that they do not truly "live by faith." Thus, the reality of our alleged faith, manifested in genuine trust with unwavering commitment, is preparing to be seriously tested in the fires of reality as persecution increasingly rears its ugly head.

It, unfortunately, helps us to understand the seemingly severe warnings to professing believers of the many who will "fall away" from the faith because they are not truly committed to what it means to identify with the Word and Ways of Christ when, as they say "the chips are down" and genuine persecution challenges their trust. This, then, is an appropriate moment to remind ourselves with the words of both our Lord and his disciples, reflecting the deeper meaning of what it means to *commit* and to *trust*.

Be not soon shaken in mind, or be troubled… as that the day of Christ is at hand. Let no man deceive you by any means: for that day shall not come, except there come a falling away first… (I Thess. 2:2-3).

My brethren, count it all joy when ye fall into divers [many] temptations [trials]; Knowing this, that the trying of your faith worketh patience [staying power]. [But] a double minded man is unstable in all his ways (Jam. 1:2-3, 8).

Forasmuch then as Christ hath suffered for us in the flesh, arm yourselves likewise with the same mind… (I Pet. 4:1).

And because iniquity shall abound, the love of many [lack of true commitment] shall wax cold. But he that shall endure unto the end [revealing his true trust and commitment], the same shall be saved (Matt. 24:12-13).

The brother shall deliver up the brother to death, and the father the child… And ye shall be hated of all men for my name's sake: but he that endureth to the end [reveals genuine faith and commitment] shall be saved (Matt. 10:21-22).

To "commit my way" to the Lord is absolute, without circumstantial change or eternal force or threat of force to the contrary. True commitment is not related to fleeting feelings, cultural pressures or painful persecution. My "heart is established," I "shall not be afraid" (Ps. 112:8). I "shall not be afraid of evil tidings" my "heart is fixed, trusting in the LORD" (Ps. 112:7).

5. **REST IN THE LORD**

Rest in the LORD, **and** wait patiently for him: fret not… (Ps. 37:7; emphasis added).

Rest is both a noun and a verb. It is both active and transitive, even in its verb form. We are advised that "there remaineth therefore a rest to the people of God" (Heb. 4:9), speaking of a final rest in the eternal presence of the Lord when the trials and testings of this world have proved our trust. But we are, at the same time and in the same chapter, exhorted:

> Let us labour therefore to enter into that rest, lest any man fall after the same example of disbelief [as did Israel] (vs. 11).

In truth, we will have no peace amid rising persecution without resting in the Lord. Yet in the same way, rest will escape us if we do not actively trust in the Lord, commit our way to Him without reserve, and delight ourselves in Him and His Word. Only then can rest be secured, if, of course, we stop fretting. Israel was prevented from entering God's rest because they did not truly believe, trusting God's Word in absolute commitment to His ways, while delighting in His presence wherein lies "fulness of joy" (Heb. 4:18-10; Ps. 16:11), but instead persistently fretted, murmuring and complaining constantly (Numb. 14:26-29; 26:63-65).

Resting in the Lord is hard work because it requires continually elevating God's Word and Will above our own fleshly wills. This is the heart of spiritual warfare. It is impossible to be victorious in spirit if we continually submit to the incessant demands of the flesh.

For this reason, Paul declared: "I am crucified with Christ" (Gal. 2:20), and "I die daily" (I Cor. 15:31). If, then, I be "dead in Christ," persecution and even death for His name's sake diminishes as a terrifying threat because I already consider myself "crucified with Christ," alive spiritually only by His Spirit.

Reaching such rest requires continual spiritual warfare, since our fleshly feelings will continually demand to be exalted over our faith in Christ and His ways. This process requires patience, and patience is the first cousin to rest and trust, resulting in a peace that passeth understanding that will prevail even amid persecution.

Patience is essential to trust, because trust is always in process. Patience, therefore, is an immense challenge to our flesh which demands immediate results. This is perhaps especially true for American Christians precisely because the spirit of American life is one of persistent action that voraciously demands results NOW! Yet if we are to be victorious in an environment of increasing persecution; we MUST embrace patience so as to endure to the end (Matt. 24:13).

"Tribulation worketh patience; and patience, experience; and experience, hope: and hope maketh not ashamed…" (Rom. 5:3-5). Tribulation involves the increasing pressure that arises from a variety of testings, trials… yes, persecution. For this reason, the apostle Paul surprisingly states: "… we glory in tribulations…" (Rom. 5:3). To many, that may appear to be a kind of spiritual masochism, but in reality, with a biblical adjustment of our viewpoint, such pressures actually serve God's eternal purpose to forge us into a *diamond* that more accurately portrays His glory.

Jesus' brother James well understood the necessity of patience in God's perfect plan.

> My brethren, count it all joy when ye fall into divers [many] temptations [trials and testings];
>
> Knowing this, that the trying of your faith worketh patience.
>
> But let patience have her perfect work, that ye may be perfect and entire, wanting nothing (Jam. 1:2-4).

The end result of such patience is God's perfect will for each of our lives that must, of necessity, be produced under pressure, including persecution. Consider well the fruit of such faith-enforcing tribulation.

> Blessed is the man that endureth temptation [testings and trials threatening faith]: for when he is tried, he shall receive the crown of life, which the Lord hath promised to them that love him (Jam. 1:12).

Do you truly love the Lord? Then, plan to be tested and tried. Only then will your alleged faith be revealed in spiritual reality from God's viewpoint. Thereby we emerge victorious as did our Lord, for as He said: Remember…

The servant is not greater than his lord. If they persecuted me, they will also persecute you… (Jn. 15:20).

Therefore, let patience have its perfect work that you might be
perfect and entire, lacking nothing in your faith.

*Wait on the LORD: be of good courage, and he
shall strengthen thine heart: wait, I say on the
LORD (Ps. 27:14).*

Chapter 6
PROBING THOUGHTS for PROPHETIC TIMES

1. Why does the very word *victory* imply a preceding battle?
2. In what ways have American professing Christians been progressively prepared to be un-prepared since the early 1970s?
3. What is a Christian's most important weapon in the battle for victory over the world and its deceitful pressures?
4. If persecution arises primarily because of "the offense of the Cross," will you personally be more prone to lay down his cross or to "take up His cross and follow," despite the likelihood of persecution? Don't answer too quickly! Consider this soberly!
5. How would you summarize God's prescription for victory in perilous times?
6. Is it possible to be victorious in spiritual warfare if we persist in yielding to the demands of our flesh?
7. Why is patience essential to trusting God?
8. In what ways does "tribulation work patience" resulting in real hope?

Chapter 7

PREVAIL… OR FAIL

"For the true believer, there is no alternative but to prevail in and by faith."

THERE IS NO SUBSTITUTE FOR VICTORY! There is no compromise with evil. There can be no attitude or action of compromise with the forces of an increasingly godless culture nor accommodation to its demands so as to achieve a modicum of purported peace to evade persecution! Loyalty to Christ and Christ alone is not negotiable. That must be our heart and mindset or our faith will fail.

Failing in Fear

Fear is the heartthrob of spiritual failure. For this reason, God continually urges both Israel and Gentile believers to "fear not." As it is written:

> There is no fear in love; but perfect love casteth out
> fear: because fear hath torment. He that feareth is not
> made perfect in love (I Jn. 4:18).

For a true follower of Jesus, Yeshua HaMaschiach, our Savior and Redeemer, failure through fear is not an option. Again, as the beloved apostle John proclaimed:

For whatsoever is born of God overcometh the world:
and this is the victory that overcometh the world,
even our faith (I Jn. 5:4).

But faith is not only something we *have* but something we *do*. We are told by Jesus' brother:

But be ye doers of the word, and not hearers only,
deceiving your own selves (Jam. 1:22).

The "doings" of **faith** are driven by our **trust** based on our **belief** revealed in our **obedience**. When any or either of these facets of Christian "faith" are weak or non-existent, we will find ourselves facing the eternal precipice of faith failure. Again, this is why our Lord emphasized:

But he that shall endure unto the end, the same shall
be saved (Matt. 24:13; Matt. 10:22; Mk. 13:13).

To *endure* is to persevere faithfully and patiently. We are exhorted to:

…lay aside every weight, and the sin which doth so
easily beset us, and let us run with patience [endur-
ance] the race that is set before us,

Looking unto Jesus the author and finisher of our
faith; who for the joy that was set before him endured
the cross….

For consider him that endured such contradiction
[hostility-persecution] of sinners against himself, lest
ye be wearied and faint in your minds (Heb. 12:1-3).

The Psalmist and prophet David, as a man after God's own heart, had to stand fast in faith against continual persecution. Listen to his cry…

> LORD, how are they increased that trouble me! many are they that rise up against me. Many there be which say of my soul, There is no help for him in God.
>
> **But** thou, O LORD, art a shield for me; my glory, and the lifter of my head [Emphasis Added].
>
> I cried unto the LORD with my voice, and he heard me….
>
> [Therefore…]
>
> I will not be afraid of ten thousands of people, that have set themselves against me round about (Ps. 3:1-6).

David always replaced his natural, fleshly fear with declarations of heart-felt trust, choosing rather to fear the Lord rather than man. David reveals how we can run the race before us victoriously, not denying fear in our flesh but shifting that fear of man to the eternal promise of the fear of the Lord. Find yourself in David's shoes, think identificationally through his thoughts and how terrifying conflict became the foundation for spiritual confidence.

> What man is he that feareth the LORD? him shall he teach in the way that he shall choose. His soul shall dwell at ease….
>
> The secret of the LORD is with them that fear him; and he will shew them his covenant.

O keep my soul, and deliver me: let me not be
ashamed; for I put my trust in thee.

Let integrity and uprightness preserve me; for I wait
on thee (Ps. 25:12-21).

Fear of man inevitably results in spiritual failure. Fear of man leads
to a host of spiritual maladies that scream for false prescriptions to
resolve our troubled minds and hearts.

Prevailing In Faith

To deny that we are living in a time of increasing anxiety is to
prepare to fail. When Jesus, the one who not only was victorious over
death and the grave but who, through the Father's grace, endured the
cross, refusing to escape its pain and reproach by willingly accepting the undeserved persecution that would lead to our redemption,
warned that one of the great signs preceding His return would be

Men's hearts failing them for fear, and for looking
after those things which are coming on the earth…
(Lk. 21:26).

Great persecution arose against the early church for the name of
Christ (Acts 8:1). That persecution became the divinely ordered vehicle through which the gospel was quickly spread throughout the then-
known world. All of the apostles, including Peter, James, John and Paul,
suffered death or exile as a privilege to be named as a follower of Yeshua
the Messiah. Paul, apostle to the Gentiles, made it abundantly clear that:

All that will live godly in Christ Jesus shall suffer persecution (II Tim. 3:12).

Peter, who is said to have been crucified upside down, lovingly
encouraged us, saying:

Beloved, think it not strange concerning the fiery trial
which is to try you, as though some strange thing
happened unto you:

But rejoice, inasmuch as ye are partakers of Christ's
sufferings, that, when his glory shall be revealed, ye
may be glad also with exceeding joy.

If ye be reproached for the name of Christ, happy are
ye; for the spirit of glory and of God resteth upon
you: on their part he is evil spoken of, but on your
part he is glorified (I Pet. 4:12-14).

How, then, do we face such times in faith and not in fear? We must
change our viewpoint concerning persecution. While we do not seek
persecution, neither should we see it as outside the scope of God's will
in and for our lives. Our viewpoint concerning persecution may well
determine the course of our destiny. If fear dominates over faith, we are
sure to fail. In order to avoid persecution, our flesh will demand negoti-
ation with evil. It will require masterful rationalization to justify whatever we deem required to evade or avoid the possibility of persecution;
therefore, we must be prepared for such ultimate spiritual warfare.

For the true believer, there is no alternative but to prevail in and
by faith. For "...this is the victory that overcometh the world, even
our faith" (I Jn. 5:4). Remember—"The just shall live by his faith"
(Hab. 2:4).

Disquietude Determines Destiny

Victory will not tolerate entertaining disquietude in our hearts.
We cannot prevent the test of worry or anxiety from attacking our
fleshly minds, but we cannot provide hospitality for its existence there.
To do so is to live by fear rather than by faith. And "without faith it is
impossible to please him [God]," as we well know (Heb. 11:6).

A quick portrait of disquietude will help us more clearly identify the seductive enemy of our faith and trust in these troubled times. Consider the probative power of these words in diagnosing what often ails us spiritually:

Alarm	Disturbance	Storm
Angst	Fear	Trouble
Anxiety	Foreboding	Turmoil
Care	Fretfulness	Uneasiness
Concern	Nervousness	Unrest
Distress	Restlessness	Worry

These words tell a familiar tale, don't they? They correspond to such words as:

Upsetting	Unsettle	Annoy	Perplex
Unhinge	Upset	Perturb	Vex

Note how these words, both individually and collectively, describe much of our thoughts, attitudes and responses to the troubling and rapidly-rising problems that assault our sensibilities as Christians. But must we allow them to set the course of spiritual failure in the face of persecution?

The psalmist David, second king of Israel, opens a window into his severe trials, their powerful challenge to his faith and trust, and to how we must likewise embrace his victorious resolution. We now visit David again in the midst of agonizing rejection and persecution. How does he gain victory when his soul is overwhelmed? Enter with David, a man after God's own heart, into these several vignettes of overcoming victory.

VIGNETTE ONE (Ps. 42)

My tears have been my meat day and night, while
they continually say unto me, Where is thy God?

When I remember these things, I pour out my soul in me.

Why art thou cast down, O my soul? and why art thou disquieted within me?

David then answers the fleshly torment in his mind.

Hope thou in God: for I shall yet praise him for the help of his countenance.

VIGNETTE TWO (Ps. 43)

Judge me, O God, and plead my cause against an ungodly nation: O deliver me from the deceitful and unjust man.

For thou art the God of my strength: why dost thou cast me off? why go I mourning because of the oppression of the enemy?

O send out thy light and thy truth: let them lead me.

[But] Why art thou [yet] cast down, O my soul? and why art thou disquieted within me?

David then speaks faith to his fleshly mind, will and emotions.

Hope in God: for I shall yet praise him, who is the health of my countenance, and my God.

VIGNETTE THREE (Ps. 27)

The setting of this Psalm begins in verse 12 describing David's painful dilemma.

Deliver me not over unto the will of mine enemies:
for false witnesses are risen up against me, and such as
breathe out cruelty.

And in response, David proclaims one of the greatest declarations of faith and trust in the pages of Scripture, even ensconced in one of the most glorious and classic songs in church history.

The LORD is my light and my salvation; whom shall
I fear? the LORD is the strength of my life; of whom
shall I be afraid?

Though an host should encamp against me, my heart
shall not fear: though war should rise against me, in
this will I be confident.

For in the time of trouble he shall hide me in his
pavilion: in the secret of his tabernacle shall he hide
me; he shall set me up upon a rock.

Hear, O LORD, when I cry with my voice: have
mercy also upon me, and answer me.

…leave me not, neither forsake me, O God of my
salvation.

David resolves his fleshly agony in favor of a victorious declaration of faith.

Wait on the LORD: be of good courage, and he shall
strengthen thine heart: wait, I say, on the LORD.

This was the continued pattern of David's life as revealed through-out the Psalms. All humans will be tested and tried with varying circumstances and degrees of severity. The looming question hovers over each of us as we see the Day of the Lord rapidly approaching.

How should we then live?

The Peace That Prevails

Jesus exhorted His disciples saying, "Let not your heart be troubled" (Jn. 14:1). Yet that same Jesus admonished the same disciples, saying: "In the world ye shall have tribulation: but be of good cheer; I have overcome the world" (Jn. 16:33). It is fascinating, though, that Jesus prefaced that warning by also saying: "These things I have spoken unto you, that in me ye might have peace." Jesus had begun his extended warning to the same disciples, telling them He did not want them to be offended by what they would have to endure, thus depriving them of the peace that only a faithful walk with Christ can give. And then He lowered the boom with a severe warning of persecution coming.

> They shall put you out of the synagogues: yea, the
> time cometh, that whosoever killeth you will think
> that he doeth God a service (Jn. 16:2).

As it was with Jews and their synagogues, so it will be with Gentiles and their churches which will have progressively become "of the world." The peace of Christ is clearly not a peace dependent on circumstances but on our unswerving trust in Him, for "He is our peace" (Eph. 2:14).

There is no negotiated peace with the world through diplomacy. We are *in* the world, but not *of* it. Our peace is secured by the Prince of Peace, not by compromising with the princes of this world for power, perks and position—even in the name of Christ. To seek to evade persecution by political maneuvering is to assume spiritual defeat. We either prevail in the spirit or fail in the flesh.

Have You Decided?

Sometimes the songs of yesteryear help to provide needed focus in times like these. Prayerfully and soberly consider the lyrics of this oft-sung song of the generation last passed. Perhaps its powerful import can here experience a resurrection, enabling us to stand in peace amid an onslaught of persecution. Remember, our Lord not only calls us to *believe* in Him but to *follow* Him.

> I have decided to follow Jesus;
> I have decided to follow Jesus;
> I have decided to follow Jesus;
> No turning back, no turning back.
>
> Tho' none go with me; I still will follow.
> Tho' none go with me; I still will follow.
> Tho' none go with me; I still will follow.
> No turning back, no turning back.
>
> The world behind me, the cross before me;
> The world behind me, the cross before me;
> The world behind me, the cross before me;
> No turning back, no turning back.

We must either prevail… or fail. He that with patience follows faithfully, enduring to the end, shall be saved (Matt. 24:13). "And fear not them which kill the body, but are not able to kill the soul: but rather fear him which is able to destroy both soul and body in hell." "But whosoever shall deny me before men, him will I also deny before my Father which is in heaven" (Matt. 10:28, 33).

> *Hear my cry, O God; attend unto my prayer…*
> *when my heart is overwhelmed: lead me to the*
> *rock that is higher than I (Ps. 61:1-2).*

Chapter 7
PROBING THOUGHTS for PROPHETIC TIMES

1. To what extent do you find yourself confronted with fear or anxiety in response to national or world developments?
2. Are you "tormented" by fear? In what ways?
3. Do you retreat from the battle with fear and anxiety, or do you actively engage in the battle, and if so, how?
4. Do you agree with Jesus' disciple John, that if we are embracing fear and dominated by it, it should cause us to reconsider the degree to which we truly love the Lord? If you disagree, why?
5. Are you prepared, given your current state of mind and heart, to "endure to the end" in the face of a dramatic increase of persecution that may well affect you and your family… or congregation?
6. How would your family or friends evaluate your faith and trust amid these trying times?
7. Are you truly prepared to be victorious even in the face of perhaps violent or threatening attack?
8. What are you doing to strengthen your faith and trust so that you will truly **prevail** in this evil day?

PART 3

PROVISION FOR PERILOUS TIMES

"Worldly conformity so colors our spiritual perception as to blind us to the need for the provision the Lord promises."

GOD IS NOT IGNORANT of the ravages of persecution that will increasingly sweep the earth immediately preceding Christ's return. Christ himself warned of both the fact of such persecution and the supreme testing it would present to His followers (Jn. 16:2).

Jesus made every reasonable effort both to warn of that which would come and to prepare the minds and hearts of those who would claim to be His disciples. He put things into ultimate perspective, helping us to properly perceive the comparative value of preserving fleshly life on earth as compared to eternal life rooted deeply in faith. Showing that He, himself, would lead the way, He announced that His own hour of suffering ultimate persecution had come, but then applied the necessary mind and heart-set to endure to those who would follow. Here are His words.

> He that loveth his life [more than his eternal life]
> shall lose it; and he that hateth [loves much less by

comparison] his life in this world shall keep it unto life eternal.

If any man serve me, let him follow me… if any man serve me, him will my Father honour (Jn. 12:25-26).

We must perceive and value God's provision for perilous times. But in order to truly *perceive* and *value* God's provision, we must first come to not only cognitively admit but to also spiritually embrace the promised reality of the perilous times now sweeping across our world that will soon become a veritable tsunami.

PERILOUS TIMES ARE PERILOUS!

The perilous nature of our times is well understood and is being experienced throughout the non-western world. But in the western world, historically known as "Christian" Europe and "Christian" America, the reality of the true nature of the word *perilous* has not yet been either admitted or experienced to a degree recognized as truly perilous. That presents a clear and present danger for professing Christians to be continually absorbed and conformed to the rapidly degenerating ways of the world and cultural mandates. That worldly conformity so colors our spiritual perception as to render us blinded to the need for the provision the Lord promises to those who love Him. We don't perceive it as *provision* precisely because we do not yet perceive the perilous nature of our times.

We now purposely expose our hearts and minds to the true nature of perilous times, but only for the express purpose of understanding and embracing the spiritual nature of God's provision.

Though I walk in the midst of trouble, thou wilt revive me… thy right hand shall save me (Ps. 138:7).

Chapter 8

A PRICE TO PAY

"We must honestly look at aspects of our alleged faith we have either inadvertently, negligently… or intentionally overlooked."

"JESUS PAID IT ALL," we say and correctly sing. "All to Him I owe." "Sin hath left a crimson stain," declared the hymn, but "He washed it white as snow." Here is a beautifully simple expression of the gospel or good news, but it is not the complete story. It is the rest of the story that is so often missing in our fervor to market salvation as a product. Such "marketing" invariably leaves out what Dietrich Bonhoeffer called "the cost of discipleship."

The cost of discipleship has been largely lost, if not totally abandoned, in the promotion and marketing of westernized Christianity over the last two generations. If we do not perceive and embrace the true cost of what it means, from Jesus' viewpoint, to be His follower, it becomes virtually impossible for us to see the need for His promised provision in perilous times that we do not yet perceive as truly *perilous…* only uncomfortable or disconcerting to varying degrees. It is necessary, then, that we honestly look at aspects of our alleged faith we have either inadvertently, negligently… or intentionally overlooked.

What Is A Christian?

In attempting to honestly answer this question, it becomes necessary to gingerly step around many theological landmines. These landmines, in their various open or hidden expressions, have resulted in at least 2200 denominations plus cults in the United States and over 20,000 denominations throughout the world. Do we all embrace our Lord's viewpoint as to what it means to be His follower? If not, does Jesus have a different standard or expectation for belief, life and practice for each separate denomination? And what of those increasingly "independent" of denominational control and theological belief systems?

For our purposes here, it is not needful that we attempt to parse the purported differences dividing these multitudinous "Christian" systems claiming to define the Kingdom of God and His Christ. Rather, we must attempt to distill, from our Savior's viewpoint and that of His initial disciples, the essence of what it means for all who are allegedly "Christian" to truly be His disciples. It is only to those true followers or disciples that promise is made for provision in these perilous times.

Sound-bite Christianity

In this purportedly modern or post-modern world, including our immediate moment in time and that of the last 50 to 75 years, it has been the increasingly popular way of expressing serious or fundamental principles by reducing them to *sound-bites.* A sound-bite purports to reveal a truth in the most distillable way possible, so as to take little time of expression in an increasingly impatient and non-serious world and culture.

But if, as the apostle Paul warned, "… in the last days perilous times shall come," who was he warning? Was he warning the world at large? Was he warning pagans and professing believers in Christ alike? Was he warning cultural "Christians" born in America and "Christian" Europe? Or was he warning American pew-sitters who have never been converted but have been embraced with open arms in America's mega churches through church-growth and seeker-sensitive marketing, leaving the Master as little more than a religious Mascot?

These are rhetorical questions to which our answers should be obvious—but often aren't. But why are the answers now glaringly obvious? It is because we have, in hyperinflated pursuit of church growth since the 1970s, been in headlong and marketable pursuit of purported "converts," failing at Jesus' most fundamental command to make disciples, "teaching them to observe [obey] all things whatsoever I have commanded you" (Matt. 28:20).

Thus, the Great Commission has become the great "omission," thus dissing the very call to discipleship. Jesus had said "I will build my church," you make disciples (Matt. 16:18), but we, in western Americanized wisdom, decided it better and more marketable to build churches and dismiss discipleship which was deemed relatively unmarketable. And now we find ourselves in a serious dilemma.

Who Are Jesus' Disciples?

To whom are our Lord's promises of provision amid perilous times directed? Can we honestly, with integrity and a "straight face," extend these sobering promises to those who are unconverted but are filling our church-growth pews? Can we pander with holy promises to people whose lives do not remotely reveal their genuine faith requiring discipleship?

This presents an obvious and serious burden upon pastors, priests and para-church leaders who have lightly esteemed Christ's call to discipleship and now, of necessity, find themselves having to preach the fulness of the gospel as revealed in Jesus' own words to their constituents who will likely face shock at the truth.

Consider the following twenty sound-bite expressions often used to define a Christian. Are they absolutely true, and if true themselves, are they lacking "the rest of the story" that makes them truly TRUE?

1. A Christian is one who is "born again."
2. A Christian is one who believes Jesus Christ is God's son.
3. A Christian is one who is a "person of faith."
4. A Christian is one who opposes abortion.
5. A Christian is one who goes to church regularly.

6. A Christian is one who was raised in a Christian family.
7. A Christian is one who prays over a meal.
8. A Christian is one who believes in God.
9. A Christian is one who is nice.
10. A Christian is one who gives to the poor and disenfranchised.
11. A Christian is one who is against racism.
12. A Christian is one who believes the Bible (Whether or not he/she reads it).
13. A Christian is one who has memorized a lot of the Bible.
14. A Christian is one who believes in the family.
15. A Christian is one who lives a clean life.
16. A Christian is always a peacemaker.
17. A Christian always obeys the government.
18. A Christian gives his or herself to poverty.
19. A Christian loves everybody and is inclusive and accepting.
20. A Christian is generous.

Here is the ultimate question. Can one conclude absolutely from any of these assertions that the person described is truly a disciple of Jesus Christ? Your answer should, and must be, a resounding NO. But why?

> **FIRST**—There is no indication of *confession* of sin requiring reconciliation with the Father through Christ.

> **SECOND**—There is no indication of *repentance* of sin and a resulting walk of righteousness.

> **THIRD**—There is no clear indication of commitment to *obey* the Word, Will and Ways of Christ and the Father essential to the very definition of discipleship.

In other words, brethren, we must prepare those we may have led to believe they are entitled to embrace our Lord's promised provisions to actually be qualified as His disciples. As Jesus once said,

> "Not every one that saith unto me, Lord, Lord, shall enter into the kingdom of heaven; but he that doeth the will of my Father which is in heaven" (Matt. 7:21). And again He saith, "Because strait is the gate, and narrow is the way, which leadeth unto life, and few there be that find it" (Matt. 7:14).

The Cost of Discipleship

While God extends His grace and mercy freely, which no one can claim to merit, there is nevertheless a price to pay for following Jesus. Jesus refers to this *cost* as "taking up His cross."

> If any man will come after me, let him deny himself, and take up his cross, and follow me (Matt. 16:24).

What, then, does it mean to "take up your cross"? It is not an idle one-time blithe confession of the full-fledged exchange of a person's previous unregenerate life for the life of Christ which, after repentance, is defined in summary as:

1. "Doing the will of my Father" (Matt. 7:21; Mk. 3:35), and
2. Willing to suffer persecution for His name's sake, even to losing one's life (Mk. 8:34-35; Mk. 13:9-13; Lk. 9:22-24).

This "taking up of one's cross" is not merely a one-time intention, but is rather a daily, life-directing and motivating conviction of mind and heart, as our Lord clearly admonished:

> If any man will come after me, let him deny himself, and **take** up his cross daily, and follow me. (Emphasis added.

> For whosoever will save his life shall lose it: but who-
> soever will lose his life for my sake, the same shall save
> it.
>
> For what is a man advantaged, if he gain the whole
> world, and lose himself, or be cast away?
>
> For whosoever shall be ashamed of me and of my
> words, of him shall the Son of man be ashamed, when
> he shall come in his own glory, and in his Father's,
> and of the holy angels (Lk. 9:23-26).

We are well reminded of this price to pay in following Jesus by Dietrich Bonhoeffer in his famous 1937 book *The Cost of Discipleship*, first published in German and then by 1951 in English. Bonhoeffer distinguishes between what he calls "cheap" and "costly" grace.

> Cheap grace is the preaching of forgiveness without
> requiring repentance, baptism without church dis-
> cipline, Communion without confession…**Cheap
> grace is grace without** discipleship, grace without the
> cross…. (Emphasis added).

Cheap grace, Bonhoeffer says, is to hear the gospel preached as fol-lows: "Of course you have sinned, but now everything is forgiven, so you can stay as you are and enjoy the consolations of forgiveness." The main defect of such false theology, argues Bonhoeffer, is that it con-tains **no** demand for discipleship—to truly follow Jesus.

He points out that as Christianity spread, the Church became more secularized, accommodating the demands of obedience to Jesus to the demands of society. "In this way 'the world was Christianized, and grace became its common property'." Grace was thus cheapened and obedience to Christ was gradually lost…even abandoned.

If those conditions were true in Bonhoeffer's day, how would he, or you, describe the condition of the western church—the American church—today? The so-called "grace awakening" of the last generation has virtually abandoned, even rejected, the call to obedient discipleship, all in the marketing of purported cheap grace for church growth and a non-confrontive gospel of good feelings undermining the fulness of Christian faith.

How then shall such purported behavior stand in the evil day, facing persecution without true grace (God's enabling power) to do His will when life itself is on the line? Who is therefore entitled to claim or have reasonable expectation to receive God's promised provision in perilous times? And what is the nature of those promises? Will they satisfy the expectation of the "cheap grace" generation?

*Hear my voice, O God, in my prayer: preserve my
life from fear of the enemy. Hide me from the secret
counsel of the wicked… (Ps. 64:1-2).*

Chapter 8
PROBING THOUGHTS for PROPHETIC TIMES

1. Do you agree that the "cost of discipleship" has been largely lost over the last two generations? If so, how or why do you think this has occurred?
2. Why might it be necessary to evaluate whether one is a true "Christian" if we are going to discuss any provision God might have made for provision in perilous times?
3. How has "sound-byte" Christianity watered down the serious essence of what it truly means to be Jesus' follower?
4. How would you define a true disciple of Christ?
5. In considering your own life, do you feel confident that you are "taking up your cross daily" in following Jesus?
6. How would you define "cheap grace"?

Chapter 9

PROVISION AMID PERSECUTION

*"If we would purport to 'stand on the promises,' we must
first have standing through faithful obedience to claim them."*

GOD'S PROMISES OF PROVISION in these perilous times are
reserved only for true followers or disciples of Jesus as Savior and
Messiah. True followers are those who not only make some confession
of faith but who, as Jesus said, "…do the will of my Father which is in
heaven" (Matt. 7:21). If we would purport to "stand on the promises,"
we must first have standing through faithful obedience to claim them.
We must, from God's viewpoint, be true disciples.

The Psalmist clearly proclaimed this requirement of standing for
the right to be heard and for provision to be made "in the day of trouble" (Ps. 50:15-23).

> …I will deliver thee, and thou shalt glorify me.
>
> But unto the wicked {speaking to Israel as heirs of the
> promises] God saith, What has thou to do to declare
> my statutes, or that thou shouldest take my covenant
> in thy mouth?
>
> Seeing thou hatest instruction, and castest my words
> behind thee.

…thou thoughtest that I was altogether such an one as thyself: but I will reprove thee….

Now consider this, ye that forget God [those who neither fear nor obey Him], lest I tear you in pieces, and there be none to deliver.

…and to him that ordereth his conversation aright [heart and life ways in obedience to God's will] will I shew the salvation of God.

Hand of God—Heart of Man

The divine hand of God is reserved and promised only to protect and provide the sincere and faithful disciple in troubled and perilous times. God's hand is linked to man's heart revealed by a person's trust as confirmed in and through obedience. We are saved by grace that works by faith through love both for God and the brethren.

Cavalier Christianity will not cut it with God as we rapidly approach the Second Coming of Yeshua whose purpose in coming to earth was to finally "do the will of the Father" so that He could be our sinless Savior. After His resurrection and before His ascension back to the Father, Jesus said to His disciples: "…as my Father hath sent me, even so send I you" (Jn. 20:21). If it is true that without holiness "no man shall see the Lord" (Heb. 12:14), why should we have any realistic expectation of God's protection and provision amid perilous times of persecution unless we are living holy lives?

In other words, there may well be a necessary spiritual preparation in each of our lives as professing Christians to have any true level of confidence of God's provision and protection as unprecedented trials and testings explode on our world, yes, even in America. Whatever our lot, we yearn to be able to say: "It is well, it is well, with my soul." Indeed, the hand of God's provision is predicated, from His perspective alone, on the preparation of our hearts and homes.

Promises To A People

It is generally shocking to our western, Greco-Roman minds, that the promises of God are directed primarily to a *people* rather than to individual *persons*. That "people," throughout the Tanakh or Old Testament, is Israel—the physical descendants of Abraham, Isaac and Jacob. Any promise by which Gentile believers in Yeshua as Messiah become authorized to claim Israel's promise is by reason of our being grafted in to the original "olive tree" which is Israel, as the apostle Paul so clearly (and perhaps troublingly) portrayed in Romans 11:11-29.

It then becomes necessary for all who contend to have standing to claim God's promises, including promises related to rising and foretold persecution, to comprehend how God views and applied His promises to Israel. For just as persecution is promised to believers in Yeshua as the Jewish Messiah, even so is persecution known as *antisemitism* promised to Israel or the Jewish people.

Consider the implications. The prophet Zechariah powerfully, and without any effort to minimize the serious nature of the world's ultimate antagonism toward Israel, declared:

> Behold, the day of the LORD cometh....
>
> For I will gather all nations against Jerusalem to battle; and the city shall be taken, and the houses rifled, and the women ravished; and half of the city shall go forth into captivity, and the residue of the people shall not be cut off from the city (Zech. 14:1-2).

Zechariah then gives hope for Israel. "Then shall the LORD go forth and fight against those nations, as when he fought in the day of battle," yet then tells us, "And Judah also shall fight at Jerusalem..." (Zech. 14:3, 14). Here is what we must consider when we purport to claim the Lord's promises of provision and protection in the face of the rising, inevitable and formidable battle against both Israel and against Gentile Christians. If the Lord fights for Israel, but Judah is also fighting, will any Jews not survive the battle? If some do not survive or suffer injury, has God not fulfilled His promise of victory?

Throughout Scripture, God often promises victory amid battle and provision amid difficult times, but did Israel believe that none would suffer loss despite victory? Absolutely not! They well understood, and to this day continue to believe, that the promises were to a people—NOT to individuals. In our individualistic thinking in the western, Greco-Roman world, we have come to misappropriate or misapply God's promises as if they are primarily to individual persons, and thereby have somewhat perverted or distorted the meaning and implication of those promises.

Here, then, is the problem we face amid the pain of persecution. The western, and particularly the American Christian mind, thinks inwardly: "I myself, will not truly suffer or die, because God has promised victory." Thus, individualism has, to a significant degree, set up professing believers for lack of preparation of heart and life to endure suffering. But of even greater concern is that untold numbers will fall away both for their lack of spiritual preparation and for the profound sense that God has somehow betrayed them by not keeping His promises.

That, then, is the inevitable consequence of the light, "bubble gum" faith that has been served increasingly in our churches since the early 1970s through the church-growth movement, then the seeker-sensitive movement, and most recently the emerging-church movement, all of them progressively exalting the lordship of feelings over genuine faith.

How to Embrace God's Promises

If promises are extended primarily to a people rather than to individuals, how then are we to embrace or appropriate those promises with confidence and with spiritual integrity? This is a supremely challenging question for westernized Christians simply because we are so profoundly individualized by our cultural "DNA."

To help our understanding in this regard, perhaps we should first broadly consider the various categories of God's promises (other than that of eternal salvation) as those promises pertain to times of intensifying persecution. Broadly speaking, we might outline those promises as:

Promises of Provision
Promises of Protection
Promises of Fearlessness
Promises of Courageousness.

While these promises are given to a people claiming to be the Lord's followers—His children—they must also be embraced individually. How, then, are we to embrace them? They must be embraced, as with salvation itself, by grace through faith which correspondingly requires our trust and faithful obedience revealing that trust. It is critical to all of us that we understand that we cannot embrace or claim provision or protection cavalierly—a mindset that is so common among American Christians.

Something is required of us daily, and that is trust revealed in obedience to the Spirit and Word of God against the loud, daily demands of our flesh or carnal nature. In other words, receipt of God's provision and protection in times of intensifying persecution requires us also to be persistent overcomers in the equally intensifying battle of our flesh against the Spirit. This, my brothers and sisters, becomes our moment of truth in the valley of daily decision. Will we be prepared to "endure to the end" (Matt. 24:13)?

Failure to understand our participatory role will, unfortunately, lead many to feel betrayed by God and to turn from Him when they do not feel that "God is coming through" on His promises. That same sense of betrayal will likely manifest when many fail to understand promised provision and protection from God's viewpoint.

Now, after such a seemingly long preparatory foundational discussion, we proceed to embrace the promises to a holy people of

Provision, Protection, Fearlessness and Courageousness as persecution presses upon us.

Promises of the "I AM"

God proclaims Himself to be our "I AM." When Moses inquired as to whom he should say had sent him to the Children of Israel as they came out of Egypt, the "house of bondage," He responded "I AM THAT I AM" and you shall say to Israel, "I AM hath sent me unto you" (Ex. 3:14).

In other words, by declaring Himself the I AM, God summarizes who He is in practical, definable terms which He later identifies throughout the Torah, including the more familiar descriptive names:

Jehovah Jireh—Jehovah our Provider
Jehovah Rapha—Jehovah our Healer
Jehovah Nissi—Jehovah our Banner
Jehovah Shalom—Jehovah our Peace
Jehovah Ra-ah—Jehovah our Shepherd.

God, by declaring Himself to be our I AM is, in effect, proclaiming…

I AM your Provider;
I AM your Healer;
I AM your Banner;
I AM your Peace;
I AM your Shepherd; and
I AM your "Commander in Chief" of My Kingdom
army of righteous warriors in which you serve.

That, dear brothers and sisters, is our incredible umbrella of protection under which lay all of God's promises of

Provision

    Protection

        Fearlessness and

            Courageousness.

To reinforce the overarching solemnity of God's self-described identity for humankind, God opens His Word in Genesis 1:1 by declaring Himself Creator and Elohim. The title Elohim is superlative in substance, meaning "supreme one" or "mighty one"—the infinite, all-powerful God who is not only Creator but is also Sustainer and Supreme Judge of the world. Elohim is the primary title used for God in the Old Testament or Tanach, and is used 2599 times throughout the Bible.

When Elohim speaks, His promises are sure when properly understood. Therefore, we can rest upon those promises when we have proper standing before Him and rightly comprehend the purpose and extent of those promises. We begin by embracing Elohim's promises of Provision.

Promises of Provision

When God promises to provide, He declares He will make available everything necessary to accomplish His will, as defined solely by His own viewpoint. His promises to provide our needs are made to a people group He alone identifies as called by His name and who purport to be His people.

In order for us to individually claim any of God's promises, including the promises of provision, we individually must belong to the group or people to whom the promises are made. Only then, by implication, can we claim those promises as individual persons or families. In other words, all broad promises are inclusive only to the people group to whom they are given.

It is critically important to understand this basic fact concerning God's promises so as not to find ourselves individually or as families claiming promises to which we have no entitlement to claim as seen or determined by God. We must have *right standing* with God, walking faithfully in His Word, Will and Ways, to claim such eligibility. When we do not conduct our lives with integrity according to God's expectation, we are likely to lay claim to promises anyway and thus believe that we have somehow been betrayed when we believe those promises have not been met. This sense of betrayal will likely cause millions of fringe "believers" to fall away from their alleged faith, claiming God cannot be trusted, leading them to cast their trust on the promises of a counterfeit savior—the Antichrist and his global beast system.

What Level of Provision is Promised?

Our Father's level of provision is both broad and narrow. It is broad in that the promise is made to the entire people group to which the promise is made. It is narrow because the nature of the specific fulfillment of the promise is somewhat unique for the individuals within that people group.

God is a Father and desires to provide for His children—the true family of God—just as a true earthly father should provide for his own flock. Each child is provided sufficiently for his or her needs, but the needs may be somewhat different depending on age, maturity or other need-specific situations for each child, such as the life/health challenges faced. It is not that one is loved more or less, but rather that the unique needs regarding health, education and relative life directions differ, thus requiring the father's wisdom to righteously discern those differences without playing favorites. God, as Father, is very acutely aware of our specific needs, depending upon His purposes and plan for our individual lives.

God's economy does not mandate absolute equality of provision, but rather sufficient provision for each to accomplish his or her life purpose in the Father's household/Kingdom. God, as our Father, has not committed Himself to a communistic standard of "equity" so as to level out all in His family to absolute sameness. Genuine *equity* and *equality* have been dramatically perverted in our generation to remove all human motivation to contribute meaningfully either to the family or to society at large... or to His Kingdom purposes. Such leveling has clearly created a selfish sense of entitlement rather than profound and humble sense of gratitude essential to God's Kingdom purposes.

God, even in the face of growing persecutions, has promised to provide all our needs and an abundance for every good work He requires of us (Phil. 4:9; II Cor. 9:8). However, as persecution rises, it places increasing pressure upon otherwise normal circumstances and the provisions to which we have become accustomed. For those who are not spiritually prepared to endure rapidly expanding persecution, their faith in the Lord will quickly become frayed, seriously testing their trust in God, and thereby many will fall away and apostacize from their once-claimed faith, shifting their trust to the temporal promises of the rising beast empire of the counterfeit christ.

Coming levels of persecution will try and test the faint of heart whose faith is not deeply rooted. For those who have grasped the severity of this hour of history and have purposed to exercise their faith in preparation, they will be strong in the Lord and in the power of His might to endure the tsunami of legal, health and economic trials that will test their faith, perhaps even to death.

Remember—God will never leave you nor forsake you, but you can forsake Him. No man, woman, power or authority can take you out of the Father's hand so long as your faith still holds to the solid rock which is Christ Jesus—Messiah. Faith demands trust, and trust is evident in obedience, without wavering. There is no other way! Let the joy of the Lord be your strength notwithstanding the avalanche of persecution coming upon us (Neh. 8:10; Heb. 12:2; Jam. 12:2).

One can almost hear the thundering hoof beats of the apocalypse approaching. The resounding rumble of the chariots of Heaven and Hell reverberate through the spiritual and political machinations of man throughout the earth, awaiting the grand finale as the clash of the Sword of the Lord and the swords of the Antichrist echo the resounding chords announcing the end of history. The Father is preparing to send His Son to sit on the throne of David as the long-expected divine Potentate to rule this planet in righteousness. People get ready! Anchor the seatbelts of your chariots for the roughest ride ever to challenge the likes of men since Creation.

Resting On God's Provision

God, as a righteous Father, has promised to provide all of our needs, not necessarily our desires (Phil. 4:19). Our actual needs may vary according to circumstances and God's purposes to be accomplished in and through our respective lives as His true family of genuine, believing followers. And He has assured us that He knows our needs even before we ask (Matt. 6:8).

Yet the very apostle Paul who assured us that God would provide our needs made clear that such provision, depending upon God's purposes in our own individual lives and the circumstances surrounding those purposes, may not always match our own desires or expectations, and that such failure to meet our own definition of "need" did not merit our feeling that God has not fulfilled His promises. Listen carefully to Paul's attitude toward God's provision.

> I know both how to be abased, and I know how to abound: every where and in all things I am instructed both to be full and to be hungry, both to abound and to suffer need (Phil. 4:12).

> I can do all things through Christ which strengtheneth me (Phil. 4:12).

> I have learned, in whatsoever state I am, therewith to be content (Phil. 4:11).

> But my God shall supply [as He does for Paul] all your need according to his riches in glory by Christ Jesus (Phil. 4:19).

Rejoice in the Lord always: and again I say, rejoice (Phil. 4:4).

Be careful [anxious] for nothing; but in every thing by prayer and supplication **with thanksgiving** let your requests be made known unto God (Phil. 4:6; emphasis added).

And the peace of God, which passeth all understanding, shall keep your hearts and minds through Christ Jesus (Phil. 4:7).

The message is clear. Trust the Lord in everything. Lean not on your own understanding or fleshly perception. Rest in the Lord, in every situation, and wait patiently for Him and His provision, for which you and I must give thanks—always—and Rejoice.

Provision, from God's perspective, seems invariably to be predicated on our deep trust in His overarching purposes. Sometimes needed provision comes from advance preparation, sometimes from unsuspecting places, and sometimes through miraculous intervention. Yet in every situation, the Lord reminds us as He did Paul: "My grace [enabling power and favor] is sufficient for thee: for my strength is made perfect in weakness" (II Cor. 12:9).

How Does God Provide?

It is very difficult for western Christians, and particularly for American Christians, to recognize and embrace God's provision when our current cultural standards and expectations are not met. We are not accustomed to any serious measure of having to endure any discomfort or sense of lack according to our current cultural expectations in the "land of plenty." But an environment of intensifying persecution through unexpected incarceration and various forms of economic pressure and deprivation rapidly changes our perception of need. It is precisely these threats that will compel the vast majority to capitulate to the promises of global government and to receive the "Mark of the Beast" without which no man may buy or sell (Rev. 13:17). Perhaps now we can better understand Jesus' warning:

> But he that shall endure unto the end, the same shall be saved (Matt. 24:13; Mk. 13:13; Matt. 10:22).

So… how does God provide? His promises issue directly from both His character as a Father and His very being as Elyon—the most high God. For this reason, whether or not we as westerners are satisfied, God expresses His promises of provision broadly in more generic terms that require our trust to embrace. Here is a sampling as to how the character and essence of Elohim as Jehovah Jireh or Jehovah Rapha was embraced by saints or declared by God in both Old and New Testaments.

Ps. 9:9—The LORD also will be… a refuge in times of trouble.

Ps. 9:10—They that know thy name will put their trust in thee: for thou, LORD, has not forsaken them that seek thee.

Ps. 33:18-22—Behold, the eye of the LORD is upon them that fear him, upon them that hope in his mercy; To deliver their soul from death, and to keep them alive in famine.

> Our soul waiteth for the LORD: he is our help and our shield.

> For our heart shall rejoice in him, because we have trusted in his holy name.

Ps. 46:1-2—God is our refuge and our strength, a very present help in trouble. Therefore will not we fear…

II Cor. 12:9—My grace is sufficient for thee: for my strength is made perfect in [your] weakness.

Phil. 4:19—But my God shall supply all your need according to his riches in glory by Christ Jesus.

Heb. 4:16—Let us therefore come boldly unto the throne of grace, that we may obtain mercy, and find grace [favor and enabling power] to help in time of need.

Heb. 13:6—The Lord is my helper, and I will not fear what man shall do unto me.

Promises of Protection

Once again, God's promises of protection; as with provision, are generic but must be embraced specifically, depending upon the circumstances we face. There are many ways in and through which our lives may be endangered, but persecution is a prevailing cause. These promises can only be embraced by faith through hope wrapped securely in the comfort of the Father's love, but always resting in the Lord's greater purposes. Here is a representative sampling to strengthen our understanding.

Ps. 59:16—I will sing of thy power… of thy mercy… for thou hast been my defense and refuge in the day of my trouble.

Ps. 60:11-12—Give us help from trouble: for vain is the help of man.

Through God we shall do valiantly: for he it is that shall tread down our enemies.

Ps. 62:2, 8—[God] only is my rock and my salvation; he is my defense; I shall not be greatly moved.

Trust in him at all times; ye people, pour out your
heart before him: God is a refuge for us.

Ps. 7:10—My defense is of God, which saveth the upright in heart.

Ps. 3:1-7—LORD, how are they increased that trouble me! many are
they that rise up against me… which say of my soul, There is
no help for him in God.

But thou, O LORD, art a shield for me… I will not
be afraid of ten thousands of people, that have set
themselves against me round about.

Ps. 17:5, 7-8—Hold up my goings in thy paths, that my footsteps
slip not.

O thou that savest by thy right hand them which put
their trust in thee…. Keep me as the apple of the eye,
hide me in the shadow of thy wings.

Ps. 18:2-3—The LORD is my rock, and my fortress, and my deliverer;
my God, my strength, in whom I will trust… my high tower.

I will call upon the LORD… so shall I be saved from
mine enemies.

Ps. 27:3, 5—Though an host should encamp against me, my heart
shall not fear….

For in the time of trouble he shall hide me in his
pavilion: in the secret of his tabernacle shall he hide
me; he shall set me upon a rock.

Protection From Fear

Ps. 27:1—The LORD is my light and my salvation; whom shall I fear? the LORD is the strength of my life; of whom shall I be afraid?

Ps. 46:1—God is our refuge and strength, a very present help in trouble.

Ps. 56:1-4—Be merciful unto me, O God: for man would swallow me up; he fighting daily oppresseth me. [But…]

> What time I am afraid, I will trust in thee… I will not
> fear what flesh can do unto me.

Ps. 112:1, 7-8 Blessed is the man that feareth the LORD, that delighteth greatly in his commandments.

> He shall not be afraid of evil tidings: his heart is fixed,
> trusting in the LORD. His heart is established, he
> shall not be afraid….

Provision of Courage

Courage is manifested by our choice in time of challenge and conflict. Courage is proven, not in the absence of persecution, but in the face of persecution. Perhaps this is why the writer of Hebrews reminds us of the nature of true faith that is often missing or ignored.

> Now the just shall live by faith: but if any man draw
> back [fail to advance courageously], my soul shall have
> no pleasure in him.

> But we are not of them who draw back unto perdition
> [shrink in the face of persecution]; but of them that

believe [act courageously by faith in the face of serious trials] to the saving of the soul (Heb. 10:38-39).

It may be shocking, but is true. GOD NEVER PROMISES COURAGE! Rather, God expects us to live courageously as a clear and convincing demonstration of our alleged faith. In spiritual reality, courage wanes when our faith wanes and our trust in God, His character and His promises, is absent when tested.

"Courage arises in response to the call of duty. But duty is no longer easily defined because we have done cultural violence to the sources from which duty flows.

> To the extent that I step out from under any authority in my life, I lose my sense of duty that arises from that relationship. If I step out from under God's authority, either by direct decision or by my behavior over time, I lose my sense of the duties that emanate from that relationship.[49]

As I gradually shed my ultimate allegiance to God's absolute authority, I then claim increasing rights while shedding corresponding responsibility to conform to God's Word, Will and Ways, thus losing my sense of obligation to live courageously when confronted by whatever seems to threaten my professed allegiance to God.

Courage requires absolute confidence in God's plans and purposes so as to face fear in the face of persecution. Courage therefore is revealed, not in the absence of fear, but when confronted with the test of fear. For this reason, we are, as with Israel, enjoined repeatedly to "fear not." It is not the Lord who removes fear, but it is we, who absolutely place our trust in Him, who choose at any particular moment of challenge, to respond in fear or in courageous faith. This is the prevailing pattern by which we find ourselves challenged throughout

Scripture to live courageously notwithstanding potentially fearful consequences. The Holy Spirit is encouraging us to re-establish courage NOW for the promised times of testing encompassing the earth… including the apostatizing West and America.

Let us embrace with courage the encouragement that the Lord gave to others before us who faced daunting and fearful circumstances.

Josh. 1:5-9—Be strong and of a good courage… only be thou strong and very courageous… that thou mayest prosper whithersoever thou goest.

> Have I not commanded thee? Be strong and of a good courage; be not afraid, neither be thou dismayed: for the LORD thy God is with thee withersoever thou goest.

Deut. 20:1-4—When thou goest out to battle against thine enemies… and shall say… Hear, O Israel… let not your hearts faint, fear not, and do not tremble, neither be ye terrified because of them;

> For the LORD your God is he that goeth with you, to fight for you against your enemies, to save you.

Ps. 27:1, 3, 14—The LORD is my light and my salvation; whom shall I fear? the LORD is the strength of my life; of whom shall I be afraid?

> Though an host should encamp against me, my heart shall not fear:

> Wait on the LORD; be of good courage, and he shall strengthen thine heart: wait, I say, on the LORD.

What is Your Courage Quotient?

Courage is not much needed to do what I want, but it is much needed to do what I ought. Courage is forged in the crucible of faith-infused conscience. When the conscience is seared by disobedience, in whole or in part, the Word, Will or Ways of God as expressed in His Word, courage has a hollow ring. "Conscience in the soul is the root of all true courage," reflected J.F. Clarke. "If a man would be brave, let him learn to obey his conscience."[50]

Courage is the backbone of moral character and genuine faith. When courage weakens, the back slumps. When courage leaves, the back is broken. And the moral back of the American church is slumping seriously. Courage is inextricably linked to all aspects of character and moral behavior. The simple truth is that courage links all of character, morality and faith into a single operative body that enables a man or woman to "take a stand."

"A decline in courage may be the most striking feature which an outside observer notices… in our days," wrote Aleksander Solzhenitsyn. "From ancient times, decline in courage has been considered the beginning of the end."[51] We must take courage! So, taking honest inventory, what is your courage quotient? Are you known in your family and among those with whom you associate as courageous… or as a compromiser? How might Heaven rate your courage quotient? Are you able to truly stand in this increasingly evil day, regardless of the consequences? Does persistent fear paralyze your faith? Will rising persecution prove your lack of courage? And what must change to prepare your heart for the persecution Christ promised would try His followers as we approach the very end of time?

The ancient sage Goethe left us words well worth our serious personal and collective consideration amid the advancing times that will "try men's souls."

Wealth lost, something lost;

Honor lost, much lost;
Courage lost, all lost.[52]

O God, be not far from me: O my God, make
haste for my help. Let them be confounded… that
are adversaries to my soul (Ps. 71:12-13).

Chapter 9
PROBING THOUGHTS for PROPHETIC TIMES

1. Why is it so hard for western, especially American, Christians to comprehend that the promises of God are primarily to a *people* rather than to *individuals*?
2. If I, as a professing Christian, am walking in continuous and unrepentant disobedience to God's Word, Will or Ways, do I have any reasonable right to claim His promises? Why... or why not?
3. When God promised victory to Israel when they took the Promised Land or when they were later attacked by enemies, did all Israelites survive the battles, or did many actually risk their lives that victory might be gained by the nation in fulfillment of God's promises?
4. Has God promised equal provision or equal protection to all individuals within either Israel or His Church?
5. If God's general promises of provision and protection cannot be claimed with absolute certainty as to what I personally expect the promise to mean to me, in what way are we to understand the names by which God has chosen to reveal Himself?
6. Why is resting on our Lord's ultimate plans and purposes in the broader scope of His Kingdom essential for our true trust in Him, regardless of how things may seem to pan out for us personally in the short term?
7. To what extent are you tormented by fear? What is it that leads you to fear?
8. How can we, how can you, resolve the potentially paralyzing conflict between *fear* and real *faith*?

Chapter 10

PREVAILING FAITH AMID PERSECUTION

"Persecution will test our patience, but
Genuine faith will enable us to prevail."

"THIS IS THE VICTORY that overcometh the world, even our faith"
(I Jn. 5:9). Without such faith, "it is impossible to please" God. We
must not only believe IN God or that He exists, but rather we must
truly believe Him—that He is truly "a rewarder of them that diligently
seek Him" (Heb. 11:6). Yet the spiritual battle against our souls, both
from within and without, is raging. Spiritual survival demands victory.
Here, then, is the true test of our faith.

The Battle Lines Are Drawn

For decades, perhaps generations, we, as professing Christians,
have faced varying levels of what might be best described as spiritual
skirmishes. Yes, these entry-level skirmishes have presented challenges
to the broader body of Christ, but for western professing followers
of Jesus as Messiah, they have been relatively minor in light of biblical prophecy. Such preparatory skirmishes exploded to biblically prophetic proportions in many non-western nations.

The levels of persecution experienced throughout the non-western
nations is now dramatically metastasizing throughout the Western purportedly "Christian" nations, reaching blasphemous levels supported

shockingly by American popular culture and politics. Manifestation of these changes within the United States have become clear as revealed in the unprecedented political and cultural divide into what is commonly identified as "blue" states and "red" states. While those are generic, broad-brush designations describing the *political* divide, at root they more accurately describe the *spiritual* divide.

It is not a spiritual divide only, but is rather a spiritual war that now rages throughout the "Land of the Free" that is now increasingly becoming only the "Home of the Brave." The violence coursing through America's and Europe's streets is a litmus test revealing Jesus' warning that "as it was in the days of Noah, so shall it be in the days of the Son of man [the period just preceding Christ's return]" (Lk. 17:26). Lawlessness prevails, preparing the way for exacerbated persecution against those who follow God's laws of righteousness.

As recorded in Genesis 6:5, "God saw that the wickedness of man was great in the earth, and that every imagination of the thoughts of his heart were evil only continually." As sexual perversion, immorality and all manner of licentiousness has now become normative and even celebrated, often now even in our churches, only the blood of the saints will soon satiate the explosive rage oozing through the pores of popular culture and its representative politicians who despise both biblical and constitutional authority, incessantly screaming "I'll do it my way!"

The battle lines are being drawn, almost with precision. The "Fear of the Lord" has been not only abandoned but despised throughout America and the West. Therefore, those whose lives are guided fundamentally by "The Fear of the Lord" and biblical authority are to be despised and rejected at best, and to be ultimately driven from society as the enemies of global peace through persecution. He that hath ears to hear, let him hear!

Only Faith Can Prevail!

Remember again—"This is the victory that overcometh the world, even our faith" (I Jn. 5:4). Some may perceive the intensity of this focus on coming persecution to be unpleasant—even morbid—but how we choose to receive it depends largely on whether we are viewing things primarily through our feelings or through faith. Faith looks forward, embracing God's viewpoint in every situation, regardless of how it seems to my flesh in the short term.

Faith is not primarily a "religion" or an assertion of the truth of certain biblical facts. Rather, faith is a walk or life of persistent trust in the Lord, regardless of circumstances. Genuine faith births genuine hope, and such hope "maketh not ashamed" (Rom. 5:5). As we will soon learn, faith demands patience. And for now, until the return of Christ—the blessed hope of the Church (Tit. 2:13)—Paul exhorts us.

> Now the God of hope fill you with all joy and peace
> in believing, that ye may abound in hope, through the
> power of the Holy Ghost (Rom. 15:23).

Just as we are saved by grace alone, through faith alone, in Christ alone, even so we live and run the race before us with patient endurance, by grace alone, through faith alone, in Christ alone, pressing persistently toward the mark for the prize of the high calling of God in Christ Jesus (Phil. 3:14). Persecution will test our patience, but genuine faith will enable us to prevail, that we also might be included in the annals of faith just as those who are recorded in Hebrews 11.

While many of the saints celebrated for their faith in that great faith chapter received recognition for how they lived, others received recognition for how they died, yet "these all, having obtained a good report through faith, received not the [ultimate] promise:

> God having provided some better thing for us, that
> they without us should not be made perfect" (Heb.
> 11:39-40).

Prevail... or Fail

No man or woman now knows the level of testing he or she will ultimately face as history marches toward its prophetic culmination.

What we do know and of which we can be confident is that God's grace—His favor and enabling, sustaining power, are sufficient for every situation notwithstanding our own felt inability to stand strong and courageously. If we do not fall back in spiritual paralysis, but rather persist in pressing toward the mark of God's high calling, we can and will endure every trial and threat thrown against us.

Yet it is we who must endure. It is we, armed by God's Spirit and His Word, who must prevail. No weapon formed against us will prosper so long as we trustingly place ourselves daily in the Father's hand. To prevail we must endure whatever persecution comes, even to the end of life itself. We are not promised relief from human persecution and any accompanying pain, but we are promised that through it all our trust will be strengthened and proven and that as we prevail in faith, we will not be exposed to the final outpouring of God's wrath on the "children of disobedience" (Eph. 5:6; Col. 3:6).

William Penn, founder of Pennsylvania, gave up status as a favored lawyer to seek first the Kingdom of God and His righteousness. Much to the heartbreak of his father, he gave up his brilliant future to join with the Society of Friends, or Quakers, who were greatly scorned and ridiculed.

Young Penn became a preacher and writer for which he suffered imprisonment three times for his faith. He was once imprisoned in the Tower of London for eight months where many men met their demise through execution. It was there that Penn wrote the classic book, *No Cross, No Crown.*

"Christ's cross," he wrote, "is the way to Christ's crown."

He boldly wrote:

> [The false notion] that they may be children of God, while in a state of disobedience to his holy commandments; and disciples of Jesus, though they revolt from his cross, and members of his true church, which is

without spot or wrinkle, notwithstanding their lives are full of spots and wrinkles; is, of all other deceptions upon themselves, the most pernicious to their eternal condition. For they are at peace in sin, and under a security in their transgression.[53]

William Penn, who had experienced so much religious persecution for his faith in England, established the colony of Pennsylvania as a land of religious freedom for all Christians. "No people can be truly happy," he wrote, "though under the greatest enjoyment of civil liberties, if abridged of… their religious profession and worship."[54] "True Godliness doesn't turn men out of the world, but enables them to live better in it, and excites their endeavours to mend it."[55]

It was Penn, who later wrote to Peter the Great, Czar of Russia, declaring words that have endured the centuries:

Those who will not be governed by God will be ruled by tyrants.

Tyrants Will Indeed Rule

Lamentably, tyrants have and will continue to rule, culminating in history's most terrifying tyrant governed by Satan himself—the Antichrist. His relatively short-term dominion shall, as Daniel prophesied and the Apocalypse confirmed, "… the same shall make war with the saints, and prevail against them" (Dan. 7:21). That "fourth beast" that completes mankind's final effort to rule the planet in absolute power shall persist in tyrannical domination over all who are perceived to stand in opposition for a period of 3½ years until the kingdom and dominion "shall be given to the people of the saints of the most High, whose kingdom is an everlasting kingdom…" (Dan. 7:27).

During that interim 3½ year period of absolute tyrannical reign by the counterfeit christ—Satan's chosen emissary—the Antichrist "shall speak great words against the most High, and shall wear out [persecute with a vengeance] the saints of the most High, and… they shall be given into his hand until a time and times and the dividing of time" [3½ years] (Dan. 7:25).

It should be clear beyond doubt, therefore, that those who the Scriptures describe as saints are specifically to be prepared for persecution. The word *saints* is not relegated solely to the Old Testament, referring, as some contend, only to purported Jewish saints, but refers even more expressly to believers in Jesus Christ as repeated at least 60 times throughout the New Testament epistles, including 13 times in the Apocalypse—the Book of Revelation.

When the end-time tyrant gains prominence and power, it will be by the permission and persuasion of the ungodly. That immense satanic power and purpose will then be directed by a spiritualized laser force against all who purport to be in resistance, either in principle or practice. It is called PERSECUTION!

The Challenge to Prevail

It is in the face and force of that unprecedented global persecution that genuine followers, saints of Christ, must prevail… or fail. Here, then, are the heart-challenging questions requiring sincere response manifested in our lives and choices.

1. What does it mean to prevail in the face of unprecedented persecution?
2. Who is it that must prevail?
3. What is required of each professed saint to prevail?
4. When will the pressure of persecution end?
5. Why will the pressure of persecution persist and seem interminable?
6. Where will persecution be most severely focused? AND…
7. What are the consequences of failure to prevail?

We must remember, and intentionalize and teach Jesus' warning words to those we love and serve—"But he that shall endure to the end shall be saved."

> *Out of the depths have I cried unto thee, O*
> *LORD. Lord, hear my voice… be attentive to the*
> *voice of my supplications (Ps. 130:1-2).*

Chapter 10
PROBING QUESTIONS for PROPHETIC TIMES

1. Is it hard for you to grasp the extent to which persecution of Christians has multiplied… even exploded… throughout the world? Why?
2. Have you or any friend or relative experienced some level of persecution for your or their faith in Christ? Give specifics.
3. Can you see how the abandonment of the Fear of the Lord has led to a spirit of lawlessness undergirding growing persecution? How?
4. How do you think you will be able to stand, without compromise, if you were to face severe persecution? Have you considered such a moment of truth and testing?
5. Why could the apostle Paul declare so definitely that "All who live godly in Christ Jesus will suffer persecution?" Didn't Jesus say almost the same thing?
6. Have you been taught or led to believe that you will not have to face significant persecution? Do you truly believe such teaching to be true? How might such teaching prepare you for feeling betrayed?
7. How might such a feeling of betrayal affect your faith?

PART 4

PATIENCE for
PERILOUS TIMES

"… an inbred level of impatience leaves us perhaps
the most unprepared people in world history."

IMPATIENCE IS OUR NATURAL INCLINATION! If our flesh inclines naturally to impatience, our ability to endure triumphantly amid escalating persecution will demand a level of patience dramatically contrary to the response patterns most characteristic of westerners and particularly of Americans who have been culturally seduced to expect everything to happen instantly… or else.

This ever-deepening cultural expectation for instantaneous response to ever-intensifying demands has paved the way for what is now commonly identified as an *entitlement* mentality now pervasive among the most recent three generations within the last fifty years, with each successive generation claiming ever-greater entitlement. Rather than being a people relatively well prepared to endure difficulties, we have inbred a level of impatience leaving us perhaps the most unprepared people in world history.

If that be even close to the reality of our cultural milieu, what then should we expect to be the condition of those who profess to be saints—true, sincere and serious followers of our Savior? Scripture gives us a clear answer… if we have "ears to hear."

Cause me to hear thy lovingkindness in the morning; for in thee do I trust: cause me to know the way wherein I should walk; for I lift up my soul unto thee (Ps. 143:8).

Chapter 11

PATIENCE OF THE SAINTS

"Patience is essential to perfection of our faith enabling us to 'endure to the end'."

PATIENCE IS NOT TANGIBLE. It cannot be discerned with our five senses, yet we are able (at least to some extent) to discern patience from others when in our presence. Interestingly, it seems a fact of human nature to expect a level of patience from others we do not expect of ourselves. Yet our Lord expects us, as His genuine followers, to be characterized by a dimension of patience imitating His patience with us.

But why does God expect us to manifest patience as a life pattern? There are a few reasons, each of which may appear to be a corollary of the others.

FIRST—Patience is a manifestation of the Father's love for us as revealed in His Son, and we are enjoined to be "… followers [imitators] of God, as dear children; And walk in love, as Christ hath loved us…" (Eph. 5:1-2).

SECOND—Patience is a fruit of the Spirit, which is revealed in love, joy, peace, longsuffering [patience], gentleness, goodness and faith… (Gal. 5:22). If the "fruit of the Spirit" is not manifest in and through our life, one could rightly question whether we are truly governed by God's Spirit at all.

THIRD—Jesus' brother, James, advised us that we must "let patience have her perfect work, that we may be perfect and entire, wanting [lacking] nothing (Jam. 1:4).

FOURTH—Patience is required to endure temptation (Jam. 1:2).

FIFTH—Patience is essential to endure persecution and the ultimate testing of the coming Mark of the Beast (Rev. 14:9-12).

Patience—Cousin of Endurance

When Jesus both warned and exhorted that "he that shall endure unto the end, the same shall be saved" (Matt. 24:13), He was speaking of a life of patient pressing forward, without any turning back, as the apostle Paul also expressed so poignantly:

> I count not myself to have apprehended [arrived]: but this one thing I do, forgetting those things that are behind, and reaching forth unto those things which are before, I press toward the mark for the prize of the high calling of God in Christ Jesus (Phil. 3:13-14).

The *pressing* that Paul embraced demanded patient endurance through "many dangers, toils and snares," including persistent persecution. For this reason, the "patience of the saints" is frequently in modern translations, referred to as the "endurance of the saints." This patience or endurance of the saints—of true followers of Jesus, Yeshua HaMashiach—is perhaps the most important focus required if we are to be victorious in faith as we face the coming tsunamic wave of persecution.

Patience's Perfect Work

Jesus' brother, James, well understood what we now face with the promised severe testing of our faith through flagrant persecution. His instructions are simple, yet simply profound—if we are to live victoriously when the assaults against the faithful are vast, defying our comprehension.

My brethren, count it all joy when ye fall into divers [many] temptations [trials];

Knowing this, that the trying of your faith worketh patience [endurance or staying power].

But let patience have her perfect work, that ye may be perfect and entire, wanting [lacking] nothing (Jas. 1:2-4; emphasis added).

Patience is essential to our faith being perfected so that we are able to "endure to the end." Endurance does not come naturally. It must be developed or perfected by testing and by facing resistance, pressure or opposition. Many begin a race, but may also quit. Many enter college, yet many never graduate.

Training for Patient Endurance

Permit me to personalize this demand for patient endurance. Before commencing law school, which would demand four years of my study all while working full time, we were all solemnly informed in a group orientation that we would face two major obstacles. FIRST—nearly half of those who began would not complete the four-year course. SECOND—nearly half of those currently married would no longer be married by the end. Those warnings proved true. A large percentage of those pursuing their desired goal failed to reach it by reason of inability to endure with patience and yet persist with the other demands of life. Marriages then, and now, fail for lack of patient endurance, capitulating to temporary pressures and temptations crying for relief. With gratitude and fortitude, my wife and I have pressed on now since 1966.

For nine years before graduating from law school, I was a public-school teacher. Before commencing the all-consuming study of law, I found myself engaged in some significant mountaineering; climbing peaks, hiking, and rock climbing, all of which tested my physical endurance but also my mental and emotional ability to press through often challenging circumstances involving risk, fear, cardiovascular and muscle strength, and the mental and spiritual fortitude to endure despite a body sometimes screaming for relief and the temptation to quit.

Gratefully, I had a patient climbing partner who was endowed with a DNA of fearlessness and an undauntable cardiovascular system. And so, he patiently endured and encouraged me when I was physically and mentally tested and tried, thus lifting my spirits, just as we in the body of Christ are called to do when faced with persecution. What an amazing four-year lesson God provided to enable me to share the spiritual calling of patient endurance with you. And that was just the beginning. So, take courage, and press onward! You undoubtedly have your own story to tell of testing to develop patient endurance.

Pressing Toward the Mark

The calling to patient endurance is of far greater significance than what American Christians may believe and are willing to embrace. This fundamental weakness in our purported faith is due primarily to having become accustomed to a life of relative ease and to the unwillingness of our pastors, priests, broadcasters and publishers to truly teach the necessity of patient endurance amid serious testing, including persecution and its attendant suffering. In summary, suffering does not sell. It is perceived as an unmarketable message, rendering most American professing Christians drastically and dangerously unprepared for the waves of persecution now advancing even throughout a historically "Christian" based nation.

The apostle Paul faced immense persecution over and over again, yet he did not waver in faith despite the death-blows he received. It is he who encourages us not to give up, not to waver, not to apostacize, but rather to press forward the more so. Let his words become your testimony both now and until Yeshua returns.

> I press toward the mark for the prize of the high calling of God in Christ Jesus (Phil. 3:14).

> I know both how to be abased, and I know how to
> abound… both to abound and to suffer need.
>
> I can do all things through Christ which strength-
> eneth me (Phil. 4:12-13).

Pressing toward the mark demands effort and patient endurance. To *press*, is to press on notwithstanding adverse circumstances. And to aid us in this spiritual challenge, we need one another.

Sin in our lives impairs our ability to press on in faith amid adversity. It is like a virus or a cancer that weakens our spiritual immune system, rendering us unable or unwilling to master the spiritual fortitude to press on with true confidence in faith. And we must remember that it is not just what we may regard as major sin that becomes an unbearable weight. More often, it may be the aggregate of many things we think are relatively insignificant compared to others that become the weight that "doth so easily beset us," for it is "the little foxes that spoil the vines" (Song of Solomon 2:15). Therefore, to run with *patience* we must run in *purity*, which requires repentance.

A Cloud of Witnesses

The writer of Hebrews exhorts us much like a coach confronted with the final game of the season. It is the "make-or-break" game for eternity. And so he reminds us that the stands are full, that "we are compassed about with so great a cloud of witnesses" to watch us press on victoriously as the clock runs down toward the end of life's "game"—the return of Jesus, Yeshua HaMashiach. Let your spirit embrace the passion of his plea to each of us.

> "…let us lay aside every weight, and the sin which
> doth so easily beset us, and let us run with *patience*
> [endurance] the race that is set before us,

Looking unto Jesus the author and finisher of our faith, who for the joy that was set before him *endured* the cross....

For consider him that endured such contradiction [persecution] of sinners against himself, let ye be wearied and faint in your minds" (Heb. 12:1-3; emphasis added).

I wait for the LORD, my soul doth wait, and in his word do I hope (Ps. 130:5).

Chapter 11

PROBING THOUGHTS for PROPHETIC TIMES

1. What is patience?
2. Why does God expect us to manifest patience as a life pattern? Do you?
3. Why is patience required to endure temptation and testing?
4. In what way or ways is patience the "cousin" of endurance?
5. Why might the calling to patient endurance be of far greater significance than most American Christians may believe or are willing to embrace?
6. What does it mean, as the apostle Paul states, to "Press toward the mark for the prize of the high calling of God in Christ Jesus?" Do others in your sphere of influence see you as "pressing toward the mark?" What do you think, and why?
7. What weights are besetting you, preventing or frustrating you from seriously, patiently and consistently "pressing toward the mark?"

PENULTIMATE PERSECUTION

"God has prophetically decreed a profound consequence for those who seek to escape this penultimate expression of persecution...."

PERSECUTION'S FINAL PRESENTATION is coming sooner than most American and western Christians are willing to consider. For many followers of Christ in areas of the world already experiencing severe persecution, this coming final era of persecution may not appear more severe, but for Christians worldwide, it will be pervasive and troubling beyond anything yet experienced.

What "Penultimate" Means

The word *penultimate* is not a word commonly used in everyday conversation for good reason. It is a compound word combining the word *ultimate* with the prefix *pen*. It is an adjective describing that which is final but that which has become final through a series of events preceding, leading to a culminating event. In this chapter we are challenged with personally confronting what the Scriptures describe as the penultimate persecutorial event that will truly "try men's souls."

We find this potentially terrifying event described in the *Apocalypse*—the Book of the Revelation of Jesus Christ—unveiling the final events of human history as those events connect with God's prophetic purposes on our planet and with all people that then inhabit it.

As the message was delivered to the apostle John on the Isle of Patmos in the later portion of the first century AD, it begins with these words:

> The Revelation of Jesus Christ, which God gave unto
> him, to shew unto his servants things which must
> shortly come to pass… (Rev. 1:1).

Consider for a moment the word *shortly*. Since the Book of Revelation was written approximately two thousand years ago, it is perhaps difficult for us to comprehend how God could properly and rightly use the word *shortly* for that which has not yet come to pass. However, when we realize that God does not live within time as do we humans, and that "…one day is with the Lord as a thousand years, and a thousand years as one day" (II Pet. 3:8; Ps. 90:4), we discover we are now approaching only "two days" since the Apocalypse was written. What then should we rightly, yet perhaps reluctantly, expect to manifest relatively shortly as persecution's penultimate expression, thus bringing prophecy to consummation?

Painting the Picture of Prophecy

Prophecy is, in reality, a divine picture of the future that, from God's perspective, is essential for His servants, true believers, to understand for the conduct of their lives. Prophecy, although provided with somewhat broad strokes of the divine brush, is sufficiently revealing so that we can, if we are willing, perceive God's purposes and align our lives accordingly. Such is the case with the revelation of a coming "mark" which will be mandated by a rising "beast" government as a pledge of allegiance and trust in its godless and God-defying system of divine replacement.

God has, for our preparation, painted for us the picture of a rising "beast" empire led by a "beast" personage to which the dragon [Satan] gave him his power, and his seat, and great authority (Rev. 13:2). God is thus allowing Satan to exercise the authority that Adam granted to Satan in accepting Satan's will over God's in the Garden of Eden six thousand years ago (Gen. 3); leading to the most historic "cover-up" of all time (Gen. 3:7-13).

The world will worship this beast and his rising beast empire, and because of his false prophet, and the "beast," the population of our planet will be drawn in awe and reverence, even as he "opens his mouth in blasphemy against God" (Rev. 13:4-14). The beast will gain global dominion and unprecedented allegiance because he appears to be the great peacemaker craved by the world amid unprecedented chaos and seems unusually powerful and clever, ultimately gaining power through flattery (Dan. 7:23-25; 11:21). His rise to prominence will be characterized by unprecedented political chicanery.

Ultimately, as the penultimate expression of planet-wide persecution, a plan will be conceived by the false prophet to prepare an "image" of the beast capable of speaking and consigning all who refuse to accept a designated "mark" on their right hand or forehead should be killed. The means whereby the mark will become mandated will make it impossible, by way of a globally-controlled economic system, to buy or sell or conduct any business, thus preventing access to the necessities of life. For most, the consequences will compel them to capitulate in order to avoid the mass execution for failure to pledge allegiance to the satanically-empowered global government (Rev. 13:11-18).

The satanically-conceived plan will, in the eyes of many, seem to require a self-decided fate, thus leading to a claim that "We did not persecute you, but you persecuted yourself" by failing to conform to the final government promising world peace and prosperity. Consider solemnly the choice to be made by parents, grandparents and even pastors who will seek, by any means, to rationalize or justify receiving the Mark of the Beast, claiming inevitably… "But I had to. What else could I do?"

(Note: To understand in greater depth this counterfeit christ—the Antichrist, read *ANTICHRIST: How to Identify the Coming Imposter* by Charles Crismier, available via saveus.org).

The Promised Consequences

Since the rise of the Imposter Christ will be accomplished seemingly over a period of 3½ years or 42 months, the mandated mark may take a while before "push comes to shove" and a deadline will be established to pledge your trust and allegiance to the beast for providing your needs through the new, globalized, digital financial system. But better it would be to choose now than later when the pressure builds.

God, however, has prophetically decreed a profound consequence for those who seek to escape this penultimate expression of persecution by fearfully receiving this blasphemous mark of allegiance to Satan's global government.

We journey then to the clear consequences expressed in Revelation, chapter 14, immediately following the profound prophetic warning of the blasphemous mark mandated to be received by the masses in chapter 13. Before these dire consequences are declared, the Lord sends a final warning to all earth dwellers. The warning is simple, yet its implications are eternal, portraying an extremely rough ride down the homestretch of human history.

> And I saw another angel fly in the midst of heaven, having the everlasting gospel to preach unto them that dwell on the earth, and to every nation, and kindred, and tongue, and people, Saying with a loud voice,
>
> Fear God, and give glory to him; for the hour of his judgment is come:
>
> And worship him that made heaven, and earth…"
> (Rev. 14:6-7).

This is God's final restatement of His gospel call to humankind, followed by God's final warning by means of yet a third angel which says with a loud unmistakable voice:

If any man worship the beast and his image, and receive his mark in his forehead, or in his hand,

The same shall drink of the wine of the wrath of God… and shall be tormented with fire and brimstone in the presence of the holy angels, and in the presence of the Lamb:

And the smoke of their torment ascendeth up for ever and ever: and they have no rest day or night, who worship the beast and his image, and whosoever **receiveth the mark of his name** (Rev. 14:9-14; emphasis added).

Even then, despite such a direct and dire warning, there will be those who continually revel in "loophole living" who will rationalize receiving of a mark that will define their eternal destiny by saying… "Well, I received the mark only because I had to, but I did not intend to receive it as an "act of worship." The problem with such a "finger-crossing" response is that a loving God is warning:

If you receive that blasphemous mark, you are by very definition declaring your final trust and allegiance to a counterfeit savior—the Antichrist.

Therefore, the time to choose is now, before the penultimate pressure is applied. This, friends, is the time for husbands and wives, for parents and grandparents, and for pastors and priests to seriously and directly prepare those purporting to place their trust in your leadership and under your wings of protection.

And so, this Apocalyptic warning of our Lord in the Book of Revelation concludes:

Here is the patience of the saints: here are they that keep the commandments of God, and the faith of Jesus.

…Blessed are the dead which die in the Lord [keep the faith and refuse the mark] henceforth… that they may rest from their labours; and their works [faithful obedience] do follow them (Rev. 14:12-13).

Again, as Jesus declared just before His crucifixion: "But he that shall endure unto the end shall be saved." Because "many false prophets shall rise, and shall deceive many. And because iniquity shall abound, the love of many shall wax cold" (Matt. 24:11-13).

Blessed is the man that endureth temptation [trials, tribulation and persecution]: for when he is tried, he shall receive the crown of life, which the Lord hath promised to them that love him (Jam. 1:12).

The LORD is nigh unto all them that call upon him, to all that call upon him in truth. He will fulfil the desire of them that fear him… will hear their cry, and will save them (Ps. 145:18-19).

Chapter 12
PROBING THOUGHTS for PROPHETIC TIMES

1. What does *penultimate* mean?
2. How would you distinguish "penultimate persecution" from other forms that preceded it?
3. How can we best understand what is meant by the words "that which must shortly come to pass" or similar use of the word *shortly*?
4. Why do you think the world's peoples will be so enamored with the *beast* and his empire that they will actually worship him?
5. Do you agree with the description from Revelation 14 as presented in this chapter concerning the consequences of receiving the "Mark of the Beast?"
6. What have you been doing to prepare yourself and your sons and daughters for such penultimate persecution?
7. Do you think God's final warnings have come from a heart of Fatherly love or from a mean and unforgiving, malicious spirit?
8. Why are you reluctant to seriously discuss these warnings with those entrusted to your care?

PART 5

PARENTING IN
PERILOUS TIMES

*We must, as parents and grandparents, watch and be ready lest
the cataclysm of corrupt faith take us and our children unawares.*

TIME IS DRAWING NEAR; Christ will soon appear to receive His own—the faithful and righteous remnant which is even now being courageously and passionately prepared by dedicated parents determined that their children will be prepared to face the coming persecutorial onslaught.

The great question remains, however. How will Satan, through his earthly surrogate—the beast, the Antichrist, the IMPOSTER—deceive the nations? What might, or will be, his modus operandi? Why was it necessary for Christ himself to give such grave warnings to those who profess to be His disciples… His followers… those who claim His name (Matt. 24:4, 10-11, 24)? Why did the apostles—Peter, John and Paul—also warn of those demonically deceptive days? The answer is clear!

The deception of the IMPOSTER will be so compelling to the entire world as to draw the unsuspecting, the ignorant, the fleshly motivated, the easily spiritually seduced (the condition of vast numbers of professing Christians today) into the false global kingdom of promised peace and prosperity signaled by a counterfeit Shalom.

The final stage has been set. We must, as parents and grandparents, watch and be ready lest the cataclysm of corrupt faith take us and our children unawares (Matt. 24:42-51; 25:13; I Thess. 5:1-6; I Pet. 4:7). But for what must we watch? What are the discernable characteristics of this beast imposter that render him so diabolically deceptive and seductive? And how might we discern his seemingly disarming modus operandi? What will be its features that masquerade as sincere faith? And how do we persuasively translate these things to those entrusted by God to our care in His behalf?

It is to those questions that we prayerfully devote our discussion in this part. We soberly remember Jesus' warning:

> Because iniquity shall abound, the love of many shall
> wax cold.
>
> But he that shall endure [be faithful] to the end shall
> be saved (Matt. 24:12-13).

What then, given our parental preparation, will be the likely destiny of our children as the Deceiver rages against all righteousness? God is trusting us to make this our preeminent passion as the dark clouds of end-time deception envelope not only the nations but also the professing church.

> *The eye of the LORD is upon them that fear him,*
> *upon them that hope in his mercy; To deliver their*
> *soul from death, and to keep them alive in famine*
> *(Ps. 33:18-19).*

Chapter 13

DEAR PARENTS: PREPARE... OR DESPAIR

"May all who come behind us find us faithful!"

PARENTING TO PREPARE for coming, yes accelerating, persecution is both a calling and a profound challenge. Many parents and grandparents throughout history have been confronted with this challenge, primarily from known tyrannical governments.

But the challenge now facing western Christian families, especially Americans, is perhaps even more dramatically challenging precisely because we have lived for so long under unprecedented freedoms and constitutional protections insuring a peaceful, democratic republic. But those protections and assurances have been gradually whittled away, paving the way for religious persecution, even under color of law, driven by a popular and increasingly godless culture that defies biblical authority while virtually deifying vacillating human feelings.

The Late "Christian" West

Welcome to the Late-Great "Christian" West. We are truly grateful for the blessings of liberty we have so long enjoyed, issuing from a truly godly heritage. Interestingly, however, history reveals that those very freedoms and the spirit of liberty gradually, over time, begin to lay the foundation for spiritual waywardness and moral decay, which in turn lead eventually toward either tacit or outward resistance to the ways of righteousness. And without personal and collective confession of such waywardness resulting in serious and lasting repentance, the culture continues its inevitable collapse, ultimately defying the Word and Spirit of Christ.

Therefore, anyone or family that remains diligently faithful to living a biblically righteous life eventually becomes the object of scorn and rejection, culminating in outward persecution. Whether or not we choose to admit it, this progressive pattern has now overtaken us and will determine whether we respond to the necessity of preparing our families for the times of persecution coming in rapidly like a flood. To delay is to commit to ultimate despair.

How, Then, Can We Prepare?

We have been frequently reminded that: "To fail to prepare is to prepare to fail." Few of us would care to publicly admit our intent to prepare to fail, and yet if we are honest, most actually prepare to fail precisely because they do not consciously and intentionally prepare to face the life and faith-assaulting challenges looming ahead. Yet our children and grandchildren depend upon our diligence and faithful attention to their welfare. They, by God's command and expectation, place their trust in us to do that which is true, right and pleasing to God. When we fail in this trust, we actually betray their trust… and God's. And the inevitable consequences are not pretty—often devastating—and we despair.

How, then, can we gird up the loins of our minds and hearts to prepare for advancing persecution with courage and conviction, transmitting that same courage and conviction to those we love and for which our heavenly Father has committed to our care? In summary fashion, we then explore the basis of mind, heart and practice providing at least a template upon which to design a spiritual destiny without which despair is almost determined.

PREPARE WITH PURPOSE

In order to prepare your family for persecution, you must have a sincere and serious conviction of heart that some level of persecution is both promised and forewarned by Christ himself. Jesus made it abundantly clear.

> The servant is not greater than his lord. If they have persecuted me, they will also persecute you....
>
> But all these things will they do unto you for my name's sake… (Jn. 15:20-21).

The apostle Peter likewise made the message plain. Stating that "… the end of all things is at hand." He continued:

> Beloved, think it not strange concerning the fiery trial which is to try you, as though some strange thing happened unto you:
>
> But rejoice, inasmuch as ye are partakers of Christ's sufferings (I Pet. 4:7, 12-13).

Your personal conviction, as a parent, will quickly become apparent to your children. They will be much more likely to take seriously that which Mom and Dad take seriously. Therefore, your very reading of this epistle together with your prayerful perusal of the Scriptures should be persuasive to the Christian conscience of the need for parental preparation. You, as a parent, must be prepared if you have any reasonable expectation of preparing others.

PROMOTE TRUTH

The true spiritual war we face is a war against truth itself. It is the same battle faced first by Eve in yielding to the Serpent's deception in

Genesis 3 and then faced by Adam in going along with exalting the Deceiver's word over God's Word. This fundamental modus operandi of the enemy of our souls has never changed because it is so pervasively effective, leading in its final form to persecution of those perceived to adhere to God's truth.

The driving tendency of our times is to mix God's truth with the countermanding "truths" of a godless culture, thereby compromising with prevailing culture so as to avoid being persecuted or feeling like "the odd man out." Your children face this pressure daily, through friends, teachers, television, and all social media. And we parents and grandparents… yes, even pastors… are not immune. It is spiritual warfare, and its intensity is increasing. Prepare yourself and your progeny with the "belt of truth" (Eph. 6:14).

PROMOTE FAITHFULNESS

It is one thing to claim faith **in** Christ, but is a much different thing to be faithful **to** Christ. As is so often said, "Words are cheap." What impresses God is not our alleged faith IN Christ but rather our genuinely living FOR Christ and in obedience TO Christ. In an age of "easy believe-ism," Americans have been preconditioned and are therefore predisposed to be "hearers of the Word" but not "doers of the Word," thus in reality living in perpetual spiritual deception while claiming Christ as a virtual mascot rather than as a Master (Jam. 1:22).

It should be obvious that one cannot walk faithfully unless he or she is truly living by faith, because without such continuous living faith, it is impossible to please God (Heb. 11:10). A pastor once said, "Faith is a long obedience in the same direction."

Faithfulness is essential to endure to the end (Matt. 24:13), because as Jesus said: "The love of many shall wax cold" due to the rise of "iniquity" (Matt. 24:12), "And then many shall be offended, and shall betray one another, and shall hate one another" (Matt. 24:10). Is it any wonder, then, that the apostle Paul warned of a great falling away (apostasy) from the faith (II Thess. 2:3). Such "falling away" from the faith once professed is even now provoking despair by parents and grandparents who would never have believed such a thing to happen in their family.

It should go without saying that we must teach and display faithfulness. Faithfulness is persistent allegiance both by belief and obedience to the Word, Will and Ways of the Lord. The spiritual cousin of faithfulness is holiness, and without holiness "no man shall see the Lord" (Heb. 12:14). May all who come behind us find us faithful!

PROMOTE PERSEVERANCE

It is fascinating that in consulting the *Oxford American Dictionary* ©2006, the word *perseverance* follows the words *perplexity* and *persecution*. It is indeed true that perseverance is required in the face of increasingly perplexing times characterized by intimidating persecution.

Jesus warned that, along with signs in the heavens, there would be "distress of nations, with perplexity." He further warned of "Men's hearts failing them for fear, and for looking after those things which are coming on the earth…" (Lk. 21:25-26). The Apostle Paul spoke of facing distress and perplexity amid persistent persecution:

> We are troubled on every side, yet not distressed; we are perplexed, but not in despair; Persecuted, but not forsaken; cast down, but not destroyed (II Cor. 4:8-9).

Paul, admonishing us to follow his example as he followed Christ's (I Cor. 11:1), then concluded that despite all the trials, tribulations and persecutions; "… we faint not;"

> But though our outward man perish, yet the inward man is renewed day by day.

> For our light affliction, which is but for a moment [relatively speaking], worketh for us a far more exceeding and external weight of glory (II Cor. 4:16-17).

The question for us as parents and grandparents should then be obvious and hopefully persuasive as to God's calling for us before our children in these times of growing perplexity. Am I, are we, demonstrating and conveying that same spirit of perseverance as did Paul, and Christ before him?

What, then, is this *perseverance* demanded by times of perplexity and persecution? What is this intangible yet powerful state of mind, heart and spirit we must faithfully impart with loving determination to those in our charge before the Father?

A dictionary definition should suffice in its simplicity. **Perseverance** is "steadfastness in doing something despite difficulty or delay in achieving success." For we and our children to persevere, therefore, requires that we all, both by precept and example, continue in a course of action of trust, obedience and faith precisely because of the perplexities and foreboding persecution we face, always…

Looking unto Jesus the author and finisher of our faith;

Who for the joy that was set before him endured the cross….

For consider him… lest ye be wearied and faint in your minds (Heb. 12:2-3).

As a parent of three, a grandparent of ten and a great grandparent, I must join with you in realization that if we do not persevere in faith without fear or compromise, our children's faith will likely fail. What then will their future be?

PROMOTE COURAGE

Our children must be trained both by precept and example to live courageously, not for self-glory but for God's glory. In order to persevere faithfully, without capitulation to either the ways of the world or the demands or threats of persecution; they must learn how to stand in the evil day... and to keep on standing notwithstanding the cost.

Courage is not displayed in the absence of fear or intimidation but rather in the very face of fear. If we, as parents, do not display this spiritual discipline when facing challenges in our decisions in seemingly small things within our family life, how, then, can we expect those raised within our sphere of influence to grasp the gravamen of courage when confronted with choices that may cost us as Christians.

Just as God, as Father, exhorted... yes commanded... Joshua to be "strong and of good courage" while facing his life calling to replace Moses and to lead an unruly bunch of the children of Israel to wage a generation of battles so they might take dominion of the Promised Land, even so we fathers must do the same with our sons (Josh. 1:6). And mothers, in their role, must also convey the same courageous spirit to their daughters.

God's exhortation to Joshua was repeated three additional times to Joshua, reinforcing the seriousness of courage in the face of unprecedented challenge both for himself and those who would follow his leadership.

> Only be thou strong and very courageous... (Josh 1:7).

> Have I not commanded thee? Be strong and of a good courage; be not afraid, neither be thou dismayed: for the LORD thy God is with thee whithersoever thou goest (Josh. 1:9).

Other than by precept and parental example, one of the best ways to convey the call to courage is by intentionally exposing our sons and daughters to various accounts, stories and books that demonstrate real courage by both young and old when confronted by threats against their persons by way of persecution. Reading such accounts should be followed by parent-led discussion with the family. The apparent commitment of Mom and Dad will clearly confirm to the kids the solemnity of the subject. Prepare for many questions, but do NOT shrink from this godly responsibility. Remember—if you or your children faint in the day of adversity, your faith is small… and maybe non-existent… setting the stage for entering a profoundly unpleasant eternal destiny.

Here are a few suggestions for starters. The Bible itself contains many such examples of courage.

GIDEON—in the battle against the Midianites is found in Judges 6-8.

DAVID—in his confrontation with a 9 ½ foot tall giant called Goliath (I Sam. 17).

ASA—leading Judah to follow the Lord by ridding the people of idols, even removing his idolatrous mother from being queen (II Chron. 14:15).

HEZEKIAH—a 25-year-old king courageously calls his nation back to God (II Chron. 29-30).

NEHEMIAH—boldly gathered Judah together to rebuild Jerusalem in the face of their enemies—after which he courageously called the people to repentance (Neh. 4).

ISAIAH—courageously warned Judah and Jerusalem to come back to God, at great risk (Isa. 1).

DANIEL—Purposed at great risk, when held captive, to follow God's ways (Dan. 1).

Again, under threat of lions, stood firm not to betray his God to appease a king and political enemies (Dan. 6).

THREE YOUNG MEN—Refused to bow down, at a king's command, to an image of a false god, notwithstanding the horrific threatened consequences (Dan. 3).

JESUS—Excoriated the hypocritical religious leaders despite their hatred and potential consequences (Matt. 23).

STEVEN—the first Christian martyr who boldly proclaimed his trust in Jesus as savior in the face of death, refusing to recant (Acts 6-7).

PETER & JOHN—Arrested by the religious governing priests for preaching and teaching in Jesus' name, boldly and courageously standing firm despite threats (Acts 4).

PAUL—Continuous suffering and persecution as a result of his calling due to his conversion to Christ after persecuting Christians (II Cor. 11:23-27).

HEBREWS—Many righteous suffered horrifically, yet courageously, that they who suffered after them might "receive a good report" at the Judgment (Heb. 11:36-40).

Other very impactful and classic books and resources include *Fox's Book of Martyrs*, the films *Chariots of Fire* and *Man for All Seasons*, or books regarding the life of Jim Elliot who was martyred in the 1950s by the Auca Indians in Ecuador and his wife, Elizabeth, who later returned to that same tribe at great risk to fulfill their marital commitment to carry the gospel.

The importance of discipling in courage cannot and must not be underestimated if we have any real hope of seeing the children God has charged to our care truly "endure to the end." Perhaps the words of William Wilberforce, the persistent and courageous Christian who fought vigorously in England against the slave trade, might be of exemplary encouragement.

> What a lesson it is to a man not to set his heart on low popularity when after 40 years of disinterested public service, I'm believed by the bulk to be a Hypocritical Rascal.

> O what a comfort it is to have to fly for refuge to a God of unchangeable truth and love.

> I long, if it might be the will of God, yet to do something more for his Glory and for the credit of my Christian professions.[56]

If courage is lost, all is likely lost!!! "Only one life, twill soon be past. Only what's done [courageously and faithfully] for Christ will last" and enable us all to endure these perilous times.

PROMOTE GODLY FEAR

A child who does not learn the fear of the Lord will quickly learn to fear man. A parent who does not truly fear God will insidiously communicate the fear of man in and through his or her responses to the issues of life and as a result to the children.

So foundationally important to genuine Christian living is the very concept and embrace of *the fear of the Lord* that we are told: "The fear of the LORD is the beginning of wisdom…" (Ps. 111:10). We are also informed that:

> The secret of the LORD is with them that fear him;
> and he will shew them his covenant (Ps. 25:14).

On the contrary, we are warned that "The fear of man bringeth a snare:" BUT—"whoso putteth his trust in the LORD shall be safe"

(Prov. 29:25). In truth, the fear of the Lord is the foundation stone of every promise of God in His Word, and of that fact both we and the flock under our wings must be convinced both in spirit and in truth. So great is the heart embrace of this fear of the Lord in order to develop a true love FOR the Lord that our Lord Jesus himself, born as a man, had to first learn the fear of the Lord as a foundation for obeying the Father.

Listen carefully to the prophetic words of Isaiah concerning the Messiah soon then to come.

> And the spirit of the LORD shall rest upon him, the spirit of wisdom and understanding… and of the **fear of the LORD**;
>
> And shall make him of quick understanding in the **fear of the LORD** (Isa. 11:1-3; emphasis added).

I urge you, as a parent or grandparent, to avail yourself of my recent book, *The Secret of the Lord: The Hidden Truths That Define Your Destiny*. As you share these "secrets" for the spiritual strength and survival of your family, they… and you… will discover:

The Secret of a United Heart
The Secret of Sure Blessing
Finding "Perfect Love"
History's Final Act
Man's Final Mark
God's Final Message, and
The Saving Secret.

Consider well the true spiritual condition of our professing "Christian" young people over the decade last passed. Reports of the most respected Christian researchers have confirmed that only 20%

of those who claim to be Christian actually believe that Jesus Christ is "the only way, the only truth and the only life—the only way to the Father."

It is unfortunate but true—80% of professing Christian young people have actually embraced multiculturalism and religious pluralism because of cultural pressures, revealing that they do NOT fear God as GOD. They are therefore primed to receive the infamous "Mark of the Beast," believing that their "good intentions" will save them from eternal damnation.

PROMOTE HOPE

Hope and *Trust* walk together. Without unwavering trust in God, hope is faltering and will soon fail.

Our children are becoming desperate for real hope. There is a reason why anxiety is mounting throughout the world and suicides are burgeoning, especially among teens. It is largely because of increasingly perceived hopelessness. So then, as Christian parents, what must we do… and do quickly?

We must become purveyors of genuine hope. But is that even possible given the wicked and dangerous trajectory of our world and nation? The answer is a resounding "Yes," but it requires a whole new mind and heart-set, since western Christians have nearly lost all realistic comprehension of both the expectation and normalcy of the very concept of suffering and persecution from God's viewpoint. And in very truth, our highly deceived and distorted viewpoints are endangering the eternal destiny of those entrusted to us.

Hope is the outflow of genuine trust. Just as our trust in the Lord and in His Word develops and deepens as we are tested, even so hope is increasingly secured by that deepened trust. Both trust and hope are totally intangible and cannot be produced in any enduring spiritual sense by the senses. Both trust and resultant hope are dependent upon faithful and persistent relationship. Therefore, if our children are to be heralds of hope in a darkening world, they must have ever-deepening trust in the God of truth, both tested and tried, revealed in and through ever-deepening relationship with the Lord.

And so, my fellow parents, what do your children and grandchildren perceive from your life patterns? Do they perceive unwavering trust in the Lord purveying deepening security in the family? Or do they experience murmuring, fear, anxiety and worry creating an atmosphere breeding not hope but an aura of despair and insecurity. It is our lives that must not only preach but portray genuine hope.

The Word of God is both a message of ultimate hope but also of temporal reality we must endure as we persist in hope. If we would rest in hope, we must persist in hope through ever-increasing trust. Here, then, is the divine record concerning hope as proclaimed by God's Holy Word.

Without God there is no hope in this world (Eph. 2:12).

If in this world only we have hope, we are of all men most miserable (I Cor. 15:19).

Christ in you is the hope of glory (Col. 1:27).

It is through patience that we might have hope (Rom. 15:4).

We lay hold upon the hope set before us: which hope we have as an anchor of the soul, both sure and stedfast (Heb. 6:18-19).

Be of good courage, and he shall strengthen your heart, all ye that hope in the LORD (Ps. 31:24).

They that fear thee [God] will be glad when they see me; because I have hoped in thy word (Ps. 119:74).

And now, because of our tried and tested trust, as parents, we display a hope that "maketh not ashamed" to those young ones who look to us for real hope amid the world's horrors (Rom. 5:5). We do not "let our hearts be troubled" because we wholly trust Christ's ultimate promise that HE goes to prepare a place for those who truly trust and hope in His mercy (Jn. 14:2; Ps. 33:18). Here, then, is our challenge until Christ's return:

FIRST - We are to look forward to that blessed hope, and the glorious appearing of the great God and our Savior Jesus Christ (Tit. 2:13).

SECOND - If we truly have this hope of Christ's return, then "Every man that hath this hope in him" will purify himself even as Christ is pure (I Jn. 3:3).

THIRD - And finally, we must "gird up the loins of [our] mind[s], be sober [serious minded], and hope to the end for the grace [favor and enabling power] that is to be brought unto [us] at the revelation of Jesus Christ (I Pet. 1:13).

But as he which hath called you is holy, so be ye holy in all manner of conversation [your life] (I Pet. 1:15).

Penultimate Parenting

As parents and grandparents we have never faced a greater challenge or calling. Preparing our families for these perilous times requires great courage and deep conviction coupled with a level of commitment that has become scarce among western and American Christians. This is undoubtedly our penultimate moment as parents and must therefore command our utmost passion, for the eternal destiny of those placed by our Creator in our charge is at ultimate risk.

This is not a time and calling to be satisfied by cheap spiritual mantras and non-negotiable God-bless-you's, nor of ritualistic "salvation prayers" or frolicking youth programs. We must "gird up the loins of our minds" with a rare measure of sobriety long lost in our society so that we might faithfully and legitimately hope to the end for the grace—favor and enabling power—that is to be made available until the return of our Lord (I Pet. 1:13).

This penultimate parental calling is a nondelegable duty. We cannot hope that merely taking our children to church, enrolling them in a Christian school or college, or punting our parenting off to a pastor or priest will fulfill the call to courageous righteousness needed to meet God's expectations as our Father. There will be an eternal accounting.

As parents we will either submit ourselves to the perceived extraordinary spiritual pressure of seriously preparing our sons and daughters, or we will painfully watch their succumbing to the rising pressure of persecution culminating in the notorious Mark of the Beast. And do not yield to the temptation of embracing the Pollyanna view that as Americans we are somehow exempt. To delay is to despair!

Just ask Eli, the priest, who God appointed to judge Israel for 40 years and to righteously father his sons. Yet God confronted Eli, even as a priest, for disregarding the spiritual discipline of his sons, consigning both Eli and his entire progeny to destruction, leaving only a grandson named Ichabod, meaning "the glory has departed" (I Sam. 2-4). My fellow parents and grandparents, do not let such a lamentable judgment be ours, but let us rather rejoice and trust our Father's promise:

"THEM THAT HONOUR ME, I WILL HONOUR"
(I SAM. 2:30).

Search me, O God, and know my heart: try me, and know my thoughts: And see if there be any wicked way in me, and lead me in the way everlasting (Ps. 139:23-24).

Chapter 13
PROBING THOUGHTS for PROPHETIC TIMES

1. Have you, your children, or your grandchildren experienced any level or form of persecution? Do you know any who have?

2. Do you consider yourself to provide strong and consistent spiritual leadership with your children or grandchildren? What does that look like?

3. How have you been preparing your kids to be courageous for Christ?

4. Have your children faced situations where thy needed to stand for righteousness when pressured by peers or even teachers?

5. How can you train your children to persevere in the face of adversity… yes even persecution?

6. Why do you think a deep "fear of the Lord" is essential for your children to stand strong amid the rising tide of evil?

7. How would you rank your current spiritual level of parenting on a scale of 1 to 10, ten being strongest, most consistent and faithful?

8. Based upon your current parenting practices, how confident are you that you have prepared your children to endure rising persecution?

Chapter 14

FATHERING IN FEARFUL TIMES

"We must accept finite disappointment, but
we must never lose infinite hope."
~Martin Luther King Jr.

INCREASING FEAR WILL DEFINE OUR TIMES. That understanding may not set well nor sell well, but it is a fact that will severely challenge our faith as fathers. The Father said it would be so.

Failing For Fear

Jesus minced no words. He was preparing spiritual sons (His disciples) for His departure, committed to leave a legacy that would last. And so, He warned them of that which was to come, whether good or bad, whether uplifting or challenging, whether godly or ungodly. These men with whom He had invested Himself (like our children) had to be forewarned so that they might be forearmed.

Jesus, sharing the Father's heart just before His crucifixion and resurrection, warned of famines, pestilences, geological upheaval and geopolitical strife that would come, yet He declared these were only "the beginning of sorrows" (Matt. 24:8). The Son of the Father was particularly concerned about the massive deception that would sweep the earth, especially among those who otherwise professed His name, "And because iniquity shall abound, the love of many shall wax cold"

(Matt. 24:02). These warnings should grip the hearts of fathers today as serious, solemn and sobering. Any lesser reaction is to play pretend - to hide one's head in the proverbial sand.

Reality is, indeed, coming home to roost for any dad whose heart is truly turned toward the Father and walking as the Son. We are living in those times so graphically described by our Lord. And just how serious are these times, both for we fathers and for those who would follow in our footsteps? Please hear the words of admonition from the Father's heart as declared by His only begotten Son.

> And there shall be signs in the sun, and in the moon, and the stars; and upon the earth distress of nations, with perplexity; the sea and the waves roaring;
>
> **Men's hearts failing them for fear**, and for looking after those things which are coming upon the earth.... (Lk. 21:25-26).

When Children Fear

If the hearts of macho men are "failing them for fear" because of what they see, feel and hear, how should we fathers expect our young who trust us to respond? This is not hypothetical. To fail to embrace the gravamen of this issue is totally hypocritical. It is nothing short of *playing pretend* with those who have rightfully placed their trust in us as surrogates of the Father.

So... as real men... as genuine, trustworthy fathers, what should we do? How should we respond amid the unpleasant realities that confront us and will increasingly plague our planet? And what will enable us to come to grips in our own minds and hearts with the truth of increasing trials and tribulations spoken of by prophets, apostles and the Father through the mouth of Jesus? Such considerations are neither trivial nor to be trifled with but rather to be seriously grafted into our thoughts so as to take hold of our hearts and our practices in our homes.

When children fear it can have a profound affect upon their faith in the Father and upon their trust in their own fathers. As trials and tribulations increase, trust must rise commensurately or faith will collapse. When true faith collapses, our sons and daughters whom we deem dear will be increasingly opened to destiny-changing deceptions that promise to temporarily allay fears but provide false hope. We fathers hold the promise of genuine hope that breeds Christ-like courage for such challenging times.

A necessary rhetorical question should even now be arcing in our minds. How am I doing as a father, standing in for the Father, in discipling my kids to stand firm in faith in exceedingly troubled times? Or are we, as a family, just continuing in a somewhat passive faith with little consideration or preparation for the rising tumult throughout our culture and the world? Are we resting our children's future faith on a *Pollyanna* view of life, leaving legacy to just take care of itself, just cavalierly embracing a *Whatever* mindset? Or, have we wrapped the future of those dear children in a fatalistic blanket expressed so well by the lyrics "Que sera, sera; Whatever will be will be; the future's not mine to see, que sera sera"?

What Should Godly Fathers Do in Fearful Times?

BUILD AN ARK OF FAITH

Jesus made clear that "as it was in the days of Noah, so shall it be also in the days of the Son of man [the days before Christ's return] (Lk. 17:26).

What, then, was it like in the days of Noah? It was business as usual, with a terrifying twist. Wickedness was great! Man's thoughts were evil continually. Corruption and violence were rampant (Gen. 6:5, 11-12). Does this not sound suspiciously familiar? Are these not the times in which we are fathering?

Yet, amid the tribulation of the times, the Father found Noah as a faithful and trustworthy father who truly "walked with God," was a "just man" and who was "perfect in his generations" (Gen. 6:9). And so Noah "found grace in the eyes of the Lord" to save mankind, his own family, from judgment (Gen. 6:8). The Father then gave Noah, His earthly father surrogate, a faith-filled challenge and calling for troubled times... "Build an ark" (Gen. 6:14). And Noah, over the next century, did exactly that, with courage and faith-filled conviction. "Thus did Noah according to all that God commanded him...." (Gen. 6:22).

Question! Are you willing to "build an ark" to save your sons and daughters... your grandchildren... those who trust you as a spiritual "father"... in your generation? This may well be the last generation given the opportunity to *build an ark*. What, then, are the building materials for an *ark of faith*?

1. Christ-like Trust—In Noah's day, the Messiah had not been revealed, so the Father spoke directly to Noah. In response, Noah did exactly what the word of the Father had instructed... he built an ark. Similarly, Jesus, in His day, did the same. He built an ark, not of wood but of faith revealed in obedience. HE did only what the Father instructed, because he trusted the Father implicitly. For this reason, Jesus Christ became the sole foundation of our faith, exemplified in loving obedience to the Father's word, will and ways.

Absolute trust revealed in obedience was the hallmark of Christ's life as did the Son. His life, death and resurrection then became the living *ark* of safety for eternal salvation for us and for our sons and daughters.

We, as the *Noahs* of our day, are to build an ark of faith-filled trust in Christ did as the only truly obedient Son, and similarly take the Father's word as absolute truth upon which we can raise our children in the same unshakeable foundation of trust and obedience. Our children are not likely to *enter the ark* with confidence unless they perceive we have done so with absolute confidence.

2. Build Christ-like Character—It is one thing to claim to have built an ark, yet it is quite another to live a life worthy of entering. Undoubtedly many a man worked with Noah and his sons to build the ark, a massive project, but none of them entered the ark. Neither their minds nor their hearts were united with Noah's as to the character of their lives that demanded that the ark be built.

Character counts. The word *character* is one way of expressing the clear connection between what we say we believe and how we live. We refer to a man whose professed belief is not reflected accurately or consistently in his life ways as a *hypocrite*. We say that he lacks *integrity*. The question then haunts our homes... What do our children or grandchildren say or think? Is my home truly a safe haven where Christ-like character guides and protects purported faith and trust? Our legacy may lie in the balance?

3. Build Christ-like Courage—Courage is the backbone of moral character. When courage weakens, the spiritual back slumps. One can barely fathom fatherly leadership without courage. Courage links all of moral character and genuine faith into a single operative body that enables a man to "take a stand."

The famous sage Goethe gave us the following words which should grip our hearts as fathers:

Wealth lost, something lost;
Honor lost, much lost;
Courage lost, all lost.

Are you willing to take a stand? In this evil day, are you doing all to stand, having your loins girt about with truth that does not sway with the tides of cultural feelings or is not enveloped by the tsunamis of godless teachings, even in the name of science, that erodes the very foundations of our faith and that of our children? Or will the winds of social pressure, employment compromise, relational infidelity, selfish ambition... or fear of loss of ministry funding or constituent support topple your moral frame, allowing onlooking children to see their father falter and fall under such minor trials and tribulation?

William Bartley Bell, a constitutional attorney of renown, prefacing *In Search of a National Morality*, wrote, "Moral courage is that most unfashionable virtue." Indeed it is! On many of the issues that men and fathers face, we lack wisdom because we lack courage.

"A decline in courage may be the most striking feature... in our days," observed Aleksandr Solzhenitsyn. "From ancient times decline in courage has been considered the beginning of the end." But we no longer, as fathers, need wander in trepidation and fear. We must take courage.

The Father, in passing the baton of leadership from Moses to Joshua in terrifying times just as the *Children* of Israel were to enter the Promised Land filled with wicked and fierce warriors, gave these words of exhortation that each of us should closely embrace for our times.

> Be strong and of good courage; be not afraid, neither
> be thou dismayed: for the Lord thy God is with thee
> whither so ever thou goest (Josh. 1:9).

BE BRAVE WITHOUT BRAVADO

The Father is looking to and fro throughout the earth for a few faithful fathers who can and will stand in fearful times. But how do we maintain the courage necessary to brave the tumultuous waves that will increasingly sweep across the hulls of our homes... the ark we are building?

Here are seven serious and sobering admonitions that will help us stand bravely, yet without prideful bravado, as we see "the great and terrible day of the Lord" approaching (Joel 2:31).

1. Fear Not

The Father repeatedly exhorted His son Israel and all his children to "fear not." We are told that "God hath not given us the spirit of fear; but of power, and of love, and of a sound mind (II Tim. 1:7). Fear not man. Neither fear rejection by an increasingly godless culture. As it is written, "The fear of man bringeth a snare, but whoso putteth his trust in the Lord shall be safe" (Prov. 29:25).

"Perfect love casteth our fear" (I Jn. 4:18). The man who yields to fleshly fear will be tormented. But "there is no fear in love." "He that feareth is not made perfect in love." The greater our genuine love for the Father, the less our fear of man. The greater our genuine, godly love for our wives and our sons and daughters, the less our fear of the wicked machinations of man. We are enabled then to be fearless and faithful without falling.

2. Fret Not

Fretting is faithless. Our propensity in the flesh to fret reveals the weakness in our spirit to trust our Father and to live by faith.

Fretting frustrates faith. And a father's fretting in the face of his family is a declaration to both wife and children of the serious weakness of his alleged faith. For this reason, we are exhorted by the psalmist David to "Fret not thyself because of evildoers…" (Ps. 37:1).

Our flesh will always demand that we fret. This helps us to understand the nature of spiritual warfare. It is a continual battle, this conflict between the flesh and the spirit. And our children need to see us victorious in faith.

3. Fall Not

Falling, alone and in an isolated instance, does not define or determine *failing*. But persistent falling reveals a propensity to fail which seriously impairs hope for a godly, lasting legacy.

As fathers, holding the Father's treasure of gospel hope in earthen vessels, we occasionally will stumble and sometimes fall (II Cor. 3:7). Yet, in our seeming weakness, by the Father's grace (enabling power and favor) we can be restored and made strong. It is always a matter of the heart. And we are called to be overcomers (Rev. 2-3).

The classic film *Chariots of Fire* drives this message home and to the heart for every sincere father. Eric Liddell, the focus of the film, finds himself in a dire circumstance as "Scotland's fastest wing." He is challenged to run a particular race to display his running prowess but is tripped up by an unscrupulous competitor, causing Eric to stumble and fall, seeming to doom him to failure. And the movie captures the moment so that every man viewing must himself enter the mind and heart of this young man as he weighs, in an instant, how to respond. Should he quit... or should he rise again to the race set before him?

Empowered and inspired by the Father's favor and amazing grace, Eric rolls on the track with the momentum of the moment, rises, shakes himself, and passionately pursues the race set before him until gloriously he crosses the finish line, having prevailed against all odds, to the glory of God. The gravity of the true account based upon the life of a truly God-loving and Father-fearing young man should grip the heart of every father to finish well. Watch it again... and again... yes with your children at your side. It is pure, and it is passionate!

Regretfully, there is a falling unto final failure and eternal loss. It involves a persistent "falling away" (II Thess. 2:3; Heb. 6:6). Such *falling away* leads not only to personal perdition but to destruction of paternal legacy. For this reason, we are given dire warning.

Fortunately, the Father is able to "keep us from falling" if we truly and sincerely follow His Word, Will and Ways (Jude 24). When we "fall into temptation," we are to "count it all joy" because our faith is being tested so that we might be perfected (Jam. 1:2-4). We are to "submit to God"... and only then "resist the devil" who will "flee from you" (Jam. 4:7). We are to "draw nigh to God [the Father]" and then "He will draw nigh to you" (Jam. 4:8).

Grace is not a prescription to sin promiscuously but rather a provision to keep us from falling. We are warned to flee temptation, especially sexual sin (I Cor. 6:18) and the "love of money" (I Tim. 6:9-11). Can I, as a husband and father, claim with a straight face that I am submitted to the Father when I am perpetually seduced by porn? "Let him that thinketh he standeth take heed lest he fall" (I Cor. 10:12).

Remember! "There hath no temptation taken you but such as is common to man: but God is faithful... and will with the temptation also make a way of escape..." (I Cor. 10:13). "Now all these things...

are written for our admonition, upon whom the ends of the world are come..." so, take heed lest you fall (I Cor. 10:11-12).

The Apostle Peter gave us a detailed prescription as to how we might prevail in these progressively evil times. We have devoted the entire Chapter 15 to applying his prescription based upon the promises of the Father. Let us remind ourselves of his final admonition:

> Wherefore the rather brethren, give diligence to make
> your calling and election sure: for IF ye do these
> things, ye shall never fall (II Pet. 1:10).

Remember this! "A just man falleth seven times, and riseth up again, but the wicked shall fall into mischief" (Prov. 24:16).

4. Forget Not

How easy it is for us as men to forget. Over and over the Father, through His Word, admonishes us not to forget but to remember. And if there was ever a time that we desperately need to embrace this warning and encouragement, it is today.

Here is a sampling of that which our Father would have us not forget.

> Take heed lest you forget the covenant of the LORD
> your God (Deut. 4:23-24).

> Beware that you forget not the LORD your God, in
> not keeping His commandments... (Deut. 8:11).

> If you do at all forget the LORD your God... I testify
> that you shall surely perish (Deut. 8:19-20).

The flip side of the Father's warning to "forget not" is His exhortation to "Remember." In order to forget not, we fathers must purpose to *remember* and practice *remembering*, both for ourselves and for our families.

> Remember now your Creator, in the days of your [relative] youth (Eccl. 12:1). This may be one of your children's deepest defenses against the godless evolutionary doctrines.

> Remember all the commandments of the Lord (Numb. 15:39).

> Remember the Sabbath day, to keep it holy (Ex. 20:8).

> Remember from whence you were fallen (Rev. 2:5).

> Stir up our minds by way of remembrance (II Pet. 3:1).

> Remember Lot's wife (Lk. 17:32).

Frivolously spent time and addictive technology are thieves we grant entrance into our homes to steal our family focus, disrupt our family faith and destroy our family joy and protection by cauterizing our memories, rendering them insensitive both to the Word and Ways of the Lord and to remembrance of his mighty acts.

Remembering is the Father's affirmative action program for all fathers. It is the only antidote to the deadly poison of forgetting in an increasingly faithless world. And we must remember out loud to our sons and daughters.

5. Fear the Lord

The fear of the Lord is foundational to fathering if we are to have hope of a godly legacy that will last. This is especially true in fearful times.

"In the fear of the Lord is strong confidence... providing a place of refuge" (Prov. 14:26). "The fear of the Lord is a fountain of life," enabling us and our families "to depart from the snares of death" (Prov. 14:27). The Father will teach the fathers that truly *fear the Lord* (Ps. 24:12).

There is great security and peace for fathers who truly *fear the Lord*. In fact, "The secret of the Lord is with them that fear him; and he will shew them his covenant" (Ps. 25:14). The *fear of the Lord* protects us and our families from "the fear of man" (Heb. 13:6, Ps. 56:11), because the "fear of man" is a snare... a trap... for our children (Prov. 29:25). And the *fear of the Lord* enables us to both identify and hate evil (Prov. 8:13).

Amid fearful times, the man who truly fears the Lord "shall not be afraid of evil tidings: his heart is fixed, trusting in the Lord. His heart is established, he shall not be afraid..." (Ps. 112:7-8). Men must seriously reconsider the Father's covenant with those who both love and fear Him.

> Blessed is the man that **feareth the LORD**, that delighteth greatly in his commandments.
>
> His seed shall be mighty upon the earth: the generation of the upright shall be blessed (Ps. 112:1-2).

Wisdom begins with the *fear of the Lord*, enabling us as men and fathers to have greater understanding as we follow Father's commandments (Ps. 111:10). Do we not need exceptional wisdom and understanding in which our sons and daughters can find hope and confidence in these troubled times?

(Note: For a more complete understanding of the all-encompassing role of the fear of the Lord in your life, you will find it in *The SECRET of the Lord* by this author, Elijah Books, 2011).

6. Follow Faithfully

If we, as fathers, are not able to faithfully follow the Father, who changes not, how can we expect our children to follow us in security and confidence? To be a father who leads to a promised legacy, I must first be a follower of the Father who made the promise. But what does it mean to be a follower? Is it cognitive assent to religious facts, or is it rather a way of life that conforms to the ways of the Father's household... as the Father alone defines those ways?

How closely do I follow the one I claim to be my Father? In Christ's most troubled and trying hour, all of his professed disciples either fled or followed "afar off" (Matt. 26:56, 58). Following demands extreme faith in fearful times. How, then, should we understand what it means to *follow* in fearful times? Here is just a brief glimpse as to the implications of the gospel for fathers who would have godly followers.

FOLLOW RIGHTEOUSNESS—"But thou, O man of God, flee these things [that cause to err from faith - I Tim. 6:3-10]; and *follow after righteousness*, godliness, faith, love, patience, meekness (I Tim. 6:11; II Tim. 2:22).

FOLLOW HOLINESS—*Follow...holiness*, without which no man shall see the Lord. "Lift up your hands which hand down, and the feeble knees; And make straight paths for your feet..." (Heb. 12:14, 12-13, I Pet. 1:13-16).

FOLLOW CHRIST'S SUFFERING—"For even hereunto were ye called: because Christ also suffered for us, leaving us an example, that ye should *follow in his steps*" (I Pet. 2:21).

"Forasmuch then as Christ hath suffered for us in the flesh, arm yourselves likewise with the same mind: for he that hath suffered in the flesh hath ceased from sin; That he no longer should live the rest of his time in the flesh to the lust of men, but to the will of God" (I Pet. 4:1-2).

"Beloved [fathers], think it not strange concerning the fiery trial which is to try you, as though some strange thing happened unto you: But rejoice, inasmuch as you are partakers of Christ's sufferings..." (I Pet. 4:12-13).

FOLLOW STEWARDSHIP—"It is required of stewards that a man be found faithful" (I Cor. 4:2). As fathers, we are appointed stewards of our children by the Father. We are the Father's surrogates—His hand extended—to raise, nurture and guide our young on behalf of the Father, both in Spirit and in Truth.

All the assets and income within our domain belong to the Father. We are trustees, delegated by the Father to use these for His glory and for the advancement of His kingdom, beginning with our families. Our talents and gifts are held by us in trust to do the Father's will. But do our children and grandchildren believe that? Do they see it borne out in our lives? It is difficult to remember in a world dedicated to SELF that our very lives are an investment by the Father in the future Kingdom of His Son.

FOLLOW WITHOUT FAIL—"Be thou *faithful unto death*, and I will give thee a crown of life" (Rev. 2:10b).

Faithfulness in following is tested in the crucible of fearful times. Our children need to learn such faithfulness both by fatherly precept and fatherly example.

Growing up as a young boy I was taught a simple, yet profound truth through the life of the prophet Daniel. Daniel, together with his three Hebrew friends, were taken captive as young men, probably in their teens. In Babylon, they were surrounded by a godless and idolatrous culture that threatened to press them into its mold. That pressure ultimately threatened each of them with their very lives. Would they be faithful... or not?

Out of this fearful environment of consummate testing came the simple lyrics of a little song...

> DARE to be a Daniel,
> DARE to stand alone,
> DARE to have a purpose firm, and
> DARE to make it known.

My young life was deeply impressed by these words that have strengthened me throughout my life in difficult times. I taught them to my daughters, and they were similarly gripped, so that when my firstborn grandson was born, he was named Daniel. A special calligraphied plaque was designed and presented to Daniel by his grandfather, this writer, and the beautifully-presented lyrics of that song have become a lasting legacy.

Several years ago, I had the privilege of speaking at a celebratory event for the largest Christian school in Ghana, Africa. Five hundred or so students from age five to nineteen were gathered, and I exhorted them to "Dare to be a Daniel" with those simple lyrics made memorable by the melody. Over and over throughout the assembly they repeated and sang those faith-building words that united the hearts of all ages into a ringing chorus of conviction. I was told years later that many were still singing and molded toward faithfulness by that chorus.

The accuser of our children is alive and well. The Deceiver seeks to destroy them daily. And we must teach them to be overcomers by our faithful example. As it is written...

And they overcame him by the blood of the Lamb, and by the word of their testimony; **and they loved not their lives unto the death** (Rev. 12:11-12).

7. Fight the Good Fight

We are at war, dads! As fathers and grandfathers, we are called by the Father to stand, and having done all to stand, to still stand. We must stand!!! Our children are trusting us to remain true... even unto death. But we can only do that by "Putting on the whole armor of God" daily, "that ye may be able to stand against the wiles of the devil" (Eph. 6:10-11). We must be lovers of the Father's truth, girding it about the most vulnerable areas of our lives.

This will demand a level of dedication seldom seen in the western world in our generation. It will require a depth of prayer, watchfulness and perseverance rarely practiced among professing Christian men today (Eph. 6:18). It will demand that, in the face of profound and discouraging adversity, we "Cast not away our confidence, which hath great recompense of reward. For we have need of patience, that after we have done the will of God, we might receive the promise" (Heb. 10:35-36).

It is time for fathers to get into the battle and "fight the good fight of faith" (I Tim. 6:12). What will you say when you face the ultimate, existential moment of your life, when you have done all you could do, said all you could say, lived all you could to define the destiny of those who will follow? Consider the convicting words of a former murderer who, in his moment of truth, knocked off his "high horse," radically committed his life to leave an eternal legacy that lasts to this day. Having his name changed from Saul—the religious murderer to Paul—the righteous-loving apostle, he declared as he faced death for his faith these challenging words for all who would follow.

> I have fought a good fight, I have finished my course, I have kept the faith:
>
> Henceforth there is laid up for me a crown of righteousness, which the Lord, the righteous judge, shall give me at that day: **and not to me only, but unto all them also that love his appearing**" (II Tim. 4:7-8).

MAY ALL WHO COME BEHIND US FIND US FAITHFUL!

> *God is our refuge and strength, a very present help in trouble. Therefore will not we [I] fear... (Ps. 46:1-2).*

Chapter 14
PROBING THOUGHTS for PROPHETIC TIMES

1. Why will men's hearts *fail for fear* in these end times in which we live?
2. Has the significance of these "latter days" gripped your fatherly heart yet? Why... or why not?
3. In what ways are you preparing your kids to stand firm in faith as the times become even more troubled?
4. How can you, like Noah, build an *ark of faith* for your family amid a mocking culture? Have you started building yet? What have you done? If you were to be tried... or fired as a builder of faith as a father, would an objective employer (God) hire... or fire you?
5. Has any warning or wooing exhortation stood out to you, in particular, as you considered these fearful times?

Chapter 15

PERSECUTION WITHIN FAMILIES

"Persecution from within… whether from family or the purported 'family of God,' is perhaps the most painful and lamentable of all…."

IT IS A TRUE SIGN OF THE TIMES when persecution arises within both the family and the church. Persecution from within is perhaps nearly as dangerous as persecution from without, but is even more troubling because of the seeming closeness of relationships and developed trust. Both Jesus and His apostles spoke of and warned concerning this insidious source of persecution. Apparently, then, it is a development in these otherwise perilous times of which we must not only be aware but for which we must prepare.

From the Outside In

How, then, does the persecutorial spirit make its way from the outside to the inside, from outside the family to invade both our immediate families and the family of God—the Body of Christ? If we truly understand the insidious nature of such persecutorial intrusion, it will at least give us a better understanding of the spiritual means by which it gradually makes its way into the very soul of family faith and trust.

The camel's nose must be given opportunity to enter the tent door, even ever so slightly. This entrance is made possible through:

1. Ignorance of the danger lurking behind the nose.
2. Impatience to achieve the prospect of immediate peace in the family or church.
3. Irresponsibility in protecting the family as a primary role of parents and pastors.
4. Implication of parents or pastors in facilitating the nose of the compromising camel into the family tent so as to make a perceived peace with the culture.
5. Improvising a temporal détente with the intrusion and established biblical standards for lack of courage to face the inherent eternal dangers emerging from the shadows that threaten both family relationships and fellowship with the Father.

Both parents and pastors have become adept at dancing through and around these dangers to preserve what they perceive to be peace in the camp to ostensibly "keep the family together," failing to realize that "a little leaven leaveneth the whole lump" (I Cor. 5:6), thus placing the entire family in jeopardy. And so, we inadvertently, though negligently, welcome the very cancer cells from the culture into our families and churches that will inevitably destroy the entire body.

The Road to Hell

"The road to hell is paved with good intentions," we are told. We believe this as a truism, but in actual truth, we act as if it is but an idle phrase, having little relevance. Though usually spoken in a jesting flair, the truth of this common aphorism should be taken to heart as an oft-repeated warning.

Few intentionally embark with gusto on the road to hell. Why, therefore, do so many find themselves on that road, accelerating to full speed on the autobahn to eternal destruction? The answer lies with good intentions. Good intentions, alone, without an absolute anchor to unmovable and unshakeable truth that does not drift, will inevitably lead down the on-ramp to the multi-lane expressway propelling all travelers thereon unsuspectingly to the abyss. Compromise becomes the engine that propels good intentions toward eternal deception and family destruction.

In reality, the road to hell begins at compromise corner. Compromise corner is at the intersection of all the major roads of our lives. The decisions we make, the turns we negotiate at compromise corner, inevitably lead toward that multi-lane expressway to destruction, even while still believing we are headed in God's general direction.

All compromise as it relates to God's truth is "compromise," and all compromise on issues of truth is deceptive and profoundly seductive. The great danger is that few travelers realize the seriousness of the seduction, because they measure themselves and the correctness of their decisions by the overwhelming majority who seem headed with clarity and certainty toward the multi-laned expressway to hell. They reason, if popular pastors, para-church leaders and the seeming majority of parents seem comfortable with this direction, it must be okay, even though deep in their heart they have this haunting suspicion that something is wrong. "It can't be wrong if it feels so right," they muse. But in the end, compromise bites like a cobra, and is deadly.

Compromise corner is found at many intersections of our lives. In fact, it is at virtually every intersection where we are called upon to make decisions, whether great or small. Small compromises are more deceptive than great ones, yet we are able to so easily justify them. We reason, Well, it's only a little compromise, not realizing that the small compromise is on a series of secondary roads leading to ever larger compromises, all similarly justified. It is not demons but decisions that are our worst enemies.

In the spiritual arena, we find ourselves "at the moment of truth, in the valley of decision" at many spiritual intersections where our decisions, whether small or great, persistently direct our destiny.

1. Our desires vs. God's desires (Eph. 2:1-3; Ps. 37:4; Matt. 6:33).
2. Our appetites vs. God's ordinance (I Pet. 2:11; Rom. 13:14; Mk. 4:19).

3. Our fears vs. Godly faith (Matt. 10:28; Heb. 13:6; II Tim. 1:7).
4. Our happiness vs. God's holiness (I Pet. 1:13-16; I Thess. 4:7; Prov. 28:13-14; Prov. 29:18; I Pet. 3:14).
5. Our pleasure vs. God's purity (Heb. 11:25; Ps. 16:11; II Tim. 3:4; I Tim. 5:6; I Jn. 3:3).
6. Our comfort vs. God's call (II Tim. 2:3; II Cor. 11:22-27, 12:10).
7. Our purposes vs. God's purposes (Gen. 45:5-8, 50:19-20).
8. Our ways vs. God's ways (Prov. 14:12; Jam. 1:8).
9. Trusting man vs. Trusting God (Jer. 17:5-10; Isa. 30:1-3).

Collective compromises on these various tests of whether we will be governed by the flesh or by the Spirit lead almost inevitably to further compromise until compromise becomes a way of life in our families. It takes radical confrontation through provocative preaching of the Word and courageous parenting, with painful application, to reverse the ingrained pattern, usually coupled with divine discipline, which is never comfortable, and which is frequently dismissed as "an attack from Satan" (Heb. 12:5-11).

Since compromise has such a corrosive effect both on our character and on our lives as Christians, perhaps we should look further at patterns of compromise and how compromise corrupts, leading deeper into deception and family destruction.

There are four distinct characteristics of compromise that collectively reveal its pattern in our lives.

1. Compromise Always Exalts Pragmatism Over Principle.
2. Compromise Always Exalts Flesh Over Faith.
3. Compromise Always Exalts Self-consciousness Over God-consciousness.
4. Compromise Always Exalts Temporal Over Eternal.

Now that we have confronted the spirit of compromise that welcomes ungodly and unbiblical patterns of thought and behavior into our homes and congregations, we now must look with lament at the persecutorial consequences of that which has invaded our families. It is this painful moment of Christ-warned truth that is the ultimate focus of our time together in this chapter.

(Note: The previous patterns of compromise and the Road to Hell, beginning at Compromise Corner, are an excerpt from my previous book, *Seduction of the Saints*).

Persecution From Within Families

Persecution from within the flock, whether from family or the purported "family of God," is perhaps the most painful and lamentable of all, precisely because it breaches what we believed were trusting relationships. Both Jesus and King David, a man after God's own heart, experienced such horrific betrayal. Jesus was betrayed by Judas, a part of the disciple family, with the kiss of death (Matt. 26:47-48). David was betrayed by Ahithophel, his deeply trusted friend, advisor and confidante, that would have consigned David to death at the betrayal of David's own son, Absolom. Here was a double betrayal—a treasonous conspiracy—against the very one upon whose eternal throne the Lord of Glory was to rule and reign.

Interestingly, almost David's entire nation—the 10 northern tribes of Israel—ultimately rose up against the continuity of David's God-ordained reign. And in the same fashion, Christ, as the seed of David, was violently rejected by His own nation of which He was the sole obedient representative. As it is written, "He came unto his own, and his own received him not" (Jn. 1:11). He came to bring life and redemption to His people, to do the will of His Father, but most wanted no part of that. They cried instead, *Give us Barabbas*—a murderer, and let Christ be crucified (Matt. 27:1-26).

Perhaps, now, we can better understand the significance of Jesus' warning words:

> The servant is not greater than his lord. If they have
> persecuted me, they will also persecute you (Jn. 15:20).

Unfortunately, the persecution of which Jesus warned was not only from without but also from within—within families and gatherings of purported followers of Christ himself. No true and faithful parent or pastor desires such painful persecution born of betrayal revealed in outright rejection of all or many aspects of the Christian faith. But it is even now shockingly being progressively revealed throughout the West and America. Individual converts to Christ have, for two millennia, experienced rejection and violent retributive reaction from family, clan and culture, but seldom have Christian families in the so-called Christian West experienced the vitriolic attitudes increasingly displayed by family members, causing perplexity among parents and serious-minded pastors.

What is happening? Why is this new phenomenon invading our homes, causing a breakdown of communication and fractured relationships, jeopardizing any binding fraternal spirit, and devastating any sincere and long-term hope for the eternal salvation of those we love? It is the intensity of this phenomena seeming to sweep like a tsunami over our homes and fellowships that reveals the reality of Jesus' warning of this very development before His return. But what faith-threatening forces are collectively amassing this assault, what are the expected consequences, and how must we respond both in spirit and in truth?

Before we can attempt an answer to these questions, we must be frank concerning our Lord's descriptive warning of this otherwise frightening scene of severe persecution from within otherwise trusting relationships. Take a deep breath, and then consider the reality many are now facing or will soon face, confident that it is God who will work in and through us "both to will and to do of his good pleasure," yes even when unrighteously persecuted.

> And ye shall be betrayed both by parents, and brethren, and kinsfolk, and friends; and some of you shall they cause to be put to death.

And ye shall be hated of all men for my name's sake.

In your patience possess ye your souls (Lk. 21:16-17, 19).

If the world hate you, ye know that it hated me before it hated you.

If ye were of the world, the world would love his own: but because ye are not of the world…therefore the world hateth you (Jn. 15:18-19).

These things have I spoken unto you, that ye should not be offended.

They shall put you out of the synagogues: yea, the time cometh, that whosoever killeth you will think [reason] that he doeth God [a] service (Jn. 16:1-2).

Let's take an honest look at the real but insidious forces invading our homes and families, creating attitudes and behaviors bringing chaos and distress, thus establishing an environment leading to eventual persecution of family members.

EDUCATION vs. INDOCTRINATION

Education establishes basic foundational truths and applications so that our young can develop lives capable of living successfully in the world in general. These include the historic fundamentals of reading, writing and arithmetic. Building upon these essentials, education then teaches students how to process ideas and choices by means of basic logic and rational thinking. All of these goals have been historically embraced under the overarching authority of God, the Creator, as revealed in and through His Word. All contrary ideas and philosophies were deemed dangerous and unwelcome in the American home.

Along came John Dewey and Horace Mann in the early 20th century, promoting progressive education and liberalism as educational reforms. Horace Mann lauded the public school system. Dewey, while raised as a progressive Congregationalist, ultimately became an atheist, replacing Christianity with a religion of his own—secular humanism—focused not on biblical principles but on pragmatism—which he described as "A Common Faith."

David Breese wrote a book called *Seven Men Who Rule the World from the Grave*. Included among them are Karl Marx, Charles Darwin, Sigmund Freud and John Dewey. Ironically, Dewey was born the same year Darwin published his *On the Origin of Species* (1859), creating and proposing a new creation story to explain in naturalistic terms the existence of all things without God. The philosophies of these four men, over the past century, have so permeated the minds and hearts of America's families, including parents and even pastors, such that our children are not now being educated but rather indoctrinated.

Thus, when our kids come home from the halls of indoctrination called public schools, colleges and universities, they are prepared to do combat with parents and grandparents who still hold onto a residue of godly principles and biblical viewpoints. The level and intensity of that combat is now dividing families, leaving no place for civil discussion, leaving parents and pastors with the apparent choice to either capitulate to the cultural pressure or to risk alienating those they have sought to lovingly raise. And as has often been said, "It only takes a spark to get a fire going." That fire will eventually take the form of Christ-warned persecution.

CULTURE vs. CHRIST

Culture is the sea of common life in which we swim. And culture becomes the ever-changing aggregate of what is being taught, the adoption of philosophies, beliefs and common practices. As the culture drifts away over time from the foundational certainties of biblical truth, exalting experience over truth and feelings over faith, the entire culture, even of a nation that persists in identifying itself as "A nation under God," literally shifts on its axis, creating pressures few are either able or willing to resist. Our choice to remain firm on biblical truth, resisting the lordship of feelings and experience over genuine and historic Christian faith will inevitably lead to unpleasant and even violent confrontation, bringing spouses against each other, children against parents, parents against children, and friends against one another just as Jesus foretold.

HAPPINESS vs. HOLINESS

Since experience and feelings have become the final arbiter of "truth" in our post-modern culture, the refrain of a Christian musician from the 1970s now reigns supreme: "It can't be wrong when it feels so right." Therefore, the entire creation ordinance of God from Genesis 1 and 2 concerning marriage, divorce, remarriage, procreation, homosexuality, transgenderism, pedophilia and now even bestiality are affirmed even within ostensibly Christian households under the banner of "love," because the pursuit of happiness trumps or supersedes our Lord's call to holiness. The very definition of what is **holy** has thus been redefined as anything that makes me, my friends, or relatives "happy." Unfortunately, refusal within a household to replace true holiness in the sexual arena with the cultural demand for feelings of happiness is approaching a virtual declaration of war in many families, resulting in various levels of persecution.

It should, therefore, be patently obvious to any and all truly Christian parents to take these signs seriously and to diligently prepare their young for times of severe difficulty yet to come. But there is yet another "family" matter that should and must grab our attention.

Offense in the Church "Family"

Jesus made clear in His High Priestly Prayer of John 17 that it is not confession of faith alone that unites people into the family of faith in Jesus the Messiah, but must include absolute commitment to His

Word which is the truth that truly unites and binds us in unity. But when that allegiance to the truth as manifested in the totality of the Scriptures is fractured through unbelief, disbelief or rejection of the truths we do not care to embrace, it causes a serious rupture in the ostensible "family" of God.

Depending upon the area of focus of such a breach, there becomes under increasing pressure of forces both outside and inside the church, the environment leading to devastating betrayal and so-called "friendly fire" taking the form of outright persecution. What may, at first, be deemed mere differences of opinion on various issues to be tolerated become intolerable to those who are not truly truth seekers but are determined to claim their opinions as "gospel" regardless of clear biblical truths to the contrary.

Thus, the "offense of the gospel" becomes not only an offense by so-called unbelievers but also offense taken by those within the church against those who are holding to, preaching or teaching the fulness of biblical truth as it bears upon those details of our lives and culture. In a culture already riding the crest of offenses, even displayed in so-called Christian communications and blogs, it is but a short step to see offenses at other Christians take a more vitriolic path leading to outright persecution.

Jesus made this dilemma plain in teaching about the Word as seed. Consider well and humbly the horrific fallout from spiritual offense due to the Word itself. In Jesus' own words, speaking of the heart as the "ground" in which the Word is sown, He warns:

> And these are they likewise which are sown on stony ground; who, when they have heard the word, immediately receive it with gladness;

> And have no root in themselves, and so endure but for a time: afterward, when affliction or persecution ariseth for the word's sake, immediately they are offended (Mk. 4:16-17).

Who, then, becomes the object of the offense? It is those who remain faithful to the full counsel of God, without wavering. This is the inevitable fruit of fifty years of birthing faith babies through mere confession of faith, without confession of sin and repentance, and without serious discipleship in the Word, Will and Ways of the household of faith in Jesus. When the true cost of discipleship is not preached, there will be a price to pay, and an unexpected source of persecution knocks at the door to our profound dismay, causing many more to fall away.

Truly my soul waiteth upon God: from him cometh my salvation. He only is my rock and my salvation; he is my defence; I shall not be greatly moved (Ps. 62:1-2).

Chapter 15
PROBING THOUGHTS for PROPHETIC TIMES

1. How might the proverbial "camel" be getting his persecutorial nose inside the tent of your family?
2. In what ways have you, as a parent, been either knowingly or unsuspectingly been trying to make "peace" in the family by brushing over things that actually may well be laying the foundation for eventual open animosity and persecution against siblings, parents or grandparents?
3. Have you perhaps lured those you love into a deeper rejection of God's ways through a pattern of progressive compromise to secure temporary comfort, unwittingly deepening their entrenchment in rebellion?
4. How did you process, or are you processing, Jesus' multiple warnings to parents and families? If this source of inter-family persecution was not of serious concern, why did our Lord bring such a seemingly negative message?
5. What is winning in your home? Education or Indoctrination? Culture or Christ? Pursuit of Happiness… or Holiness?

PART 6

PASTORING IN PERILOUS TIMES

"We have failed dramatically in presenting the cost of discipleship...."

PAUL PREPARED FOR PERILOUS TIMES. The apostle well understood the nature of persecution, having experienced it first-hand. He also well knew that such persecution and the attitudes driving it would be compounded as the growing church prepared for the coming of the Lord. And so, he boldly, and in love, without mincing words, prepared his ministry trainee pastor, Timothy, not in how to grow a big church but in how to prepare the people to endure the cost of discipleship that would come.

This revered apostle warned Timothy that "in the last days perilous times shall come" (II Tim. 3:1-7). He laid out all the attitudinal and behavioral characteristics that would combine to create such perilous times. And those characteristics are a clear-cut diagnosis of that which haunts and horrifies our world and the church today, especially throughout the West.

Declaring that the Lord Christ shall judge, Paul exhorted Timothy to "preach the word," to "rebuke and exhort." Because he warned that "the time will come when they will not endure sound doctrine" (II

Tim. 4:1-4). Our problem is that for sixty years we have failed dramatically in presenting the true "cost of discipleship" so as to meet the cultural mandates of growing mega churches and of marketing books.

The question that should haunt and hover over the mind and heart of every pastor and para-church leader is: Can I, with a straight face of holy integrity, claim before God and the holy angels that I have faithfully and diligently prepared those under my sphere of influence to endure the persecution that both Christ and His apostles promised? The judge is awaiting our answer.

Preserve me, O God: for in thee do I put my trust
(Ps. 16:1).

Chapter 16

PERSECUTION WITHIN THE CHURCH

"Persecution coming from within the church
is well-deserved to be designated
as 'a sign of the times' precisely because Jesus declared it to be so."

THE PAINFUL YET UNDENIABLE TRUTH is that throughout the past two thousand years since the "end times" began at Pentecost and the death and resurrection of Jesus Christ, massive persecution of professing Christians has come from the hearts and hands of other professing Christians and their respective theological groups, the Roman Catholic Church being the greatest offender of all. Yet Protestants and a variety of corollary groups have also participated in the open violence against Roman Catholics and various other Protestant expressions of the faith considered to be on the fringe of perceived orthodoxy that required purging to protect the perceived purity of Christian life, belief and practice.

While it is true that the Protestant Reformation triggered often violent reaction from the Roman papacy, the driving motivational forces were, in reality, only superficially religious. The underlying motivation was the preservation of papal power, perks and position through sinister political machinations coupled with deputized papal armies sent to crush all perceived to threaten the "Absolute Monarchy" that the Roman Catholic Church had become in the Middle Ages. Absolute Monarchy employed absolute tyranny through the Inquisitions,

"Recant or Burn" orders, and the "Tariff of Torture" employed by papal edict to mechanize suffering, all of which created unfathomable carnage over twelve centuries.

The result was Absolute Terror. Church and state had united again, as with ancient Rome under the absolute monarchy of the religiously empowered pontifex maximus. Terror was the tool as directed by the Supreme Pontiff, the sheer magnitude of which is almost impossible to comprehend. Purported heresies were everywhere, and papally-driven mobs were given the task to root them out wherever they may be imagined, and whoever they may be. No one was safe. Estimates of the papal carnage range from 50 million to 150 million souls. (The details of this painful yet, prophetic, history can be found in my book, *ANTICHRIST: How to Identify the Coming Imposter*, Chapter 24 "The 'ABSOLUTE MONARCHY',").

Will History Repeat Itself?

What are the prophetic implications of a history revealing massive persecution of Christians all purportedly in the name of Christ himself? Does biblical prophecy not foretell such horrors to again sweep not only Europe but the entire earth? If the Bible is God's Word and is true, history will indeed repeat itself… on steroids… and beyond all current comprehension.

Perhaps an unfortunate harbinger is that on January 17, 2019, Pope Francis consolidated and assigned all related Inquisitional duties to the "Congregation for the Doctrine of Faith."[57] It would appear the "Congregation for Universal Inquisition" established July 21, 1542, has been revived, resurrected, or reconstituted, preserved for further implementation as the streams of history and prophecy merge and surge toward the Return of Christ.

Divide to Conquer

Jesus made the principle plain. If you want to conquer a marriage, family, city, nation, or the professing body of Christ, you must first create division from within so that it cannot stand (Matt. 12:25; Lk. 11:17).

Consider well the manner in which our marriages and families which make up the Church are being divided and destroyed. Yet the full extent of that destructive division has not yet been fully manifested. It will very soon, in fact already is, becoming a reality in our homes, and what happens in our homes insinuates itself like a virulent cancer throughout the community professing to be followers of Yeshua, the Messiah. What then does such a message of internal division and discord transmit to the broader society?

Our Lord was very specific as to what we should expect as we approach the near edge of His return. His words are shocking to our western and American sensibilities. Anchor the seatbelt of your chariot as you contemplate their confrontive implications.

> Suppose ye that I am come to give peace on earth? I tell you, Nay; but rather division:
>
> For from henceforth there shall be five in one house divided, three against two, and two against three.
>
> The father shall be divided against the son, and the son against the father, the mother against the daughter, and the daughter against the mother; the mother in law against her daughter in law, and the daughter in law against her mother in law (Lk. 12:51-53).

Do these words not sound familiar as we observe the antagonism building within our purportedly Christian families as cultural mandates increasingly supersede Christ's words as Master. The unfortunate reality is that culture is becoming King in the household of faith while Christ becomes little more than a cuddly mascot. Thus, families and marriages are breaking apart with reverberating consequences throughout the greater professing community, creating the intensifying atmosphere for even greater accusations and internecine warfare resulting ultimately in persecution—yes within and against professing Christians, just as Jesus foretold.

How It Is Happening

The spiritual and cultural mechanisms through which inter-church and intra-church persecution arises remain largely a mystery to most precisely because we cannot bear to admit it is happening or are, dare we say, intentionally blind to the blatant reality. For this reason, we must look for a few moments at the means by which the atmosphere for open persecution is growing within individual congregations, within denominations, and between denominations and other independent groups.

ABANDONMENT OF TRUTH

The historical concept of *truth* as that which can be known and embraced as absolutely "true" in guiding our lives together in harmony has been gradually abandoned, particularly since the late 1960s. As has already been made clear, feelings began to replace facts and therefore the foundation of true faith, leaving only personal experience to become the accepted substitute for truth. Hence the oft-quoted phrase—"What's true for you is not necessarily true for me."

It was perhaps a decade ago that the respected researcher, George Barna, reported that only about half of adult professing Christians believed in "absolute truth" but that only 9% of professing Christian young people believed in "absolute truth." The terrifying consequences were revealed in Barna's further findings that only 20% of America's professing Christian young people actually believed that Jesus Christ is "the ONLY way, the ONLY truth and the ONLY life—the ONLY way to eternal relationship with God the Father" as Jesus himself had declared (Jn. 14:6).

And why is such disbelief terrifying? It reveals that 80% of professing Christian young people cannot possibly be truly Christians, since they believe that many philosophies, viewpoints and religious beliefs are co-equal and efficacious to qualify both themselves and their friends and relatives for eternal and joyful habitation with the Father, excluding all from Christ's judgment. And woe to anyone, whether parent, youth pastor or pastor who dares to directly disagree or confront. Such person… and church body… will become the object of angry scorn, rejection and ultimately violent resistance.

And then, in a spirit of parental protection, moms, dads and grandparents rise up to defend their child's abandonment of truth with a variety of justifications and spiritual gymnastics; thus deepening the conflict within the collective body of Christ. Pastors are therefore increasingly fearful and intimidated, unwilling to face the risk and anticipated consequences of confrontation. And so… pastors, church boards and other wealthy parishioners gradually climb on board the mutinous ship sailing contrary to the Holy Spirit given to guide us into all truth.

THEOLOGICAL DRIFT

The broader church—both Protestant and Catholic—has been drifting dramatically from theological "givens" embraced largely throughout history. This drift has been justified in the pursuit of being "modern," then "progressive" in order to dance with the cultural drift toward "post-modernism" which has led inevitably to the denial of absolute truth.

The explosive expression of the Church Growth movement in the 1970s leading to the seductive surge of the Seeker Sensitive" movement in the 1990s leading to the so-called Emerging Church" movement early in the first decade of the 2000s has defined a shockingly weak theological foundation—rejecting or intentionally ignoring the Lord's command to holy living in favor of the pursuit of happiness. Should it then surprise anyone that, as the broader professing Christian community in America and throughout the so-called Christian western world, that we are now neither *happy* nor *holy*.

Unhappy people, while claiming Christ but living in unholiness and rejecting all correction, eventually rise up in self-righteous retribution to attack the remnant still seeking to live righteously. Division is only natural, yet division will eventually not suffice due to the rising self or group-protecting rage. The remnant still bearing the righteous standard must be openly or covertly attacked so as to be purged from the newly perceived "respectable" society.

Such theological drift has long been a matter of concern, but it has now manifested in a nearly full-fledged rebellion against biblical authority clearly revealed in the progressive embrace of the culture's radically changing stance on matters of sexuality. God's creation ordinance regarding marriage, divorce, remarriage, homosexuality and now transgenderism, pederasty and polyamory, even bestiality has become the clear fulcrum over which the broader church has decided that the demands of culture supersede the commands of Christ.

That which God hates or calls abomination is now to be celebrated in pursuit of peace and unity. And woe to the one who deigns to declare otherwise, for you have become an enemy of world peace and global salvation.

CULTURE AS KING

It is nearly undeniable that culture has become king in our churches and among our purportedly Christian families. Our pastors, priests, bishops and the pope have all not only felt the pressure to conform but have decided to conform to the ever more radical demands of rebellion and profoundly unrighteous culture. Jesus tells us to "come out from among them" but we have decided to become one with them. As the phrase goes—"If you can't beat 'em, join 'em." And the alleged justification is always a counterfeit "love."

Concepts of biblical justice have been summarily replaced by the new humanistic morality of "social justice" as the mediator of salvation—not by faith but by absolute conformity to the cultural dictate. Again, according to the Barna Group, two-thirds of our high school and college grads previously claiming to be "Christian" have rejected biblical justice based upon the Creator's viewpoint and have embraced as dogma the new "progressive" social justice tenants.

Chuck Mason, who has given himself as a unique calling to confront these issues with Christian parents and pastors, writes:

> Social justice narratives provide a new form of morality, giving them the justification they need to break from a Judeo-Christian worldview to explore lifestyles of their choice. They reject faith, families, traditional perspectives, and common sense as they embark on a journey of complete self-determination.
>
> Progressives have wanted to purge the influence of Christianity from society for nearly a century… but the "bigotry" of the Judeo-Christian worldview stands in their way.
>
> … the intellectual revolution of the post-modern movement gave Progressives the justification they needed to purge Christianity's influence from the land.
>
> Kids are like intellectual sheep sent to the ideological slaughter.[58]

Yet parents, pastors, priests, popes and certainly our politicians have succumbed to and have perhaps unwittingly become co-participants in the slaughter of genuine biblical truth and faith, thus setting the stage for an unsuspected backlash of internal persecution that will ultimately separate the remnant of true followers of Christ from the masses of purported believers who are not prepared to stand in this evil day.

"A Sign of the Times"

Persecution coming from within the church is well-deserved to be designated as "a sign of the times" precisely because Jesus declared it to be so, as we have already seen. His warnings were intended to prepare His followers to not only realize what the cost of discipleship would be throughout the centuries but to also prepare His followers for the culminating intensification of persecution for carrying His name as the end of the church age drew near. And so, our Lord made clear that only those who endure to the end shall be saved (Matt. 24:13).

The problem American and European Christians have with connecting in any meaningful way with Jesus' warnings is what Grayson Gilbert has called "a weak theology of suffering," out of which comes "an inability to willingly and joyfully endure our present sufferings." As he laments, "The American gospel has so long imbibed a gospel message devoid of telling people of the cost it takes to follow Christ." We are rather inclined, he notes, to "see the kind of luxury-suffering indicative of a soft generation, as suffering for our faith." We confuse the natural results of living as a Christian in a fallen world with genuine suffering and persecution. "Many Christians confuse temptation with suffering," he observed, "and therefore have no accurate category for how to deal with legitimate forms of persecution for the sake of the gospel."

For these reasons, "… you find people who are unable to think biblically" about persecution, and the result is to totally resist either the tide or actuality of persecution so as "to avoid suffering at all costs." Such people, the western church at large, "will be completely blindsided when they actually experience any kind of suffering first-hand." "When the church is not on guard and equipped to deal with these things, it is only a matter of time before they savagely rip one another to shreds with their teeth (Gal. 5:15)." I firmly believe, and therefore write, that "we will soon see those professing to be Christians turn on other Christians in order to save themselves"—a condition that "is already beginning to happen." "What this means is that we are coming to the point where the church itself is the place where we ought to expect persecution, rather than just the culture we live in."[59]

Peter Prepares Us for Persecution

Peter, who once denied Christ thrice under pressure of fear when Jesus was arrested before his crucifixion, came full circle to realize what Jesus had warned and that Paul later reinforced—that "all that will live godly in Christ Jesus will suffer persecution" (II Tim. 3:12). And so, Peter also suffered crucifixion upside down (as held by tradition). Knowing well the ultimate cost of discipleship, the apostle Peter left us with a serious exhortation so that we might be victorious amid the victim culture preceding Christ's soon return. We conclude this chapter with his enduring words of exhortation:

> Forasmuch then as Christ has suffered for us in the flesh, arm yourselves likewise with the same mind....

> Beloved, think it not strange concerning the fiery trial which is to try you, as though some strange thing happened unto you.

> But rejoice, inasmuch as ye are partakers of Christ's sufferings; that, when his glory shall be revealed, ye may be glad also with exceeding joy (I Pet. 4:1, 12-13).

> *The mercy of the LORD is from everlasting to everlasting upon them that fear him... To such as keep his covenant, and to those that remember his commandments to do them (Ps. 103:1-2).*

Chapter 16
PROBING THOUGHTS for PROPHETIC TIMES

1. In what ways do you see the preservation of power, perks and position being a significant source of or motivation for persecution within the church?
2. How has the supposed spiritually motivated "Inquisition" been used to foster and foment persecution historically? Can you envision the possibility or even likelihood that such action could again be used?
3. Why is it deemed necessary to "divide" in order to "conquer"?
4. How do you see the foundations of truth… and truth itself, being abandoned?
5. What are some areas of "theological drift" you can identify?
6. If "culture is king," what is the natural responsive attitude toward those who truly claim Christ is King?
7. When you read the apostle Peter's admonition to us regarding persecution, how would you define your response?

Chapter 17

PREACHING DISCIPLESHIP'S COST

"We must courageously prepare those God has placed in our care for the very persecution Jesus promised…."

"BLESSED ARE THOSE who are persecuted for righteousness' sake," declared pastor H.B. Charles to close out the 2023 Southern Baptist Convention, "for theirs is the Kingdom of heaven." Was this message to thousands of pastors from Matthew 5:10-12 a wrap-up message of encouragement or discouragement… of hope or horror ahead? It well depends upon your viewpoint, and the viewpoint of most American pastors today causes them to flee the subject of persecution, the cost of discipleship, like the plague, even though Christ clearly promised such persecution.

Suffering Doesn't Market Well

American ministry has, for at least sixty years, focused largely on *marketing* the gospel rather than the complete *message* of the gospel. The message must be sweet to the ears rather than searching the heart. In reality we have concluded: "You cannot sell suffering." Therefore, the cost of discipleship rarely, if ever, hits either the ears or hearts of professing Christian believers or those unbelievers they purport to reach through well-programed marketing; always exclusive of what it truly means to be a disciple.

Two classic cases are piercingly illustrative. The first was the case of a well-known Christian musician who joined me a number of years ago on my national radio program, *VIEWPOINT*, to discuss his new book—*A Violent Grace: Meeting Christ at the Cross*. During the interview, the author interrupted the conversation saying that he needed to let our listeners know what he faced in getting the book published. And his words I have never forgotten. He told us he had presented the manuscript to numerous Christian publishers to which they ALL responded in rejecting the book stating: "The cross doesn't sell anymore."

The second case involves the subject of Hell. *USA Today*[60] carried an article posted August 1, 2009, stating, "Many Americans don't believe in hell, but what about pastors?" The Pew Forum on Religion and Public Life concluded per recent surveys that "Only 59% of Americans believe in hell, compared with 74% who believe in heaven." And so, the director of the Global Center at Samford University's Beeson Divinity School conducted a workshop for pastors to discuss "Whatever happened to hell?" He inquired as to how many had ever preached a sermon on hell, but nobody had, he said. "I think it's something people want to avoid," he said.

An attending pastor of a Wesleyan church in the South commented that pastors shy away from the topic of everlasting damnation because, as he said, "It's out of fear we'll not appear relevant. It's the pressure from the culture to not speak anything negative."

Enter now the *Los Angeles Times*[61] on hell and evangelical pastors. A well-known and trusted evangelical pastor from the most politically-conservative county of southern California was interviewed regarding preaching on the subject of hell. He affirmed his personal belief in hell, but explained that he never broaches the subject with his congregation because, as he said, Hell "isn't sexy enough anymore," that hell is being frozen out by secularism in the church.

Hell! "Well it's just too negative," said Bruce Shelby, a senior professor of church history at Denver Theological Seminary. "Churches are under enormous pressure to be consumer-oriented churches.

Churches today feel the need to be appealing rather than demanding." The Barna Research Group noted that church-shopping has become a way of life, issuing out of the Church Growth movement of the 1970s followed by the watered-down gospel of the Seeker Sensitive movement in the 1980s and 1990s. He lamented that such fickleness gave rise to consumer-driven megachurches. "Once pop evangelism went into market analysis, hell just happened," declared Martin Marty, renowned religion and culture professor.

"Perhaps more than any other pastor," concluded the *Los Angeles Times*, "the Rev. Robert H. Schuller is credited with inspiring the movement to supplant hell with a feel-good message." The founder of the dazzling Crystal Cathedral gathered pastors worldwide for many years to impart his new sinless and therefore saleable message to ministers and ministries for church and denominational growth rather than making true disciples of the Kingdom of God. Having declared that to call people "sinners" was "abusive" and that what they truly needed was "more self-esteem," his new marketable message metastasized throughout the world, but especially in America,[62]through such mega movements led by his foremost disciples commonly or popularly known as "The Purpose-Driven Life" and "The Willow Creek" movement of churches.

As uncomfortable as such a willful trajectory of drift from the demands of Christ and His disciples is revealed to be, we must humbly look at the current and seriously weakened state of our flocks that has consequentially developed over nearly two generations, leading us to the near edge of Christ's return. As we have both consciously and progressively embraced the Market to set our course, we have similarly reduced the authority and call of our Master to that of not much more than a mere mascot.

How, then, does this state of spiritual affairs, where culture now increasingly celebrates dominion over Christ, affect the readiness of those entrusted to our pastoral and prophetic care in the face of our Lord's warning of serious persecution looming ahead? Are we even willing or capable of such consideration given two generations of ministry that has seriously undermined or even denied the warnings of Christ to professing believers?

Pastors Are People Too

Please understand! Pastors are people, regardless of the various titles they choose to wear or that others attribute to them. A degree behind the name does nothing to change the calling or to alter the authority under which, in the name of Christ, they purport to serve.

It may be shocking to some, but pastors are tempted in all manner as are their parishioners… and perhaps in ways their parishioners would find difficult to comprehend. The church and cultural statistics of our generation bear out this truth, much to our collective consternation. And so, it is increasingly incumbent upon us to face up to our humanity as susceptible to social and cultural pressures that distract and even deceive us to depart from the absolute truths of Christ and His Word in order to accommodate to an increasingly resistant and rebellious culture that has made its way surreptitiously into our congregations.

The problem we now and have always faced is the challenge of pontificating from our pulpits with a degree of pastoral passion and even chutzpah while we either negligently or consciously refrain from dealing with some of the most consequential issues faced by our flocks… of which they are likely not even cognizant in any serious way. Perhaps this is a clarion call to consciously remember with what we either say, or don't say, that the Potentate of the Universe is and will judge us as to the actual integrity of our messages and as to our motivations in determining what we preach or refuse to preach in such ultimate times in which we live.

It is entirely possible some might say, "Whatever gives you the right to say or suggest such things?" "How dare you?" And to that I must respond that such is not a joyful calling to be one of a growing number of voices coming forth with the express message to "Prepare the Way of the Lord… to make His paths straight." The road ahead is far more troubling, challenging and even dangerous than many… perhaps most… pastors are willing to admit and embrace.

As for me, as your servant, I am following a call from the Lord in 1992 to "speak to His church at large, whether they will hear or whether they will forbear." In 1993 we launched Save America Ministries to "Rebuild the Foundations of Faith and Freedom" and in 1995 began a daily LIVE radio broadcast, *VIEWPOINT*, from the shores of America's birth river, the James, "Confronting the deepest issues of America's Heart and Home" from God's eternal perspective, as "A Voice to the Church, Declaring Vision to the Nation" in America's greatest crisis hour.

As a former trial lawyer, I have been called to plead the cause of a lifetime to a jury of my peers, the American people… but more specifically to the Church in America. For that purpose I have brought on thousands of witnesses to "testify" on the broadcast—over 3500 national Christian leaders, pastors, parachurch leaders, authors and publishers, to assist in bringing a full and balanced case to our listeners so that they and their families, and pastors, might prepare themselves for the times now upon us.

This unique ministry calling, while being presented and pled by a former trial lawyer, is deeply rooted in pastoral ministry. Therefore, this chapter is not written to "You" but rather to "We" the pastors. Although I have pastored from coast to coast—even while practicing law—that sojourn has now continued since the early 1980s. My father was a pastor for 50 years. His parents were both pastors in the Salvation Army, and my mother's parents were both Salvation Army officers as was an aunt.

Yes, ministry has been our purpose and passion, and we have all written our own heart "lamentations" over the clear signs of the times for four generations as the church and her leadership have progressively marched to the ever-increasing drumbeat of a godless culture. So, my pastoral brethren, we are in this together, whether or not we want to accept the choices now challenging our callings. Indeed, pastors are people too! Yet we of all people must tell the whole truth.

Telling the Whole Truth

Having now seen how we as pastors have managed to not only skirt but intentionally evade the subject of sin and hell, concluding they are no longer "sexy" or saleable, how do we suppose we have dealt with preparing the saints in the West for promised persecution?

Our current viewpoint within the western and American church reveals a belief that persecution is a curse to be avoided at all costs, including any serious conversation that might presuppose its reality other than in far-away lands. Like sin and hell, persecution will not "sell." Yet millions are likely to lose their souls for lack of courageous preparatory preaching.

Who, then, will bear the eternal consequences? Will it be only the unprepared people who have long occupied our pews, or will pastors bear judgment as well? Are we watchmen who give warning whether or not we think people will hear, thus "delivering our soul," or will their blood be "required at our hand" (Ezek. 2-3)? Will we be mere straying ministry "Levites" or the blessed "sons of Zadok" (Ezek. 44:10-15, 48:11)? Perhaps the Christ we call Lord and Messiah is lovingly, yet persuasively, seeking to get our attention as does a great coach because his team has forgotten for whom they are playing and the owner's expectations.

It seems as if pastor H.B. Charles, in delivering his 2023 closing address to thousands of SBC pastors, gave all pastors a powerfully prophetic hint when he drove home the Beatific words of Christ:[63]

> Blessed are those who are persecuted for righteousness' sake, for theirs is the Kingdom of heaven (Matt. 5:10-12).

Our attitudes of being in Christ are not reflecting the true attitudes of a genuine believer walking in righteousness, observed H.B. Charles, for Jesus, he reminded, said that such persecution should cause us to "rejoice and be glad." He made clear that "these features express and emphasize the gravity of Christian persecution" and that it is Jesus' teaching regarding a proper perspective of persecution that introduces the main body of the great Sermon on the Mount. Thus, if we are persecuted truly "for righteousness' sake," from God's viewpoint we are already blessed.

Yet if we as pastors do not embrace this viewpoint as a functioning and observable reality in our own lives, how can we communicate it to those who are trusting our spiritual preparation for the trying times to come? Or are we passively punting the persecution football down the field in the hope that some more diligent saint may, notwithstanding our refusal to include persecution in our playbook, just happen to see the light for victory while the rest of the team languishes in spiritual defeat?

The transferrable concept from H.B. Charles' message was clear. Persecution is a given—not just for pastors—but for all who live godly in Christ Jesus. So, count yourself "blessed" if and when you are persecuted "for righteousness' sake" and "be exceeding glad, for great is your reward in heaven." We want our lives and ministries to be blessed, but don't much want to pass through the stiles of persecution to get there. So brethren, what must we do? We must consciously and courageously prepare those God has placed in our care for the very persecution Jesus promised that would tear faith and family asunder if proper preparation of heart and mind has not been made. The infamous Mark of the Beast may thus swallow up massive numbers of those who have occupied our rolls and pews, notwithstanding the insulating vagaries of various theologies many have embraced to the contrary.

What Must We Do?

In order to effectively prepare our people for rising persecution, we must do some preliminary house-keeping. Obviously, we cannot teach or preach with conviction and passion on that which has not truly and passionately gripped our own hearts and homes.

Here, then, are some perhaps sobering preparatory house-keeping matters we must immediately confront if we believe in Christ's soon return.

FIRST—We must restore *The Fear of the Lord* in God's house.

If indeed, as most attest in alignment with the Scriptures that, "The fear of the LORD is the beginning of wisdom…" (Ps. 111:10), how could we have so cavalierly abandoned it over the two generations last passed? Indeed, it is fascinating that the phrase "a God-fearing man" that was commonly heard in America to describe a person who could most likely be trusted because he believed there was a God who would hold him accountable for his words and actions, has likewise been seldom heard over the past generation. As one leader once said, "We don't want our people to fear God—we just want them to love Him."

Thus, we have, in overzealously promoting the love of God since the early 1970s, to market the Church Growth movement, either neglected or rejected the very foundation of Godly wisdom, in effect leaving our people and countrymen to "do that which is right in their own eyes" without fear of either temporal or eternal consequences.

God declared His *secret* which we, in our own prideful and religious rationalization have rejected.

The secret of the LORD is with them that fear him;
and he will show them his covenant (Ps. 25:14).

The Fear of the Lord is the sure secret of His blessing. God makes no promise of blessing or protection, success or prosperity, to those who do not truly fear him. Again, as it is written: "Blessed is the man that feareth the LORD, that delighteth greatly in his commandments" (Ps. 112:1). "The fear of the LORD is to hate evil" (Prov. 8:13). Yet as we have progressively abandoned the Fear of the Lord, we have in progression redefined or rationalized evil in our midst. And evil is that which disses or dis-agrees with God's viewpoint on any or all of the issues of life. We are inherently prone to expect the Creator's favor while rebelling against His authority, thereby rendering ourselves "equal to God."

We are increasingly confronted with the question, "Hath God said?" How we answer that question will ultimately determine our place of favor... or of fearful wrath. We must return to recognize God as GOD... not the "god" we wish Him to be but the God that He is. *TIME* preempted pastors in addressing the issue with its cover story April 5, 1993, titled "The Generation that Forgot God" on the cover with the double-page spread story "The Church Search." After surveying America's "faith" landscape after Gulf War I, the reporters declared that Americans were "flooding back to church" but that "church would never again be the same." After consulting many knowledgeable sources including respected strong evangelical leaders, the conclusion was clear. Church would "never again be the same" because "Americans are looking for a custom-made God—one made in their own image."

Consider well the implications for a time of unsuspected persecution in the so-called Land of the Free. If our parishioners do not truly fear God and His wrath for their dissing His authority, they will readily succumb to the pressures of persecution, reasoning that God will wink at their rebellion. Failure to truly fear God will lead to the paralyzing fear of man, which will be an eternal snare unto their souls. And who will the Lord of the Church hold responsible? Is it not likely it will be those of us who, fearing the possible backlash of the people, will refuse to prepare them for the persecution which Christ Himself declared would surely come?

SECOND—We must preach righteousness!

It is not only that "Righteousness exalteth a nation" (Prov. 14:34), but rather that "Righteousness and judgment are the habitation of his throne" (Ps. 97:2). And furthermore, that those who "love the LORD, hate evil" (Ps. 97:10).

The greatest *evil* our parishioners face amid the coming onslaught of persecution, both foreign and domestic, is the refusal to stand courageously in the evil day now demanding that they conform to a rabidly ungodly culture, but also that they are drawn through force or threat of force to embrace the demands of a rising global government dedicated, as was the French Revolution, to eradicate Christians and Christianity from the global realm. Whether we admit it or not, that is the ultimate global design, so as to elevate transformed humanity to God-defying deity.

A brief reading of Revelation 13 and 14 should be sufficient to a serious and spiritually-minded pastor or priest to jerk us from our business-as-usual preaching emphasis to more diligently "prepare the way of the Lord" for those in our pews whose minds and hearts can be likewise stirred. There is a cost to being a mouthpiece for God, just as there is a generic cost of discipleship for all believers.

Perhaps a brief vignette may aid in deepening the issue of righteousness. Obviously, we are not referring to the issue of "standing" or "position" but righteous living as the expression of holiness "without which no man shall see the Lord" (Heb. 12:14). About 20 years ago, as I was driving to a monthly pastor's prayer breakfast, I was moved to ask the Lord a simple question: "Why do we not have revival either in America or in our city after so many years of prayer?" His answer was immediate and simple: "My pastors are not preaching righteousness." As I briefly contemplated that, He responded again: "And that's the reason your country is in the mess you are in." And again, a few seconds later, He declared: "And that's the reason my church has no power to bring change or revival."

Upon arriving at the breakfast prayer gathering, with coffee in hand, I shared that little experience with the pastor of one of the larger evangelical churches in town, having its roots a century earlier in the holiness movement. Having shared my experience, the pastor hung his head and lamented with these words: "Chuck, I don't think I even know how to preach righteousness." Do you? The Barna Report finds that if pastors even grasp the meaning of righteousness as a life requirement for genuine Christian living, only about 20% even make an attempt at preaching on the subject.

So, brethren, if we sincerely have a hope with biblical support of truly preparing our flock to stand faithfully in the face of life-challenging persecution, they must first embrace a life-guiding and guarding Fear of the Lord, which, upon a serious confrontation with the God both of Creation and history, will lead many to profound confession and repentance of sin and spiritual rebellion, causing the call to righteousness to prevail as necessary preparation for contemplating coming persecution. This is, in reality, Christianity 101, from which we have danced around for two generations in pursuit of so-called Cultural Relevance. Have we yet grasped with any level of gravity the time in which we live from God's eternal perspective? Our viewpoints may be determining the destiny of untold millions! P.S.—If the shoe doesn't fit, please don't put it on! Just check in with the Holy Spirit first.

Not A Marketing Message

When we decide to seriously embrace the necessity of preparing those God has entrusted to us for promised persecution, some may be tempted to create or search for a marketing angle so as to "promote" the message. That just happens to be the American ministry mindset that was driven into the pastoral, publishing and preaching methodology by the diversionary spirit of the Church Growth Movement followed by the Seeker Sensitive Movement. We must consciously admit this pattern and forsake all thoughts tempting us to try to "promote" a response to persecution.

Our Lord, in promising and warning of persecution, made no effort to paint persecution with a promotional brush or to diminish the gravity of its reality by making it appear relatively attractive. On the contrary, not only Jesus but Peter, James, John and Paul spoke of the severity and unescapable reality of suffering. If there was to be any glory realized by persecution, it was to be found in being willing to "take up our cross" as did Christ, and thus be identified with Him, anticipating by faith the "eternal weight of glory" that awaits us (II Cor. 4:17).

The Church father, Tertullian, once famously said, "The blood of martyrs is the seed of the Church." From that time on, the idea has persisted, that churches and people grow most under pressure. There is significant truth in that belief, but it is certainly not absolute truth to be used as some kind of promotional tool for church growth. To attempt such a "marketing" mindset is, in effect, to pervert or under-mine the spiritual gravity of the subject for individual believers, thus inevitably watering down the very message of warning preparation our Lord and His disciples clearly presented. Truthfully, the very opposite affect of persecution has been experienced in the near decimation of the once vibrant Christian faith in North Africa, the Middle East and Asia Minor over the past 100 years, where suffering has been severe.[64]

On the contrary, we know from the experience of the early church that persecution in and from Jerusalem actually caused the gospel message to be spread more rapidly—"both in Jerusalem, and in all Judea, and in Samaria, and unto the uttermost part of the earth." This was achieved not through ministerial promotion but by the power of the Holy Spirit (Acts 1:8). In this manner, God makes persecution a part of His Kingdom purpose to fulfill the Great Commission. Our job, however, is not promotional but solely preparational. What, then, might that look like?

Not to Scare, But to Prepare

Persecution can have a powerful impetus to our otherwise "Laodicean" church. While weeding out the worldly, it can awaken those whose hearts need spiritual defibrillation. While persecution can seem to have harmful effects on the church, it also purifies and empowers as the Holy Spirit is given full sway.

Prosperity, it seems, may be more devastating than persecution to God's ultimate purpose to prepare our world for the return of His Son who is not coming back for a bride, "having spot, or wrinkle, or any such thing" (Eph. 5:27). Our job, as pastors, is not to scare, but to seriously and honestly prepare a holy and steadfast bride.

How to Prepare

In order that the author's voice not appear to be the only voice sounding the trumpet, a message presented by Zane Pratt for preparation in the face of advancing persecution will form the final plea to pastors, publishers and para-church ministers. So… as the coach tells his team… "Listen up!"[65]

Suffering Is Normal in a Fallen World

"The Bible regards suffering as normal. Part of this suffering comes from the fact that we live in a fallen world, and this kind of suffering falls on Christians and non-Christians alike." "It is true that God, in His incredible mercy, undoubtedly does protect us from many of these consequences of the Fall…. However, he does not ever promise in His Word that he will protect us from physical injury or illness, and he allows all of us to die."

Suffering is Promised for Christians

"For followers of Jesus, however, the picture is even more sobering. The Bible actually promises us persecution and suffering for our faith." "In the Bible, suffering and opposition are a normal part of the normal Christian life." Persecution is coming to the West notwithstanding our Christian heritage and historic democratic freedoms.

How to Prepare for the Reality of Suffering as a Christian

1. "Christian workers need to examine their own hearts, searching for any sense of entitlement" that they might falsely promise to those who hear them. "They will do this… by concentrating long and hard on the surpassing worth of knowing Christ Jesus who is better, more valuable… than anything we lose by following him."

2. "We need to share the gospel the way Jesus did, by making the cost of discipleship clear (Lk. 9:57-62)." "And lest we fear that such a sobering presentation of the gospel will keep people from being saved, we need to realize…"
   A. In offering Jesus, we are not offering a cozy life… and
   B. "It is the power of the Holy Spirit that draws people to Jesus, not our attractive packaging of the message."
3. "We need to include the subject of suffering well in our immediate follow-up with new believers."
   - "They need to endure suffering without compromising their integrity (II Tim. 4:5; I Pet. 2:19)", so that they are not caught off guard by suffering (I Pet. 4:12)."
   - "They must love their persecutors and pray for their welfare (Matt. 5:43-47)."
   - "They are to renounce any intention to take revenge (Rom. 12:14-21)."
   - "They are to trust God in the middle of their suffering and respond by proactively doing good (I Pet. 4:19)."
   - "They are to use their experiences of suffering as a basis for comforting others who suffer (II Cor. 1:3-7)."
   - "They are to fix their eyes on Jesus (Heb. 12:1-3)."
   - "They are commanded to rejoice (I Pet. 4:13; Matt. 5:12)."

As Jesus' disciples, we do not seek pain or rejoice in suffering as a form of flagellating our flesh to achieve an exalted level of spirituality. Rather, we see persecution and suffering as a given if we truly identify with Christ as Messiah. All suffering is temporary and isn't to be compared with the glory in His presence that awaits us (II Cor. 4:16) where all pain and suffering will turn to joy unspeakable, where the half has never yet been known (Rev. 21:4; I Pet. 1:8).

We each have unique personalities and places where we are given opportunities to serve, yet none of us will be able to bear excuse before the Father if we fail to purposely prepare those who rely upon us to stand courageously and faithfully in these increasingly perilous times. The eternal implications are perhaps greater than we might choose to consider, yet both our Lord and His apostles make them plain. We are all called to the Kingdom for such a time as this! May all who rely upon us find us faithful, so that no plaintiff cry might legitimately echo before the One who will judge the earth in righteousness… "Why didn't you warn and prepare me?"

> *In thee, O LORD, do I put my trust: let me never*
> *be put to confusion. Be thou my strong habitation,*
> *whereunto I may continually resort (Ps. 71: 1, 3).*

Chapter 17
PROBING THOUGHTS for PROPHETIC TIMES

1. Do you agree that the engine of the Church Growth Movement in the 1970s became the "marketing" of the gospel into a "saleable commodity?"

2. Can you see how reducing the gospel to a "saleable commodity" so as to be "relevant to the market" undermined serious and needed discipleship?

3. Why would the "cost of discipleship" be a casualty of the Church Growth and Seeker Sensitive Movements?

4. To what degree or in what ways have you, or other pastors, priests, publishers and broadcasters succumbed to the "marketing" spirit so as to reduce your willingness to truly present and prepare those in your sphere of influence to endure persecution?

5. In what ways might the Holy Spirit have spoken to you as you have considered the challenges of this chapter?

6. What, if anything, are you inspired or convicted to do in response?

HOW PERSECUTED LEADERS LEAD

"Only one who is ready to 'go forth to die' has the authority to lead."

LEADERS LEAD BY EXAMPLE and by PRECEPT. "Christian leadership, in countless communities around the world, is forged in the heat of persecution. Five hundred million followers of Jesus Christ in over sixty-five countries face significant restrictions on expressing their faith, including limits on worship gatherings, public identification as a Christian, evangelism and/or even ownership of a Bible." "Many risk public humiliation, ostracism, beatings, prison, torture, and even death because of their allegiance to and witness for Jesus." "They understand that leadership—as an expression of discipleship—is inherently costly."[66]

Western Leaders Unprepared

In truth, as so aptly presented by his lengthy piece titled, What Can Persecuted Christians Teach Us About Leadership," Brent L. Kipfer shines a much-needed light on our unpreparedness to be effective guides through the painful pathway to and through persecution.[67] He outlines several reasons why western leaders are unprepared to truly lead our flocks as persecution now increasingly raises its ugly head.

1. "Leadership studies have been heavily centered in North America… awash in theory" and statistics, but "severe persecution of Christians [has] mostly happen[ed] elsewhere."
2. Lack of awareness that persecuted Christian leaders have spiritual insights and resources—shaped uniquely by their suffering—to contribute to the strength of the global church in increasingly perilous times.
3. Severe persecution creates barriers to getting the needed stories to those who might most profit from them, since persecuted churches and leaders must necessarily operate with great discretion—often secretly.

These barriers to genuine and effective leadership are broad and generic but do not penetrate the deeper motivations of our hearts that define our ministries—what we emphasize or de-emphasize, what we choose to focus on in our teaching and preaching, or what we seek to avoid, often with the proverbial ten-foot pole. "Robert E. Quinn emphasizes the personal cost of real leadership."[68]

- **Comfort-centered**
  By making self-survival our highest priority, we become stuck in patterns of behavior, ministry and preaching that not only diminish ourselves but frustrate the greater impact we might have for the Kingdom.

- **Externally Directed**
  We let outside pressures or the culture shape us. We do what we think is necessary to please others to get what we want, thus our flesh overrides our faith.

- **Self-focused**
  We tend to put our own interests ahead of others, which compels us to avoid teaching those things we perceive might place us in a less favourable light.

- **Internally Closed**
  We are constrained by thinking we don't need the kind of inspiration that is outside our cloistered walls, that it might be somewhat intimidating to really see persecution for what it is.

"This impulse toward self-preservation reduces a person's capacity to make [needed] changes and leads to increasing gaps in personal integrity." "Genuine leadership," according to Quinn, "is anchored in a fundamental decision (often triggered by a crisis) to fully commit to… a purpose greater than one's own survival. Only one who is ready to 'go forth to die' has the moral authority to lead."[69]

Persecution's Leadership Impact

A retired U.S. Army lieutenant general spurred debate when he said that the rise in global attacks on Christians could become "a national security threat" to the United States. "Lt. Gen. William Boykin, a former commander of Delta Force and undersecretary of defense for intelligence" "is not alone in his fear America is plunging toward an increasingly anti-Christian future," noted David Curry for Religion News Service.[70]

Sociologist George Yancey, a professor at Baylor University, said, "We no longer live in a society generally supportive of Christians."[71] "Sadly, the persecution of Christians is often denied, downplayed, overlooked or justified… that Christians deserved to be harassed, vilified or punished for adhering to their religious views."[72]

As Christians in Western democracies there seems to be a tendency to romanticize the effect of persecution on churches elsewhere in the world, believing that it inevitably leads to church growth or glorious stories to be celebrated from afar, but it appears that such persecution may be coming home to roost in American and western homes. What glory, then, shall inure to our ministries as we embrace the cross with those on distant shores?

Brent Kipfer gives us a much-needed prod in our ministerial derrieres for this time of pastoral testing. He admonishes that reality is beginning to set in—that "Christian leaders are often targeted for attack, as opponents of the gospel seek to weaken and eliminate their influence." The consequences to our impact on those trusting our leadership will either be strengthening or devastating. Will we lead by faith or succumb to fear? Consider a few of these consequential choices:

- Weakened confidence in the gospel.
- Compromise of faith, confidence and call, undermining moral authority and followers' trust.
- Conforming to the perceived demands of culture, limiting preaching, publishing and broadcasting to "safe" topics.
- Weakening marriage and family due to weak response amid persecution through insecurity and tension.[73]

As Kipfer said on behalf of Training Leaders International:

> Persecution does not, in and of itself, transform Christian leaders into super-saints or spiritual heroes.[74]

Our Calling is Clear

We conclude these perhaps provoking pages to pastors and those committed to ministry leadership roles with a provocative question as these perilous times inexorably advance upon us.

> Will I, with integrity, be able to say to all in my sphere of influence, as did Paul, "Follow me as I follow Christ?"

Brethren, "Hereunto were ye called: because Christ also suffered for us, leaving us an example, that ye should follow his steps" (I Pet. 2:21).

> *Be merciful unto me, O God: for man would*
> *swallow me up…. What time I am afraid, I will*
> *trust in thee (Ps. 56:1, 3).*

Chapter 18
PROBING THOUGHTS for PROPHETIC TIMES

1. Have you experienced anything in ministry you might truly label as "persecution" for righteousness' sake?
2. Have you witnessed others in ministry in America or the West to have experienced real persecution for righteousness' sake?
3. Have you purposed to acquaint yourself, other than through statistics, with ministry leaders around the world who have suffered severe persecution? Have you considered in your mind and heart that you might eventually find yourself in a similar position?
4. Do you have any sense that neither you nor those in your sphere of influence are likely to experience serious persecution? If so, how would you ever be prepared to lead as an example?
5. If we truly, in America or Europe, live in a society that no longer welcomes or is supportive of Christians or the Christian faith, how long do you think you might have before you must shoulder a level of leadership example you never dreamed could happen in the "Land of the Free" that is increasingly becoming the "Home…only…of the Brave?"

PART 7

THE POWER OF PRESSURE

*"It is the fear of man and the fear of death
that become the final test of our trust."*

"FEAR OF DEATH as a Christian IS NOT from God," declared a well-known pastor and broadcaster, Michael Yousef, through his teaching on his radio program, Leading the Way, as reported on one-place.com, a resource of Salem Communications carrying the broadcasts of hundreds of ministries.

Fear Has Power

The scriptures make clear that fear has incredible power. Legitimate fear can protect us from the consequences of negligent or intentional exposure to a host of dangers that occur throughout our years on a planet infested by naturally occurring threats or by the fallout of the sin that has corrupted our world through the Fall of man.

Yet there is a more dangerous and consequential fear beyond these that so easily beset us. It is the fear of man (Ps. 56:4; Heb. 13:6) and the fear of death. The fear of man is a snare to our soul (Prov. 29:25). But the fear of death defines destiny, controlling our minds and hearts, stripping us of both faith and freedom, thus securing eternal bondage.

And so, we have been forewarned so we may be forearmed against this ultimate temptation.

Forasmuch as Jesus became and took part of flesh and blood (humanity) as are we,

> ...he also himself likewise took part of the same; that through death he might destroy him that had the power of death, that is, the devil;

> And deliver them who through **fear of death** were all their lifetime subject to bondage (Heb. 2:14-15; emphasis added).

Fear of death is ultimate bondage. It compels us as slaves to do the devil's bidding, to yield to his deceptions and to conform to his counterfeit kingdom ways, thus disqualifying us by our own decisions to an eternally undesirable destiny.

It is the fear of man and the fear of death that become the final test of our trust in Jesus as our Savior and Messiah. The pressure that we allow to prevail through these two fears will painfully, yet prophetically, lead masses of professing believers to succumb to the Seducer's consummate plan to rule and reign over their lives, exchanging the hope of eternal salvation for the temporal hope of protection of physical life.

How, then, is such pressure brought to bear, like a boa constrictor crushing its prey, until we declare our trust in a counterfeit savior and thus fail the ultimate test of life itself?

In God have I put my trust: I will not be afraid
what man can do unto me (Ps. 56:11).

Chapter 19

THE HORROR OF FALSE HOPE

*As with ancient Rome, the resurrecting end-time
'Rome' will brook no opposition once enthroned.*

"WE SHALL HAVE WORLD GOVERNMENT, whether or not we like it," declared James Paul Warburg on February 17, 1950, speaking before the United States Senate. "The only question is whether World Government will be achieved by conquest or consent." In this chapter, we surgically explore the hidden depths of the final battle for dominion—a global search for hope without Christ.

Men's Dream of Dominion

World government has been the dream and dominion of men throughout the ages to this present age. From the Tower of Babel in Genesis 11 to the trumpeting of the New World Order in our generation, mankind and its various kingdoms and rulers have sought to govern the then-known world in power and glory. Inevitably, man's lust for power and glory seeks to eclipse, escape, or even defy the power and glory of the Creator.

The problem with pursuit of global government is not in the nature of government itself, for God has ordained government as "the minister of God to thee for good," to protect against evil and praise that which is good (Rom. 13:1-4). Civil government among mankind is to be conducted under the overarching fear of the God of the Bible and His governance. When humans forsake the fear of the Lord, God's ways of government and covenantal oversight and revelation are no longer available (Ps. 25:14). Man thus devises his own ways, seeking inevitably to create a utopian world order promising peace on earth—a substitute for the hope of the gospel.

The promise and hope of a global order ushering in world peace is profoundly alluring to the natural mind. After all, who in their right mind would not yearn for peace to avert a nuclear holocaust? Those under forty years of age today have haunting fears that their lives or the lives of their children will be cut short in a worldwide conflagration. The aura of fear with empty promises of peace recalls the oft -repeated phrase, "Peace, peace; when there is no peace" (Jer. 6:14, 8:11).

In this chapter we will briefly explore the advanced stage of preparation in every major sphere of man's endeavor for a One World government and a new global order. We will unveil the massive deceptions paving the way and why these are of potential eternal consequence to you and the world's inhabitants in the epic battle for *KING of the Mountain* (the Temple Mount) and for your soul, leading to unfathomable persecution that will test the faith of every professing Christian.

Daniel's Dominion Dream

While the prophet Daniel was captive in Babylon, God gave him a prophetic dream (Dan. 7). In that dream, he saw four great beasts representing the existing and future great powers of the earth that would rule until the "latter days" and the great "time of trouble." These kingdoms have been commonly interpreted as:

> FIRST: A Lion—Babylon
> SECOND: A Bear—Medo-Persia
> THIRD: A Leopard—Greece
> FOURTH: An "Exceedingly Dreadful Beast"—Rome

The fourth beast, "dreadful and terrible," "exceedingly strong," was different from all the others. It had ten horns representing governing powers. The book of Revelation describes this same beast as having "seven heads and ten horns" with "ten crowns" (Rev. 13:1). These ten horns are further described as to "receive power one hour with the beast. These have one mind, and shall give their power and strength to the beast." These ten kings or powers "shall make war with the Lamb..." (Rev. 17:12-14), tolerating no competition.

This great and fearsome fourth beast that "shall devour the whole earth, and shall tread it down, and break it in pieces" (Dan. 7:23) is generally understood to be a resurrected or revived Roman Empire. Ancient Rome, a democratic republic, was diverse in government from the monarchies that preceded it. Rome governed the then-known world with an iron fist through its legendary legions, amassing great wealth, ushering in the *Pax Romana* or "Roman Peace" even as Christ, the Prince of Peace was being born.

Rome declared the government of the world to be upon its shoulder, even as the King of kings was sent by God to re-introduce God's governance in the world.

Isaiah had prophesied:

> For unto us a child is born, unto us a son is given: and **the government shall be upon his shoulder:**
>
> **Of the increase of his government and peace there shall be no end**, upon the throne of David [not Rome], and upon his kingdom, to order it, and to establish it with judgment and with justice from henceforth even forever (Isa. 9:6-7).

The battle lines for dominion were drawn. God had promised His "Prince of Peace" (Isa. 9:6), but Satan, the dragon, would empower His counterfeit "prince" with a global government promising peace on earth. That final world government would be a composite of the previous world powers, blending the best man had to offer to blasphemously compete with the Christ of God.

> And the beast which I saw was like unto a leopard, and his feet were as the feet of a bear, and his mouth the mouth of a lion: and the dragon gave him his power, and his seat, and great authority."

> And they worshiped the beast, saying, Who is able to make war with him?

> And he opened his mouth in blasphemy against God... (Rev. 13:2-6).

The Battle for Dominion

The battle for dominion rages. The great dragon (Satan) is determined to dominate the planet to satisfy his personal vendetta against God. He is marshaling every tool at his disposal, and he knows destiny is in the balance. His determination is to "deceive the whole world" (Rev. 12:9). He is convinced his spiritual cunning and clever seduction will draw the vast majority into his final global conspiracy against the Christ of God through a counterfeit christ. That is why Yeshua (Jesus) warned us in his final words before his crucifixion, "Take heed that no man deceive you" (Matt. 24:4).

How will such diabolical deception take place? Why will the vast majority be deceived? What is the Deceiver's scheme or *modus operandi*? What is wrong with globalization? Will you be able to discern the difference between truth and deception? Between a real and a false hope?

The Moment to Be Seized

The date was September 11, 1990. U.S. President George Herbert Walker Bush stood before a joint session of Congress, a fresh wind of patriotism blowing across the country. Consider closely the words of the 41st president.

> The crisis in the Persian Gulf, as grave as it is, also offers a rare opportunity to move toward an historic period of cooperation. Out of these troubled times... a new world order can emerge: a new era—freer from the threat of terror, stronger in the pursuit of justice, and more secure in the quest for peace.[75]

That "new world," declared President George H.W. Bush, "is struggling to be born." The "opportunity" that he so eagerly desired to seize was the building of a "new-world order." Over 200 times, the senior President Bush declared this "new world order" during his administration. It was historic. It was as if the world had become pregnant and the president of its reigning superpower was deputized to announce the conception long-thought to be but the rantings of conspiracy theorists. But the gestation period was not given. The birth would come in the "fulness of time"... heaven's prophetic time and Satan's false-gospel hour to seduce the world.

It would be man's glorious gospel of self-salvation, of utopian peace and of global safety without the God of Creation and of biblical revelation. A substitute god would be prepared, designed democratically, without dogma or doctrine offensive to a multicultural, religiously pluralistic world intent on global unity. The Scriptures had warned, "when they shall say, Peace and safety; then sudden destruction cometh upon them, as travail upon a woman with child; and they shall not escape" (I Thess. 5:3). But such warnings, however dire, are deemed unworthy in the face of such lofty ambitions as a global order promising unprecedented peace and prosperity.

The very concept of a grand global order almost defies the imagination. For thousands of years, the world, its people and nations, being inherently sinful and selfish, have sought self-gain by grinding others into submission. Europe is a classic study. It's various nations and peoples have been in almost perpetual warfare from the purported fall of Rome to the end of World War II. So, what is so unusual about this moment of history? Will the world now become "one"?

"Utopian as it sounds," notes Jeremy Rifkin, "remember that 200 years ago, America's Founders created a new dream for humanity that transformed the world. Today, a new generation of Europeans is creating a radical new dream." "Romano Prodi, the President of the European Commission, has admitted that the EU's goal is to establish 'a superpower on the European continent that stands equal to the United States." When Prodi was asked to explain what he meant, Rifkin notes, "he spoke of the European vision as one of a new type of power... a new kind of superpower based on **waging peace**."[76] It is said that imitation is the ultimate flattery. If that be so, the European Union, the resurrecting bones of the Roman Empire, stands profoundly flattered, for the entire world is in hot pursuit of "waging peace" to achieve *security* and *prosperity* (Shalom) by forming regional unions in order to seize this historic moment.

Counterfeit Peace

Consider that the Hebrew word "Shalom" might be best translated "peace and security" or "security and prosperity." The divine plan was to send forth His anointed One, the Prince of Peace, to unify the "Israel of God," genuine believing Jews and Gentiles, into "one new man" in Christ," "so making peace" (Rom. 2:28-29, Rom. 9:4-8, Rom. 11:25-26, Eph. 2:12-22).

But Satan seduced the nations with his own alternative peace plan. Unite the nations, contrary to God's express command, and let them build a global "tower" system that will reach heaven, or at least create man's best heaven on earth, thus "saving" the earth from the inevitable consequence of sinful rebellion. Unwittingly, history would repeat itself. The God-dispersed tower of Babel of Genesis 11 would now become global. The world would become **one**, under the Deceiver's direction, until its final destruction.

The United Nations was thus founded in 1945. One of its earliest official acts was to partition the land of Palestine, which God had eternally deeded to Israel, into two nations, one for the Jews and one for Arabs. The partition was to transpire in 1948. The Deceiver was deft in his direction: Divide Israel, which God decreed to be united as one, and unite the nations which God had commanded to separate. The divine penalty would be severe... ultimate divine judgment (Joel 3:1-2, Zech. 12:8-9). Israel was re-born May 14, 1948, and the world has been haunted for its division to this day, and will repeat that debacle.

Just as God would breathe life into the house of Israel (Ezek. 37:1-5), so Satan would breathe life into the unifying of the Gentile nations. Satan's counterfeit is nearing completion. Again, as Jacques Delos, former head of the resurrecting Rome once said, "We must hurry. History is waiting."

Where will this process now end, and what are its implications not only for the world but for Israel and for those who profess ultimate allegiance to Jesus Christ?

On February 1, 1992, then President Herbert Walker Bush, having over 200 times announced the coming New World Order, declared:

> It is the sacred principles enshrined in the UN
> Charter to which we will henceforth pledge our
> allegiance."

The Dream of Dominion

The dream of man's dominion over man has persisted since the Fall of Man from selfless service to sinful selfishness. Refusal to submit to the Creator as Lord birthed in mankind the perverse premise that he was to be "lord" of his fellow man... to exercise dominion, whether by force or threat of force. The God who was King of Creation was displaced by the creature's pursuit of kingship over his fellows. It is clear that such was never God's intent as revealed in His dealings with Israel, His chosen people, who insisted upon having a king like all the surrounding nations, much to the prophet Samuel's despair (I Sam. 8).

"Give us a king to judge us," they cried. But the LORD responded to Samuel,

> Hearken unto the voice of the people in all that they say unto thee, for they have not rejected thee, but they have rejected me, that I should not reign over them.

Samuel spoke all the words of the Lord to the people. He declared explicitly the nature of what a man exercising dominion over his fellows would look like… the progressive taxation, oppression, loss of freedom, and enforced service. "And ye shall cry out in that day because of your king which ye shall have chosen; and the LORD will not hear you," warned the prophet.

> Nevertheless the people refused to obey the voice of Samuel; and they said, Nay; but we will have a king over us;
>
> That we also may be like all the nations; that our king may judge us, and go out before us, and fight our battles.

"And the LORD said to Samuel, Hearken unto their voice, and make them a king." Israel got her king. Indeed, several of the books of the Tanakh, the Old Testament, are historical reminders of the troubles and triumphs of Israel's kings, their most frequent godlessness and painful dominion over the people God had delivered from the bondage of Egypt. They despised the promise of the "Promised Land."

Restoring Dominion

After a thousand years of rebellion, prophetic rebuke, a divided kingdom and ultimate exile, God, in His compassion for the "people of promise,' again sent them a Deliverer to restore the years the locust had eaten and to provide for the promised "Hope of Israel." The Deliverer would restore the dominion of the Creator among a people chosen to be a light to the world. He would be the very incarnation of God Himself, in human flesh, son of David by lineage and son of Abraham by faithful obedience (Matt. 1:1). His very name, Yeshua, would declare his holy purpose… "Yehovah saves."

But again, He came unto His own (Israel) but His own received Him not (Jn. 1:11). He was "despised and rejected," again, as Israel's king, but the Jews "esteemed him not…" (Isa. 53:3). In the crucible of all history, the chief priests "cried out, saying Crucify him, crucify him" (Jn. 19:6). When a pagan governor sought to spare Him, saying, "Behold your King," they cried out, "Away with him. We have no king but Caesar" (Jn. 19:14-15). As Yeshua had already made clear by parable, the Jewish leaders would declare, in effect, "We will not have this man to reign over us" (Lk. 19:14).

Who Will Have Dominion?

A thousand years of the demeaning and enslaving dominion of earthly kings had not yet revealed the devilish nature of man's dominion, despite any ameliorating good intentions. Israel would have Caesar, however despised, as opposed to the Creator's chosen Anointed One, Yeshua HaMashiach. And so, again, for two thousand years God, spurned by His own chosen people, gave them over to their hearts' desire. "Caesar you desire, Caesar you shall have."

Even now, "Caesar" is emerging once again to claim global dominion. Will a resurrected "Rome," exercising ruthless dominion, wield a heavy hand again over Israel, seeking to sit in pontifical glory upon the Temple Mount. Will the physical descendants of Abraham, Isaac and Jacob hear again the words, "Behold your king?" Will a counterfeit Messiah present himself to a resurrected Sanhedrin for history's final question; "Will you have this man to reign over you?"

Both Israel and the Gentile world must prepare for this question. History and prophecy are now converging with breathtaking speed.

The final "beast" empire foretold by the prophet Daniel is preparing to exercise global dominion (Dan. 7). And the centerpiece, the ultimate prize, is Jerusalem, the Temple Mount and ultimately the Temple.

There are many contestants for the prize. Some will come in their perceived individual capacity while others will confederate to augment their power for the final battle for *KING of the Mountain*. The battle is epic and eternal. It began before Creation and continues to the soon Culmination. (For an in-depth look at this battle, consider the author's book, *KING of the Mountain*, Elijah Books, 2013).

Who will have dominion? Will it be China, Russia, Turkey, Iran, The United Nations, the European Union, Islam, the Vatican, Israel, or the God of Abraham, Isaac and Jacob?

The *dream of dominion* will soon become a global nightmare as the people of planet earth choose sides. Who will have dominion… over you? Choose carefully!

Violent Conflict Ahead

Two kingdoms are coming into mortal and eternal conflict. Satan, as the "god of this world" (II Cor. 4:4), is drawing the peoples of this planet into godless oneness. In drafting the historic Treaty of Lisbon as the constitution for the reviving Roman Empire, the European Union elite refused even to recognize God, having embraced the godless antipathy of the French Revolution. Rather, this expanding union chose to declare its rebellion against the Creator by adopting symbols to set itself blatantly against Christ's coming kingdom.

The twelve stars of the European Union flag set themselves against Christ's twelve disciples and the twelve tribes of Israel. The Tower of Babel, through a variety of European posters and other depictions, displays open contempt for oneness in Christ, boldly declaring man's intent to unify for his own salvation. The European Parliament in Strasburg is even architecturally designed to visually replicate, with a modern flair, the ancient Tower of Babel.

A "Radical New Dream"

But the political rebuilding of "Rome" is not yet complete. The nations, observing the seeming phenomenal success of the European Union in such historically short order, are seeking to create similar regional unions throughout the world, all for *security* and *prosperity*. The goal is "global consciousness." The first transnational political entity in history, the "United States of Europe," represents "the rise of a new ideal that could eclipse the United States as focus for the world's yearnings for well-being and prosperity [shalom], declared Jeremy Rifkin in a profound editorial analysis.[77] Rifkin noted, as an American, "Yet our country is largely unaware of and unprepared for the vast changes that are quickly transforming the Old World and giving birth to the new European Dream." His words should grip the heart and soul of every Christian believer worldwide.

> The European Dream, with its emphasis on inclusivity, diversity, sustainable development, and interconnectedness is **the world's first attempt at creating global consciousness.**

As man's godless global consciousness grips the planet, God-consciousness not only dramatically diminishes but becomes anathema to the masses, driven by demonically empowered leaders intent on cleansing the world of all apparent opposition. The very name of Jesus becomes treasonous to a resurrected Roman Empire that will brook no opposition to the ultimate deification of its new Pontifex Maximus—the counterfeit prince of peace. All those who have grown to place their trust in this false hope will find their world explode in unprecedented horror as persecution of the remnant of true believers becomes the world's frenzied occupation.

Once again, domain will determine destiny as the horror of false hope descends upon the unsuspecting occupants of earth. So the question remains. Who will have dominion… over you? Choose carefully! The choice will present itself daily, and even surreptitiously. Discernment will define the true saints who endure [persevere] to the end and the glorious appearing of our Lord and Savior, for persecution now knocks at your door.

Blessed is the man that feareth the LORD, that delighteth greatly in his commandments. He shall not be afraid of evil tidings: his heart is fixed, trusting in the LORD. His heart is established, he shall not be afraid... (Ps. 112:1, 7-8).

Chapter 19
PROBING THOUGHTS for PROPHETIC TIMES

1. Why is mankind's persistent effort to dominate others made in God's image a pernicious, deceptive device of Satan to destroy God's human creation?

2. At what point does the accelerating goal of global dominion reach the "tipping point" leading to global destruction?

3. If indeed Satan, the enemy of your Creator and your soul, is the driving and diabolical force compelling the world toward a totalitarian globalized dominion, what consequences might we rightly anticipate? Order… or chaos? Freedom… or bondage? Joy… or oppression? Peace… or panic? Love… or war? Fulfillment… or desperate finality?

4. What have been the prevailing consequences over the past 2000 years of Israel's choice of "Caesar" over "Christ"—Yeshua HaMashiach? How long will those consequences continue?

5. What would the consequences be to a Gentile or gentile nation that persists in choosing "Caesar over Christ as "king"?

6. Are you becoming increasingly able to comprehend the diabolical drama unfolding before our eyes?

7. How will you discern and decide for actual dominion over your own life and those who trust you as the pressure builds?

8. Are you able to see how persecution of the saints is inevitable?

Chapter 20

BEAST OF BLASPHEMY

*The angel said… I will tell thee the mystery of the woman,
and of the beast that carrieth her…" Rev. 17:7*

THE "PROPHET of HOPE" is the unusual title ascribed to Dr. Robert Muller, former Assistant Secretary General of the United Nations. Dr. Muller has made it clear that world unity cannot be achieved simply through political unions and alliances. Such unity, according to Muller, requires a one-world religion.[78]

A Counterfeit Body

In his book, *New Genesis: Shaping a Global Spirituality*, Robert Muller reflects: "I would never have thought that I would discover spirituality in the United Nations…! Perhaps spirituality is such a fundamental human need that it always reappears in one form or another in life and throughout history and we are about to witness now its renaissance in a global, planetary context."[79] In 1993, Dr. Muller delivered the historic Parliament of World Religion's first keynote address, calling for a "permanent institution" dedicated to pursuing religious unity.[80]

Dr. Muller believed we were entering "a new period of spiritual evolution," a period of rising planetary consciousness and global living which is expected to result in the perfect unity of the human family.

Central to his theology are views of "a divine United Nations" and a "cosmic Christ." "If Christ came back to earth, his first visit would be to the United Nations to see if his dream of human oneness and brotherhood had come true," wrote Muller. "I often visualize," said Dr. Muller, "of a United Nations which would be the body of Christ."[81]

In every chapter of *New Genesis*, writes Gary H. Kah in his *The New World Religion*, Robert Muller calls for a U.N.-based world government and a new world religion "as the only answers to mankind's problems." "Through it all," notes Kah, "Muller maintains his status as a Catholic Christian," ultimately linking the U.N.'s mission to Roman Catholicism. Note well his passionate pseudo prophecy.

> Pope John Paul II said that we were the stone cutters and artisans of a cathedral which we might never see in its finished beauty.

> All this is part of one of the most prodigious pages of evolution. It will require the detachment and objectivity of future historians to appraise... the real significance of the United Nations.[82]

The de Chardin Connection

Pierre Teilhard de Chardin was born in France in 1881. Evolution was the passion of his life. As a Jesuit priest of the Catholic Church, Teilhard pursued his first love - blending the physical and spiritual worlds under the banner of evolution.[83] The "Christ" of de Chardin was not the Christ of the Gospels. For him, Christ had to fit into the theory of evolution. According to Teilhard's concept of evolution, God had not previously evolved enough to express himself through human consciousness. Chardin's process of evolution concludes with man becoming conscious of who he is - "God."[84]

"Christ is above all the God of Evolution," wrote de Chardin. "He is the supreme summit of the evolutionary movement... evolving into a Super-Christ. Humanity is the highest phase so far of evolution... beginning to change into a Super-Humanity... the Omega Point."[85] Chardin is the most widely-read author of the New Age movement, and his ideas "gained acceptance among many Catholic leaders, including Pope John Paul II."[86]

Father Teilhard de Chardin influenced most of the prominent United Nations leaders of his day. Norman Cousins, former president of the World Federalist Association, made the connection, writing in the Forward to Robert Muller's autobiography...

> Whatever the uncertainties of the future may be... oncoming generations will need living examples of the conspiracy of love that Teilhard de Chardin has said will be essential to man's salvation. Robert Muller is involved in such a conspiracy."[87]

Muller, in *New Era Magazine*, made the final connection, saying, "It is necessary that we have a World Government centered on the United Nations." ... we can credit the coming World Government to the 'influence of the writings of Tielhard de Chardin'."[88]

Bringing all the world's religions into cooperation with the United Nations was Robert Muller's top priority. "My great personal dream," he explained, "is to get a tremendous alliance between all the major religions and the U.N." Muller, in 1997, exulted, "... during the 50th Anniversary of the United Nations... we launched again the idea of United Religions... and a meeting... to draft and give birth to a United Religions.... I will be the father of the United Religions."[89]

The March of Inter-Faith Ecumenism

Even as the vision for uniting the nations through a common religion advances through the United Nations, the systematic spirit of inter-faithism and ecumenism is marching lock step to the spiritual drumbeat of a deceptive "unity" movement worldwide. The cry of

"UNITY" in our churches, cities and throughout the various religious expressions globally, as well as through a variety of governmental and (NGO) Non-governmental yet quasi-governmental structures, is in itself becoming a common voice and unifying mantra.

It is profoundly seductive, for who, in the current market of politically-correct ideas, desires or even dares to resist the tide. And where is the deceptive danger?

Exchanging trust in the truth of God's revealed Word, the Bible, for trust in man's experience and relationships is becoming the new model of "Christian" ecumenism. It is subtle and it is seductive. To break down walls of division, the new approach is to ignore divine proposition in favor of personal testimony. As Cecil "Mel" Robeck of Fuller Seminary, an Assemblies of God minister said, "We will not get embroiled in disputes involving scripture or homosexuality because it "would have the potential to derail our effort."[90]

Cecil Robeck is on a 12-member committee for Global Christian Forum. The *Christian Century* reported, "After keeping a low profile for several years, advocates of a fresh approach to ecumenism are going public...." "About 240 leaders from the Vatican, World Evangelical Alliance, Orthodox Churches, historic Anglican and Protestant communions, and Pentecostal and independent churches" gathered November 6-9, 2007, for the Global Christian Forum, to advance the new approach based on "personal testimony." Just one month earlier, Catholic Cardinal Avery Dulles admitted the potential for harmonizing doctrines was exhausted, necessitating "an ecumenism of mutual enrichment by means of personal testimony."[91]

"How then can Christian unity be envisaged?" asked Cardinal Dulles. Testimony must trump truth so as to build trust in man. As Dulles declared, "Our words, they may find, carry the trademark of truth."[92] We would do well to remember the warning of the Psalmist.

> It is better to trust in the LORD than to put confidence in man.

> It is better to trust in the LORD than to put confidence in princes [pastors, priests, popes and presidents] (Ps. 118:8-9).

Once again, this false unity movement requires that you spiritually dance with the devil, the very Deceiver himself. Remember, there is a great eternal battle between Satan and God for the souls of men, to become *"KING of the Mountain"*... of your heart. Satan seeks to seduce your soul away from the faithful trust and allegiance in HaShem, the one true God, and His Son, *Yeshua*, Jesus Christ.

Yeshua, the "Anointed One," the Mashiach, the Holy one of Israel, is the "express image" of God's person, "upholding all things by the word of his power." He declared, "I and my Father are one" (Jn. 10:30). He said, "He that hath seen me hath seen the Father" (Jn. 14:9). And Yeshua also said, "I am *the* way, *the* truth, and *the* life: no man cometh to the Father but by me" (Jn. 14:6). Jesus made clear that the only true unity pleasing to God was that which is the fruit of being *sanctified* or set apart through God's truth as found in the Scriptures. It was this unity "through the truth" that would cause the rest of the world to "believe that thou has sent me" and would display God's glory as true followers of Yeshua (Jesus) became "one" even as Yeshua was one with the Father (Jn. 17:16-23). Never forget! It is our trust in the truth of God's Word, the Bible, that binds us in biblical oneness. Anything else is a counterfeit, however attractive it may appear and however broadly it may be embraced. We, whether Jew or Gentile, are *in* the world, but not *of* it, if we truly love the God of Creation, as revealed in Messiah.

Yet interfaith-ism and ecumenism march on to a louder and more incessant drumbeat. The Third Parliament of the World's Religions met in December, 1999, in South Africa, with 6000 delegates from more than 200 different religious groups. Catholic theologian, Hans Küng, said he maintains a "horizon of hope" that the 21st century might witness "unity among churches, peace among religions, and community among nations."[93]

The most ambitious organization in today's interfaith movement has been the United Religions Initiative (URI), founded by William Swing, the Episcopal bishop of California. Although this movement is little known to the public, "it now provides a spiritual face for globalization, the economic and political forces leading from nationalism to a one-world system," says Lee Penn, an investigative reporter. The interfaith movement "is no longer... a coterie of little-heeded religious idealists..." he says. "The URI's proponents range from billionaire George Soros to President George W. Bush, from the far-right the late Rev. Sun Myung Moon to liberal Catholic theologian Hans Küng, and from the Dalai Lama to the leaders of governmental-approved Protestant churches in China."[94] Penn warns in his *False Dawn* that the United Religions Initiative and the interfaith movement are poised to become the spiritual foundation of the New World Order - the "new civilization" proposed by Mikhail Gorbachev, the last leader of the Soviet Union.[95]

A Geo-Political Struggle

We dare not lose sight of the global context in which the accelerating move toward ecumenism and interfaith-ism is taking place. To do so is to run the risk of being assimilated into a compromised faith system that is sucking an unsuspecting and naive world into a deception from which few will be delivered. What is truly at stake is a massive geo-political struggle for governance of the earth in which religious faith is but a pawn. Again, it is mankind's rebellious pursuit of a counterfeit peace or *shalom* outside of the true claims of Yeshua, Jesus the Messiah.

Illustrative of this geo-political struggle is the historic battle between the Vatican and Russia, in which Russia symbolizes a *secular* vision and the Vatican a *spiritual* vision for a New World Order. Each, however, utilizes the counterpart, whether spiritual or secular, to achieve its long-term objective of global dominance.

Under Vladimir Putin, the Russian Orthodox Church was exalted to near unprecedented favor, with Putin having to kiss the ring of the reigning archbishop. Secular power embraced religious power in pursuit of global dominance. Moscow, thus empowered and supported by massive petrol dollars, signaled its "place in the new world order."[96]

Seeking global influence, Vladimir Putin declared Russia "Defender of the Islamic World," thus uniting the world's greatest concentration of oil and gas production and reserves in an embrace of Islam, the goal of which is world domination.[97]

The Vatican had earlier moved to neutralize the clearly growing wedding of Russian Orthodoxy to Russian nationalism being parlayed into global power. Pope John Paul II, seeing Russia as the greatest opposition to ultimate Vatican objectives, did everything he could to romance the Russian Orthodox Church back into the fold of Rome after a 1000-year schism. As of July, 2008, the Archbishop of Moscow said to Pope Benedict XVI, "the right conditions do not yet exist for Pope Benedict to visit Russia." "He needs an explicit invitation."[98] No such invitation has been given.

Looking back to the time of the fall of the Iron Curtain and the dissolution of the Soviet Union by Mikhail Gorbachev, Vatican insider, Malachi Martin, noted that "These two men [Gorbachev and John Paul II] are the only two among world leaders who not only head geopolitical institutions but have geopolitical aims. Geopolitics is their business." But, observed Martin, "for the vast majority of onlookers and for many in government... the gargantuan change being effected in the shifting ground escapes them." Malachi Martin called Gorbachev and Pope John Paul II "Forces of the 'New Order': The Two Models of a Geopolitical House."[99]

The Vatican—"A Geopolitical House"

"The newest game in the City of Man," declared Vatican insider Malachi Martin in *The Keys of This Blood*, "is the building of a geopolitical structure. Everyone who is anyone in terms of sociopolitical and economic power is engaging in it... and ultimately... all nations, great and small, will be involved. It is the millennium endgame." But where does the Vatican fit? Why would a Vatican insider be talking so seriously about geopolitics? Most people undoubtedly think of religion when they hear words like *Vatican* and *Pope*. What then is the geo-political connection?

According to Malachi Martin, since the start of his pontificate in October 1978, Pope John Paul II was a consummate geopolitician. "He heralds a new and as yet unrecognized force in the geopolitics of nations, a force that he actually claims, will be the ultimate and decisive factor determining the new world order." He further notes, "… there are no other feasible ways of rationalizing this Pope's performance on the world stage." "His Holiness has assiduously carved out for himself an international profile" which "no pope ever did on a like scale. Nor has any human being known in history attempted it."[100]

During his Pontificate, John Paul II visited 130 countries, establishing personal relationships with governmental leaders in most of them. He invited representatives of 100 of the world's largest religions to join him in Italy for the ultimate multicultural, religious-pluralistic prayer meeting, directing prayers to over 300 million gods. He was the most traveled Pope in history. He even re-established relations with Israel after 2000 years of rejection, resulting in the first official visit by an Israeli head of state to the Vatican seat of Roman Catholicism.

Vatican City is not just the locus of Roman Catholicism but is an independent state. The Vatican is "considered among the nations" whereas God declared Israel "shall not be reckoned among the nations" (Num. 23:9) and that true followers of Christ would be as "strangers and pilgrims" on the earth (I Pet. 2:11).

The Vatican lies within Rome, Italy, and is the world's smallest state, having no commerce of its own. As a sovereign state, it has its own flag, currency and postal system. It has diplomatic relations with most of the nations of the earth. The Pope, as "Bishop of Rome" known as the "VICAR of Christ," has absolute legislative, executive and judicial power, the ultimate merger of church and state. He resides in the largest and grandest palace in the world with 1400 rooms, while Christ himself had no place to lay his head (Matt. 8:20).

John Paul II was the only Pope in history, at the time of his pontificate, to actually call for a New World Order. A CNN news release from VATICAN CITY January 1, 2004, is instructive.

> Pope John Paul II rang in the New Year with a renewed call for peace... and the **creation of a new world order** based on respect for the dignity of man and equality among nations.... He stressed that to bring about peace, there needs to be a new respect for international law and the **creation of a "new international order" based on the goals of the United Nations.**[101]

It should come as no surprise that upon the death of Pope John Paul II, 4 million pilgrims and 100 heads of state gathered in Rome to mourn, surrounding hundreds of scarlet-clad cardinals and bishops shown surrounding a golden, crucified Christ. He had ingratiated himself and the smallest of all states to the world for a generation, wooing all faiths and political powers to come under papal authority.

But why did Pope John Paul II wait for 25 years before announcing his clear embrace of a "New World Order?" Perhaps the only real answer why John Paul II took this opportune moment to declare the New World Order as his objective is that the world stands at the threshold of the appearance of the first "beast" of Revelation, a beast "having seven heads and ten horns... and upon his heads the name of blasphemy" (Rev. 13:1-8).

Papal Primacy Rising

How does papal primacy join with the emerging beast empire? The reigning popes from and after John Paul II paint the picture that is vividly coming into global view. Each of these popes has called for a New World Order. Yet how might the Vatican bring about such a catastrophic union while, at the same time, seeming to the casual religious or political eye to be promoting the Kingdom of God? The papal powers well understand that it can be accomplished only by incremental steps couched in the spiritual language of religious purpose.

Hence, speeches and papal encyclicals. Please seriously consider the insidious manner in which such incrementalism is being accomplished under the "Christian" banner of caring for humanity. The underlying globalist current is sweeping nearly all unsuspectingly onto the back of the prophesied beast.

Pope Benedict XVI

Christmas 2005 "Urbi et Orbi Message of His Holiness Pope Benedict XVI"

"The life-giving power of his light is an incentive for building a **new world order** based on ethical and economic relationships." "A united humanity will be able to confront many troubling problems of the present time...."

July 6, 2009 "Encyclical Letter CARITAS IN VERITATE of the Supreme Pontiff, Benedict XVI"[102]

Translated "Charity in Truth," Pope Benedict XVI, through a carefully-crafted, 79-point encyclical framed under the rubric of *evangelization*, portrays the Vatican as the facilitating force for instituting "a true world political authority." After wading through reams of multi-paged religious rhetoric, the pope finally makes his pontifical point clear. Couching the global purpose of the encyclical under the easily and universally embraceable banner of "Charity in Truth," the masked tyranny of a proposed new global order under Vatican oversight emerges with shocking clarity.

Consider thoughtfully, whether you are Roman Catholic or a mere follower of Christ, the papal proposal in the "Vicar of Christ's" own words.

"In the face of the unrelenting growth of global interdependence, there is a strongly felt need...for a reform of the *United Nations Organization*, and likewise of *economic institutions and international finance*, so that the concept of the family of nations can acquire real teeth. This seems necessary in order to arrive at a *political, judicial and economic order which can increase and give direction to international cooperation for the development of all peoples in solidarity.*"

"To manage the global economy...to bring about integral and timely disarmament, food security and peace; to guarantee the protection of the environment and to regulate migration: for all this, *there is an urgent need of a true world political authority*, as my predecessor Blessed John XXIII indicated some years ago.?

"Such an authority would need to be regulated by law, to observe consistently the principles of subsidiarity and solidarity, to seek to establish the common good, and to *make a commitment to securing authentic integral human development inspired by the values of charity in truth* [i.e., the Vatican]."

"Such an authority would need to be universally recognized and to be vested with the effective power to ensure security for all.... Obviously it would have to have the authority to secure compliance...."

"The integral development of peoples and international cooperation require the establishment of a greater degree of international ordering...for the management of globalization. They also require the construction of a social order that at last conforms to the moral order...and to the link between politics and the economic and civil spheres, as envisaged by the Charter of the United Nations."

July 8, 2009 VATICAN CITY press release as reported in **nytimes.com/world/europe/08pope-**
"Pope Benedict XVI on Tuesday called for a radical rethinking of the global economy...urging the establishment of a **true world political authority** to oversee the economy and work for the 'common good'."

Wow!!! The secular news media did not miss the message. Never had such a global vision and intention been so clearly and unabashedly stated by the reigning *pontifex maximus.* When the New York Times and Reuters chime in with a common conclusion of the papal purpose, perhaps the world–and especially professing followers of Christ alone–should take heed. As declared Reuters news service, this was "An encyclical of the highest form of papal writing and gives the clearest indication to the world's 1.1 billion Catholics–and to non-Catholics–of what the pope and the Vatican think..." ("Pope calls for a Global authority on economy," reuters.com/article/us-pope-encyclical, July 6, 2009).

December 3, 2012
Pope Benedict XVI delivered a speech before the *Pontifical Council for Justice and Peace* in Rome in which he again called for a unified world government dubbed a "new evangelization of society." As reported by Ethan Huff for *nationalnews.com*, December 27, 2012, the pope's message called for the "construction of a world community" and for a "corresponding

authority" to guide this new world community to achieve "the common good of the human family."

"In no uncertain terms," notes the reporter, this is a clear call for a "New World Order"... "the ultimate goal of the Roman Catholic Church." As further stated by Pope Benedict, the Roman Church's responsibility is to bring about this world government to promote an "anthropological and ethical framework around the common good."

This may "initially sound benevolent," observed the reporter, but "based upon the Roman Catholic Church's sordid history of consolidating power and mandating its religion on societies through a blending of church and state, it is hard to call such a proposition by Pope Benedict XVI anything other than a call for a dictatorial New World Order guided and controlled by the Roman Catholic Church." This should "come as no surprise considering that in 2010 the Catholic Church sought the establishment of a new Central World Bank that would be responsible for regulating the global financial industry and the international money supply."

POPE FRANCIS
May 24, 2015

It was "the most anticipated papal letter for decades, published in five languages" declared John Vidal in *theguardian.com/world* June 13, 2015. The rare encyclical, called "Laudato Sii," or "Praise Be," was "timed to have maximum public impact ahead of the pope's meeting with Barack Obama and his address to...the UN General Assembly...." The encyclical's subtitle "on care of our common home" revealed the serious environmental theme in which the pope insisted that the world must "hear both the cry of the earth and the cry of the poor."

As noted by Stephanie Kirchgaessner and John Hooper from Rome on behalf of *theguardian.com*, June 16, 2015, Pope Francis echoed his predecessor, pope Benedict XVI, who in 2009 had proposed "a kind of super-UN" to deal with the world's problems. Francis called for "a new global political authority" tasked with "tackling...the reduction of pollution and the development of poor countries and regions."

As Benjamin Gill and Steve Warren wrote for *cbn.com/cbnnews*, May 6, 2019, "Pope Francis is pushing for steps toward global authority that supersedes the rights of individual countries" all with the ostensible goal of:

> "pursuing the 'common good' on issues like climate change and immigration." In other words, national sovereignty is now an obstacle to the papal visions of global government. As the editor of *First Things*, R.R. Reno noted of the pope's encyclical, in *firstthings.com*, June 18, 2015, it makes many fierce denunciations of the current global order."

February 18, 2016—Vatican City
> The *catholicnewsagency.com* reported the full text of an in-flight interview of Pope Francis from Mexico to Rome. He responded to many issues pressed by reporters and then was queried regarding the "Charlemagne Prize" he was soon to receive, in recognition of his perceived role in re-establishing the Holy Roman Empire in Europe for which Charlemagne was crowned in 800 AD. The Pope's response was prophetic of papal intentions, declaring, "I like the idea of the re-foundation of the European Union...because Europe....has a force, a culture,

a history that cannot be averted, and we must do everything...to make it go forward," referring to it as a "mother Europe."

June 2017

Speaking with Ecuador's *El Universo* newspaper, the Pope said that the United Nations doesn't have enough power and must be granted full government control "for the good of humanity."

"Disturbingly, world religious leaders are also beginning to...preach from the same hymn sheet, instructing their sheep to accept the components of the New World Order's one world government." Leaders called for "world unity" in a video message June 14, 2017, according to Baxter Dimitry on *newspunch.com*, June 23, 2017. "The call for a world government led by Pope Francis, Ayatollah Al-Milani, the Dalai Lama and Rabbi Abraham Skorka, is seen as a major step on the road to the New World Order prophesied over 2000 years ago." "It is the process of transitioning the world into a global government," and "religious leaders are playing their part in this great deception."

The unavoidable question looms large before us: "Can the IMPOSTER be far behind?"

Resurrecting the Pax Romana

The Roman Empire never fully "died." Just as with Israel, in its prosperity it was greatly weakened and decayed internally, incapable of resisting its enemies. Its citizens were, in effect, dispersed (as it was with Israel) throughout the then-known world, having largely lost their Roman identity. But the emergence of "Rom-ance" languages and Roman-esque laws, and culture and architecture over the centuries that spread throughout the European continent revealed the Roman root.

Eventually that Roman root spread across the Atlantic and Pacific to the Americas, revealed largely in laws, government, language and culture... and even in religious practices. The *Pax Romana* or "Roman Peace" was, two millennia later, identified as the *Pax Americana*. English became the lingua franca (common language) of the western world, indeed of the entire earth. America, with her glorious eagle wings spread, had become the reigning "Roman" superpower with a Roman capital and a Roman government seeking to export a Roman democracy to an ever-expanding Roman world to bring a Roman "peace on earth." Yet in her prosperity, she also progressively abandoned the Prince of Peace, the only true source of *shalom* (security and prosperity). And as with ancient Israel and Rome, she also began a precipitous internal decay. As her moral and spiritual foundations crumble, fear and fragmentation grow even as her citizens and "caesars" pump their chests in Roman pride. And so, America's President, George W. Bush, in the waning days of his presidency, reached for security and prosperity from the new and rising Roman star, the European Union,[103] envisioned as the pulpit from which the new counterfeit gospel of Satan's false Roman peace will be preached as "man's last best hope of earth."

Plea for Prophetic Perspective

A bird's-eye view or heavenly top-view perspective on earthly history reveals valuable prophetic insights not otherwise apparent on this plane of casual life experience. By analogy, it may appear like a chess game being played in three or even four dimensions at once. That may already have become apparent, but if not, it is necessary to point out that in the "end game" of geopolitics compounded by religious objectives, the actual significance or prophetic connection of historical events may not be superficially apparent or even recognizable for centuries. Deception for many arises in failure or refusal to "connect the dots" biblically.

As we complete this chapter, our difficulty, in very limited space, will be to translate, in distilled fashion, the vast historical and more recent information available in an attempt to convey the convergence of geopolitics in pursuit of a new Roman global government with the pursuit of a unified global religion that is preparing to usher in and undergird the New World Order that will set itself "against the LORD, and against his anointed" (Ps. 2:2).

Many, without prophetic perspective, will be seduced to swim in the surging stream of global-ism and of interfaith-ism, caught up in its politically-correct euphoria, unaware that deception is leading them to destruction. But those who are truly "looking for that blessed hope, and the glorious appearing of the great God and our Savior Jesus Christ" will "purify themselves even as he is pure" (Tit. 2:13; I Jn. 3:3).

E Pluribus Unum

E Pluribus Unum is a Latin phrase out of ancient Rome meaning "Out of Many, One." It was proposed by Franklin, Jefferson and Adams in 1776 as a motto for the United States. It first appeared on the Great Seal of the U.S. in 1782 and has continually appeared on America's coins. However, the official motto of the United States is "In God We Trust."

The original settlers on American shores sought to display the kingdom of God as described in the Bible in living color. What Israel had failed to do, they intended to complete for God's glory until Christ's return in the "New Canaan." Many were joined together from the European continent for one holy purpose—to spread the gospel of Jesus the Messiah across the seven seas and seven continents, as described in their founding documents. That spiritual vision gave rise to a secular dream... the American Dream, magnetizing mankind everywhere. As prosperity multiplied, trust in God waned. Discipling people to obey the commands of the Master was exchanged for an increasingly godless democracy worshiping at the feet of the Market. For the last generation, America has exported to the world the salvation power of democracy bowing to the Market. Lamentably, that model has become our global legacy, as the Market has become "lord."

As with Israel, God called America to be separate for His glory, and blessed her with power and prosperity. But as with Israel's abandonment of obedience to God in her prosperity, so it is with America. She now joins the world system with vigor and vengeance and is preparing to pass the baton to the new rising star modeling unity for the emerging global order.

"The POST-AMERICAN WORLD" was *NEWSWEEK's* shocking cover story May 12, 2008. "Over the last 20 years, globalism has been gaining depth and breadth," wrote Fareed Zakaria. "To bring others into the world, the United States needs to make its own commitment to the system clear." "For America to continue to lead the world, we will have to first join it," he notes. He closed the article with this painful observation: "… when historians write about these times, they might note that by the turn of the 21st century, the United States had succeeded in its great, historical vision—globalizing the world."[104] Having abandoned our unity "Under God," we have sown the seeds of a false trust. We have exchanged our divine call of globally preaching the "Great Commission" for a mess of globalizing material "pottage." The baton of leadership is being passed.

The European Union now models the new global mantra. "Unity in diversity" is the motto of the European Union. According to the EU website, the motto means that Europeans are "united in working together for peace and prosperity." It should therefore come as no surprise that America should embrace the DEI movement, "Diversity, Equity and Inclusion," all to mimic the EU mantra.

Notice the continual recurrence of the words "peace and prosperity" or "security and prosperity." These have become the marketing mantra for the coalescing of nations in pursuit of global government. God desires that we enjoy *peace and prosperity* in pursuit of Him.

When we seek the fruit without the root of righteousness in Christ, it becomes idolatrous… and insidiously dangerous.

When men or nations collectivize themselves in idolatrous pursuit, rejecting God's governance, God rejects them and despises their efforts as open and notorious violation of the first three of the Ten Commandments. That is what brought God's judgment on the builders of Babel and what will bring His judgment on Europe's end-time effort to "union-ize" the world into a godless democracy.

Godless unionizing of the world is an act of collective rebellion against the rule of the Creator. And that is why the European Union, in establishing its constitution, refused to even give God a polite "goodbye" or "au revoir," refusing even to recognize His name in a historical sense or to acknowledge Him or the Christian faith in historically "Christian" Europe.

From Constantine to Charlemagne

To understand the European Union's prophetic role today, it is necessary to recall Europe's papal past. This becomes a sensitive matter for those raised within or currently embracing the Roman Catholic Church and its Vatican governance through absolute papal authority and the "Holy See." Yet to remain pure and escape the seductive snare being laid for your soul, it cannot be avoided. Please read prayerfully rather than through the lens either of tradition or of political correctness. We are about to pull back the curtain, beginning the final ACT of an unfolding historical drama that will reveal the Deceiver's choreography of a masterful counterfeit to deceive the nations and consign the seduced masses to eternal perdition. It will lead us to solve the "Mystery of the Woman."

We begin this final dramatic ACT by looking back over the shoulder of history to the ancient Roman Empire. Let us now fasten the seat belts of our chariots and return to ancient Rome whose *Pax Romana* promised peace, stability and security (shalom) to the world just as God's "Prince of Peace" was being born.

In 63BC, Julius Caesar, who had been elected *Pontifex Maximus*, became emperor of Rome and was vested with the governmental office of Roman emperor and ultimate priestly powers. From that time forward, the title *Pontifex Maximus*, which had been used solely among the pagan priesthood, was appropriated by the Roman Caesars. The Caesars not only merged the role of supreme governmental ruler with that of supreme religious leader (Pontiff), but also claimed to be deity or god in the flesh and were worshiped as such.

In 376 AD, Gratian became the first Roman Emperor to refuse the idolatrous title of *Pontifex Maximus* and presented that role to the Bishop of Rome. By this time, Roman bishops had gleaned substantial political power, and in 378 AD, Bishop Damasus was elected *Pontifex Maximus*, the first pope in history to bear the title. All the pomp and ceremony that had characterized Rome's pagan worship was imported into the Roman version of Christianity.

Historian Will Durant in *Caesar and Christ* succinctly describes the transfer of the power of Rome's decaying government to the increasingly politically powerful Roman version of the Christian Church.

> The Roman See increased its power.... Its wealth and ecumenical charities exalted its prestige.

> By the middle of the third century, the position and resources of the papacy were so strong that Decius vowed he would rather have a rival emperor at Rome than a pope. The capitol of the Empire became the capitol of the [Roman Catholic] Church.

> Rome absorbed a dozen rival faiths and entered into Christian synthesis. It was not merely that the Church took over some religious customs and forms common in pre-Christian Rome—the stole and other vestments of pagan priests, the use of incense and holy water, the

burning of candles... the worship of the saints... the law
of Rome as the basis of canon law, the title of *Pontifex
Maximus* for the Supreme Pontiff, and... the Latin language as the enduring vehicle of Catholic ritual.[105]

Durant, in concluding his history of the growth of the Roman
Catholic Church, makes secular observations that have had profound
spiritual implications echoing down to this fulcrum moment of world
history. He notes that "as secular failed," Roman government "became
the structure of ecclesiastical rule." Consider well his concluding
remark and its implications for our time.

> The Roman Church followed in the footsteps of the
> Roman state; it conquered the provinces, established
> discipline and unity from frontier to frontier. Rome
> died in giving birth to the [Roman Catholic] Church;
> the Church... inheriting and accepting the responsi-
> bilities of Rome.[106]

The prophetic pattern emerging from the merger of political and
spiritual authority in the pope is best captured in the lives of two
emperors, Constantine and Charlemagne.

Constantine is credited with declaring Christianity to be the official religion of the Roman realm. In the Edict of Milan, he granted
toleration to all religions and increasingly showed favor to Christians,
"But as the Roman Empire became Christian, Christianity in turn
became imperially Roman."[107]

Despite his ostensible "conversion" to Christianity, Constantine
was a consummate politician deeply rooted in a pervasively pagan
empire. "He treated the bishops as his political aides; he summoned
them, presided over their councils, and agreed to enforce whatever
opinion their majority should formulate." observed Will Durant,
"A real believer would have been a Christian first and a statesman

afterward; with Constantine it was the reverse. Christianity was to him a means, not an end." "Constantine's support of Christianity was worth a dozen legions to him...."[108]

"Constantine aspired to an absolute monarchy; such a government would profit from religious support," noted Durant in *Caesar and Christ*. "Perhaps that marvelous organization of bishops and priests could become an instrument of pacification, unification and rule."[109] Perhaps, as we await the return of Christ, the visionaries of global government will again utilize the power of the Roman church to gain and authenticate power for a resurrected "Rome." Constantine, while claiming to be a "Christian," maintained the pagan title of *Pontifex Maximus*. His coins were inscribed: "SOL INVICTO COMITI" (Committed to the Invisible Sun). During his reign, Constantine blended pagan worship with worship of the Creator, ordering the Roman realm and the Roman Church to change the biblical Sabbath of the Fourth Commandment so that all would worship "on the venerable day of the Sun," Sunday.

In a powerful sense, surrounded by a profound aura of mystery, Rome never truly expired in 476 AD as often written in the obituaries of nations. Rather, Rome was revived in 800 AD when Pope Leo III, in desperation, fled to Charlemagne for protection. On Christmas Day, with Charlemagne at Rome, Pope Leo III crowned Charlemagne emperor of the Holy Roman Empire. He was the first in a line of emperors that continued for the next one thousand years. But if Leo conferred a great honor on Charles that Christmas morning, he conferred a still greater honor on himself: the right to appoint, and to invest with crown and sceptre, the Emperor of the Romans. Here was something new, even revolutionary. No pontiff had ever before claimed for himself such a privilege—not only establishing the imperial crown as his own personal gift, but simultaneously granting himself implicit superiority over the emperor whom he had created.[110]

Take note, ye leaders of this leasehold of mankind on earth. That dominion which was sown under Constantine and consolidated by the papacy under Charlemagne is about to be claimed in a culminating act of dominion by this world's ultimate consolidation of church and state, the Vatican. In exercise of this papal precedent of power to anoint and appoint the Emperor to govern the state, so the pope, claiming to be "Christ in the flesh," will assert his "lordship" to anoint, appoint and affirm the one who shortly will grant the sceptre to rule over the world's ultimate and final global order. Consider well.

> The reaction in Constantinople to the news of Charles's (Charlemagne) coronation can easily be imagined. To any right-thinking Greek it was an act not only of breathtaking arrogance but also of sacrilege. The Byzantine Empire (eastern half of the Roman Empire) was built on a dual foundation: on the one hand, the Roman power; on the other, the Christian faith. The two had first come together in the person of Constantine the Great, Emperor of Rome and Equal of the Apostles, and this nuptial union continued through all his legitimate successors. It followed that, just as there was only one God in Heaven, so there would be but one supreme ruler on Earth; all other claimants to such a title were imposters and blasphemers as well.[111]

> From then on, the power of the Papacy steadily grew, and before long it was generally agreed that every new emperor must be anointed by the pope personally, in Rome.[112]

And that vision was revived under Pope John Paul II, the "geopolitical" pope, throughout his papacy from 1978 to his death in 2005 AD. The world's near universal obeisance and adulation at his Vatican state funeral by Protestant, Catholic, Hindu, Buddhist and a hundred other faiths revealed that the scarlet-robed bishops led by the *Pontifiex Maximus* ruled a global "Roman" world. As the *BBC News* noted, it was "history's largest funeral," attended by millions and broadcast worldwide to billions. The then leader of the free world, George W. Bush, eulogized the pope as "a hero of the ages."

Indeed, as Nigel Rodgers notes in *Roman Empire,* "The Catholic Church, with its hierarchy and universalist ambitions, is the most obvious inheritor of ancient Rome."[113]

All Roads Lead to Rome

A British newspaper headline read, "Pope declares EC (European Community) heaven sent." In 2004 AD, Pope John Paul II began the process of canonization for Konrad Adenauer, Alaide de Gasperi and Robert Schuman, founders of the European Union. Indeed, it is "extraordinary" for a politician to be canonized, declared the Catholic newspaper, *The Tablet. The Daily Telegraph* quoted one attending the canonization synod as saying, "The European Union is a design not only of human beings but of God." He added that the canonization of the politicians would show that the European Union was "built on a rock,"[114] the very biblical words used to describe the pre-figured Messiah of God.

Why the historical and accelerating role of the Roman Catholic Church in global political matters? Why did Pope John Paul II make history with his journeys to 130 nations and the building of connections with heads of state worldwide. What are the goals of the smallest nation-state, the Vatican, and its *Pontifex Maximus*, increasingly seeking to merge the religious role with political power? Indeed, it appears that all roads are leading inexorably to Rome, setting the stage for the great apocalyptic showdown between a prostituted religious power and the global political powers that pimp her for personal gain until she is cast away in disdain. The great contestants claiming "KING of the Mountain" are showing their colors.

The Treaty of Rome in 1957 established the European Economic Community now known as the European Union. In 2004, the

European Parliament presented to the member states of the EU the text of a proposed constitution to be ratified. EU leaders agreed in Brussels that the constitution should be officially adopted in Rome in November 2004; if ratified by all member countries, it would replace the Treaty of Rome (1957).

Also in 2004, the Vatican received additional political power as a representative of the United Nations. Rome now has the right to be heard at the UN General Assembly.

The Vatican sees its role in the United Nations as essential to fulfill its geopolitical ambitions. The UN sees the pope as the world's greatest "moral leader" to persuade global citizens of the glories of the New World Order. Each needs the other. The matter of religion in the global scheme is taking "front row-center." In his final address before the U.N. General Assembly September 21, 2006, Secretary General Kofi Annan warned of a "new war of religion on a global scale" and declared only the United Nations can solve the world's problems.

Israel has become complicit. President Moshe Katsav visited Pope Benedict XVI at the Vatican on November 17, 2005. It was the first official visit by an Israeli head of state to the seat of Roman Catholicism after John Paul II had recognized Israel for the first time in history. Israel, as with the world's nations, fears catastrophe and seeks global religious union. On February 19, 2006, *Arutz Sheva*, Israeli National News, delivered this news brief:

> Israel's Ashkenazi chief rabbi, Yonah Metzger, meeting with the Dalai Lama, a Buddhist monk... suggested that representatives of the world's religions establish a United Nations in Jerusalem, representing religions instead of nations, like the UN currently based in New York.

> "Instead of planning for nuclear war... it will invest in peace," Metzger said. [115]

The Woman Rides the Beast

In the 1990's, unusual biblical symbolism began to appear throughout Europe. Britain issued a stamp to commemorate the European Parliamentary elections. The stamp depicted a woman riding a beast. Paintings and statues of the woman and the beast appeared in official Brussels' circles and on a poster. A mural of the woman and the beast even decorated the Brussels' airport lounge.

"The woman on the beast is now the official picture of the EU," according to Rev. Dr. Ian Paisley, a Northern Ireland minister who was also a member of both the Westminster and European parliaments. He said that when the multibillion-dollar new parliament building in Brussels, Belgium, was completed, at the end of where the parliament meets is a dome. On the dome is a colossal painting, three times life size, of the woman riding the beast.

In Strasburg, France, the rival new headquarters of the parliament, designed like the Tower of Babel, is a painting of a naked woman riding the beast. When designs for the new Euro coin were unveiled, there was the woman riding the beast on the back of the Greek euro-coin. In 1992 a German ECU coin was issued showing Europa and the beast. In the new Brussels building of the Council of Europe is a bronze statue of the woman riding the beast.

A United Airlines' seat-pocket magazine contained this headline in German, "Good morning, Europe." The article began with these words.

> This May, a daring picture appeared on the cover of
> *Der Spiegel*, one of Europe's most prestigious news
> magazines: a pitch black bull, horns lowered, charging
> straight at the reader. On its back sat a young woman
> draped in dark blue cloth and waving the blue flag
> of a United Europe. The cover was a delight for
> European readers since the woman was the very
> popular French supermodel Laetitia Casto, who had

also recently been selected as the "Marianne 2000" in France - the feminine personification of the French Revolution...[116]

According to tradition, Europa is the Great Goddess, mother of the European continent. According to mythology, Zeus, also known in Rome as Jupiter, fell in love with Europa, the beautiful daughter of a Phoenician king. He seduced her attention by assuming the form of a white bull. When she sat on his back he whisked her away, returned to his normal form, and she bore him three sons. This supreme deity of mythology also bore other names including *Pater* (father) and *Soter* (Savior).

All this may be fascinating history, but why should we be concerned about mythological figures even if they have been adopted for the identity of the resurrecting Roman Empire? The reason is simple. The Bible gives specific description and warning concerning a woman sitting upon such a beast which figuratively depicts the merging of religious power and political power ushering in the grand finale of Satan's deceptive drama of the ages. Shockingly, the final ACT of this drama is now happening before our eyes, and most, whether rich or poor, and regardless of status, race, color or religion, are predisposed to embrace the coming counterfeit salvation offered by a false "Christ" bearing false promises of *security* and *prosperity*. What, then, has God said concerning this mystery woman? The answers are found in the book of Revelation, chapter 17.

MYSTERY OF THE WOMAN

Revelation 17 and 18 are perhaps the most explicit prophetic chapters of Scripture. They may also be the most dramatic. The sheer scope of their historical applications and prophetic implications is breathtaking as well as heart-rending.

God despises "whoredom." God actually "hated" Esau because he prostituted his birthright for a mess of temporal pottage (Mal.

1:1-6; Rom. 9:13; Gen. 27, 28:1-9). He ultimately dispersed Israel, the "apple of his eye," throughout the nations because of her spiritual whoredoms (Jer. 3:1-3). Our Creator is pure and holy. He despises those who, for personal or institutional gain, will compromise their principles. He hates those who will exchange eternal favor and power with God for temporal favor and power with man. Consequently, when the Scripture speaks of a great whore," we should universally take notice.

THE GREAT WHORE

According to Revelation 17:1-2, this *whore* is like no other in the spiritual monstrosity of her prostitution. She is a "great" whore! And she sits on "many waters." The sheer magnitude of her influence and those with whom she has prostituted herself are global. Both the kings and political power brokers of earth as well as the world's common inhabitants are dramatically affected by her spiritual fornication and have become, in one way or another, complicit in it.

A WOMAN of SCARLET and PURPLE

The great whore of Revelation 17 is "arrayed in purple and scarlet" and "decked with gold and precious stones...," "having a golden cup in her hand." The cup is "full of abominations and filthiness of her fornication" (vs. 4).

MOTHER of HARLOTS

This "great whore" is not content with her own prostituted life and ways but seeks to birth others who will likewise prostitute themselves as she, so that she can bring them in under her mothering wings, claiming them as her own. She is "THE MOTHER OF HARLOTS." Her home is also the seedbed, supply center, and seductive cover of "ABOMINATIONS OF THE EARTH," all under the cover of "sainthood" (vs. 5).

PERSECUTOR of TRUE SAINTS

The "Mother of Harlots" fiercely protects her global prostitution ring and will brook no opposition. True saints cannot be tolerated, since the true gospel light of their lives shines into the dark corner, revealing the shocking spiritual debauchery characterizing the "Great Whore's" prostitution system. Persecution of true saints is inevitable for the Mother of Harlots to maintain the global spiritual brothel that decks her with "gold and precious stones" and vast wealth. Throughout history, she has become "drunken with the blood of the [true] saints, and with the blood of the martyrs of Jesus" (vs. 6).

She is a great mystery. The political leaders and peoples of the planet stand in amazement, "with great admiration" at her immense earthly power and glory (vs. 6). They seek her influence, long for her prosperity and lust for her power, The Whore needs them, but they need her. Can this brothel relationship persist indefinitely, or will one prevail?

The Woman and the Beast

The Great Whore sits upon "a scarlet colored beast, full of the names of blasphemy, having seven heads and ten horns" (vs. 3). These ten horns or powers would appear to be the same "ten horns" spoken of by the prophet Daniel in describing the "fourth beast" and final world empire, Rome (Dan. 7:7-25). Just as Rome seemed to rise triumphant, fall into obscurity, and now resurrect with astonishing vitality, so the world is wondering with amazement at the dramatic rise of the European Union now merged with the Mediterranean Union which the nations now regionally strive to emulate. It is "the beast that was, and is not, and yet is" (Rev. 17:8).

Here is "the mystery of the woman, and of the beast that carrieth her" (Rev. 17:7). This "mystery" is made historically and prophetically manifest to those with an eye to see; an ear to hear; and with a mind, heart and will to understand. Please contemplate with conviction of heart and conscience the inherent warning of this prophetic passage:

...they that dwell on the earth shall wonder, whose names were not written in the book of life from the foundation of the world, when they behold the beast that was, and is not, and yet is (Rev. 17:8).

The Beast

The beast that carries the woman is something to behold. It will captivate the entire world, the overwhelming majority of the earth's population. It is a global political or governmental system "which hath seven heads and ten horns" (verse 7). The "ten horns" are component governmental powers that give global governing power to "the beast" which is the fourth and final world empire (Dan. 7:16-25). The ten horns are "ten kings" (governing authorities) which have not had ongoing historical existence but rise throughout the earth in the final season ushering in the end of the age, and they receive power one hour (a short time) with the beast." "These have one mind, and shall give their power and strength to the beast" (Rev. 17:12-13).

The spirit and purpose of this beast that carries the woman is not only secular but in serious rebellion against God, having declared evolution as the "creator" so as to vacate all vestiges of divine dominion. All who truly submit to the God of Creation, in obedience to His Word and commandments, and who walk faithfully in the spirit and truth of Jesus, Yeshua the Messiah, will be seriously persecuted, as they were in ancient Rome, in the beast's "war with the Lamb" (Rev. 17:14, 14:12, Dan. 7:21). But "he that shall endure unto the end, the same shall be saved" (Matt. 24:13).

The mushrooming power of "the beast" and of the "ten horns," from whence it receives power, are inadequate, by themselves, to fully convince the world's citizens of the great glory and authenticity of their enterprise. Once again, as with ancient Rome, so it is with the final emerging global "Rome." The power of the secular is seen as insufficient. A religious power must be embraced. They will accomplish global dominion together. The woman "drunken with the blood of the saints" will ride the beast (Rev. 17:6-7), out of which partnership each hopes to gain preeminence to become *KING of the Mountain*, to rule the world.

The Whorish Woman

The "kings of the earth have committed fornication" with the "great whore" that rides the beast (Rev. 17:1-2). Each has, historically, and will, prophetically, use the other for illicit self-gain. That is the nature of prostitution. Each seeks to gain through geopolitical intercourse the perceived power and favor of the other to gain ultimate power and favor with the people.

The beast is described as having "seven heads and ten horns" (Rev. 17:7). The "horns," we have seen, are political governing powers. The "seven heads," however, are "seven mountains on which the woman sitteth" (Rev. 17:9). This woman that rides the beast into global power "sitteth on many waters" (vs. 1). The "waters" are "peoples, and multitudes, and nations and tongues" (vs. 15). The whore's influence is vast, multicultural and perceived as the most globally influential religious power.

The "beast," despising the God of Creation, determines to use the "woman," and her feigned and prostituted faith, to establish the beast's global authority, until she is no longer needed. The "ten horns," then, "shall hate the whore," and "shall make her desolate and naked," and "shall eat her flesh," and "shall burn her with fire" for "God hath put in their hearts to fulfill his will" (Rev. 17:16-17).

We must now establish the woman's identity. Her identity is established geographically and geopolitically. God makes her identity historically recognizable so that no one of honest heart, "keeping God's commandments" AND "having the faith of Jesus" (Rev. 14:12), could mistake His message. The identification is an implicit warning to beware and not participate overtly or covertly in the whore's deception.

> The woman which thou sawest is that great city, which reigneth over the kings of the earth" (Rev. 17:18).

The seven heads are seven mountains [hills] on which the woman sits" (Rev. 17:9).

The "great whore" is also symbolically described as "Babylon the great" (Rev. 18:2). Many of the same descriptions given of the "woman" that rides the beast in Revelation 17 are given of "Babylon the great" in Revelation 18. "The kings of the earth, who have committed fornication and lived deliciously with her, shall bewail her, and lament for her, when they shall see the smoke of her burning... saying, Alas, alas, that great city Babylon, that mighty city, for in one hour is thy judgment come" (Rev. 18:9-10).

The global merchants that have participated with the beast in prostitution with the "great whore" shall weep and wail, saying, "Alas, alas, that great city, that was clothed in fine linen, purple and scarlet, and decked with gold and precious stones...! They "cried when they saw the smoke of her burning, saying, What city is like unto this great city" (Rev. 18:15-18).

The "Great City"

The rhetorical question of Revelation 18 echoes to our time... "What city is like unto this great city?" Is there any historical and continuing city on earth that matches the geopolitical and religious descriptions of Revelation 17 and 18?

There is only one city on earth that for more than 2000 years has been known and identified globally as the city on seven hills. That city is Rome. And the Bible unambiguously declares that the "great whore," the woman that rides the geopolitical "beast," is "that great city, which reigneth over the kings of the earth" (Rom. 17:18). She has prostituted eternal truth for temporal power and prosperity, [117] becoming the wealthiest institution on earth. Much of her wealth has been acquired through the sale of salvation. Under her proclaimed power to mediate heaven and hell, millions gave untold billions, thinking they could purchase heaven on the installment plan, not by the free grace of God but by the forceful merchandising of a false gospel by "His grace," the Pope.

There is only one city in history that could be characterized globally as fornicating with the kings of the earth, mixing the persuasive power of religion with the power of politics to gain dominion over the world's people. It is Vatican City. *The Catholic Encyclopedia* states: "It is within the city of Rome, called the city of seven hills, that the entire area of Vatican State proper is now confined."[118] The words *Vatican* and *Rome* are used interchangeably. When one speaks of *Rome*, the most common reference is to the hierarchy that rules the Roman Catholic Church.

The Pope, claiming to be the "Vicar of Christ" (in essence, "Christ in the flesh") has absolute monarchal rulership over Vatican State, the world's smallest political state, yet "reigning over the kings of the earth" (Rev. 17:18). Popes have claimed dominion over kings and kingdoms throughout history and claim their word and that of the Roman Catholic Church, which the Pope mediates, has authority over and supersedes the authority of the Scriptures. And now, at the end of the age, the Vatican seeks to bring the entire "Christian" and pagan world under its whorish motherhood.

The Scriptures describe her as "MYSTERY, BABYLON THE GREAT, THE MOTHER OF HARLOTS..." (Rev. 17:5). The Roman Catholic Church describes herself as "The Mother Church." But having prostituted herself for earthly wealth and power with political suitors, she became the "MOTHER OF HARLOTS." She presents herself as a great "MYSTERY" to the world, claiming global moral authority while committing global fornication; claiming to be a bearer of the truth while embracing treachery in her heart. Her prostituted power reigns supreme through threat of political blackmail. Hell hath no fury like the "great whore's" scorn mediated by the *Pontifex Maximus*.

The Pope has become the most powerful ruler on earth today. Ambassadors from every major country come to the Vatican to do obeisance to "His Holiness." As Pope Gregory IX thundered, the pope was lord and master of everyone and everything. As one historian noted, the papacy in Rome is "a single spiritual and temporal authority exercising powers which, in the end, exceed those that had ever lain within the grasp of the Roman Emperor."[119] One historian has called the papacy *"ABSOLUTE MONARCHY."*[120]

Usurpation of Authority

In the name of Christ, the Roman Catholic Church has, in effect, usurped God's authority in the earth. With blasphemy of the highest order, the Pope, claiming to be "The Holy Father," has declared his pontifications to be co-equal with or superseding the very Word of God. The Scriptures admonish: "Ye shall be holy: for I the LORD your God am holy" (Lev. 19:1-2). But the Pope claims the title, "YOUR HOLINESS." Jesus Christ is declared "King of kings and Lord of lords" (Rev. 19:16), yet the Pope is coronated, with the accolade: "Father of princes and kings, Ruler of the world...."

The Deceiver's culminating act to defy God's authority in the earth is to exalt his counterfeit as "Father of princes and kings, Ruler of the world," bringing every tongue, tribe and nation under his dominion and authority in religious defiance of what God hath said. The Roman *Pontifex Maximus* is about to proclaim that authority and dominion as the woman rides the beast into global glory and power. It has begun in Europe.

Religion - The New Politics

A veteran European journalist wrote: "what is emerging in Europe is a Holy European Empire, an attempt to rebuild the old empire united under the pope. This is becoming blatant: The stained-glass window of the Council of Europe at Strasbourg Cathedral features the Virgin Mary under a halo of twelve stars, the same stars you see on the EU flag. The Vatican is playing a major role in the creation of a new Holy European Empire." "The pope repeatedly called for religious unity in Europe. This means a united Catholic Europe, which was consecrated to Mary by the Vatican in 1309 AD."[121]

Otto von Habsburg, head of the house of Habsburg, whose family dominated Europe for centuries as the continent's leading Catholic layman, wrote in *The Social Order of Tomorrow*:

> Now we do possess **a European symbol which belongs to all nations** equally. This is the crown of **the Holy Roman Empire**, which embodies the tradition of Charlemagne, the ruler of a united occident....[122]

How then does this "European symbol which belongs to all nations" extend the "Holy European Empire" to become a global "Holy Roman Empire?"

On May 29, 2008, the former British Prime Minister, Tony Blair, declared, "I'll dedicate the rest of my life to uniting the world's religions." "Faith is part of our future... an essential part of making globalization work." He said faith could be a "civilizing force in globalization."[123]

In December 2007, Tony Blair converted to Catholicism, after meeting numerous times in private with the pope. On May 30, 2008, Mr. Blair formally announced the Tony Blair Faith Foundation. He declared, "Into this new world, comes the force of religious faith." His goal is to bring the six leading faiths together: Christian, Muslim, Hindu, Buddhist, Sikh and Jewish. "Religion is the new politics," declared the new Catholic convertee. "Religious faith will be of the same significance to the 21st century as political ideology was to the 20th century."[124]

Blair, who serves also as Middle East peacemaker—the official emissary of the United States, the European Union, the United Nations and Russia—told *TIME* he "converted to Catholicism to fully share his family's faith. But he plainly enjoys being part of a worldwide community with shared value, traditions and rituals." "In a sense," observed *TIME*, "**The Catholic Church has long embodied the attributes of globalization** that now engage Blair."[125]

The rising spirit of globalism is compelling and profoundly deceptive. It is drawing business and corporate leaders, political leaders and spiritual leaders, yes, even professed Christian leaders and Protestants of every stripe. It has become the "IN" thing, a mark of modern savvy and of market and ministry success, but the Master becomes little more than a mascot in pursuit of secondary agendas that wed the world in counterfeit unity or oneness.

A classic, but by no means exclusive, example of this global fever is the cover story of *TIME*, August 18, 2008. The cover title reveals the globalizing spirit: "THE PURPOSE DRIVEN PASTOR—RICK WARREN—America's most powerful religious leader takes on the world." But the title of the feature article goes straight to the heart of the matter: "The Global Ambition of Rick Warren."[126] In the seeming righteous pursuit of ridding the world of material poverty, an unrighteous wedding, "unequal yoking," of religious pluralism is embraced to accomplish the secondary agenda (II Cor. 6:14). The *purity* of the faith once delivered to the saints is inevitably compromised. The apparent "goodness" of the global agenda becomes a subtle substitute for the God who commands us to care for the poor. We may be "purpose driven" but not "purity and principle—driven." The *good* has seductively replaced *God* in the pursuit of a compromised and more universally acceptable *global gospel...* all in the name of Christ. It lures world leaders, not to the foot of the Cross, but to a counterfeit faith rooted in false unity.

As Tony Blair declared, "Religion is the new politics." The global spirit uniting religion and politics is also politically uniting Protestants under the *Pontifex Maximus*. The British *TIMESONLINE* reported "Churches back plan to unite under Pope."[127] These efforts are well under way as the report set forth.

Radical proposals to reunite Anglicans with the
Roman Catholic Church under the leadership of the
pope were published... and have been agreed by senior
bishops of both churches. In a 42-page statement
prepared by an international commission of both
churches, Anglicans and Roman Catholics are urged
to explore how they might reunite under the Pope.

Rome has already shown itself willing to be flexible
[on doctrinal issues]. In England and Wales, the
Catholic Church is set to overtake Anglicanism as
the predominant Christian denomination for the first
time since the Reformation....

The document titled *Growing Together in Unity and Mission* significantly reported:

The Roman Catholic Church teaches that the ministry of the Bishop of Rome [the Pope] as a universal
primate is in accordance with Christ's will for the
Church and an essential element of maintaining unity
and truth.

We urge Anglicans and Roman Catholics to explore
together how the ministry of the Bishop of Rome
might be offered and received in order to assist
our Communions to grow towards full, ecclesial
communion.[128]

Reports throughout the Protestant and Charismatic world show
a similar pattern of pastor, priest and people drifting toward and
embracing the catholicism of Rome, ultimately leading to papal primacy and submission to the *Pontifex Maximus* who embodies both

the spirit and substance of the resurrecting Roman Empire, leading the Roman Church to ride the Roman political beast to world domination and ultimate destruction. The Deceiver's seductive system is clever but will prove cataclysmic.

"Come Out of Her"

The "King of kings and Lord of lords," Jesus Christ, Yeshua HaMashiach, will not countenance a counterfeit that seeks to usurp both His glory and His authority. He will not tolerate those who trifle with His truth. He cannot and will not bless those who blasphemously claim authority to change His eternal Word for political or pontifical gain or to arrogate themselves to change even His Ten Commandments, proudly declaring the papal magisterium's authority to change the very "times and laws" God hath put in His own hand (Dan. 2:21, 7:25).

The "great whore" is seducing kings and kingdoms, both political and religious. Her bed is spread with "purple and scarlet, and decked with precious stones... having a golden cup in her hand full of abominations and filthiness of her fornication" (Rev. 17:4). As she lures many into her lair, she becomes "THE MOTHER OF HARLOTS" (Rev. 17:5). She has gathered to herself the very colors worn by Roman Caesars and with which Christ was mockingly clothed. *The Catholic Encyclopedia* declares her golden chalice "the most important of the sacred vessels... of gold or silver... and the inside surfaced with gold."[129]

For more than fifteen hundred years, the Roman Catholic Church, under the *Pontifex Maximus* exercised both religious and civil control over Rome. The Pope abolished the Roman Senate and placed all authority under his hand. The *Curia Romana* that once governed Rome was adopted by the Roman Catholic Church as the "Roman Curia" that is now "the whole ensemble of administrative and judicial offices through which the Pope directs the operations of the Catholic Church."[130] That usurped authority is once again being merged as the "woman" rides the "beast" of a resurrecting global Roman empire.

Her symbolic name is "Babylon." "Catholic apologist Karl Keating admits that Rome has long been known as *Babylon*. Keating claims that Peter's statement 'The church here in Babylon… sends you her greeting' (from I Pet. 5:13) proves that Peter was writing from Rome. He further explains, "Babylon is a code word for Rome."[131]

To all, whether Catholic or Protestant, or of whatever religious or political persuasion, the God of Creation warns from heaven…

> "COME OUT OF HER, MY PEOPLE, that ye be not partakers of her sins, and that ye receive not of her plagues. For her sins have reached unto heaven, and God hath remembered her iniquities" (Rev. 18:4-5).

He that hath an ear to hear, let him hear what the spirit saith to professing Christians, Jews and Gentiles across this shrinking globe. The horrific persecution historically manifested by and to preserve papal power in the past will soon again become the horrendous means by which that ultimate power over the planet will be secured as "The Woman Rides the Beast." Will you be prepared to persevere when this global betrayal of Christ rides to temporal glory over the souls of men?

> *The angel of the LORD encampeth round about them*
> *that fear him, and delivereth them (Ps. 34:7).*

Chapter 20
PROBING THOUGHTS for PROPHETIC TIMES

1. What do you think is the significance of the "United Religions" campaign under the United Nations?
2. How is the continual call to "unity" propelling the world into a "spiritual force for globalism?"
3. Did you know that Pope John Paul II called for "the creation of a new world order" based "on the goals of the United Nations?" How does that reflect upon a *geopolitical* role for the Vatican as opposed to a *spiritual* role?
4. Can you see how the political and spiritual history of Rome and of the Vatican connects the prophecies of Daniel and Revelation? Does this history reveal the nature of the final "beast" empire? In what ways?
5. Historian Nigel Rodgers noted, "The Catholic Church, with its hierarchy and universalist ambitions, is the most obvious inheritor of ancient Rome." How does this provide foundation for massive deception, particularly among Roman Catholics?
6. In what ways do you think Tony Blair was right in declaring: "Religion is the new politics?"
7. Does it appear to you that the promoters of global government and the Roman Catholic Church (The Vatican) are working in concert, each for their own purposes of global dominion?
8. What should be the attitude and response of true followers of Christ? Of Jews? Of the Gentile World?
9. Are you able to accept that the massive papal persecution of the past will again be exercised in pursuit of the New World Order in mankind's final effort to take false dominion over the world, all under a false "Christ"?

Chapter 21

PRESSURE –ENGINE OF PERSECUTION

"Envy comes in subtly, but in the end it bites like a
serpent… and becomes a violent engine of persecution."

PRESSURE HAS IMMENSE POWER! Pressure creates but it also destroys. It creates diamonds but also has explosive power, accomplishing a task in quick order that otherwise might take hours, decades or centuries.

A gun has explosive power to kill or defend, to hunt or create horror, precisely because of the instantaneous pressure ignited in its firing. A bomb, whether atomic or nuclear, does its duty due to the immense pressure created instantaneously, yet nuclear power under control can electrify an aircraft carrier for a generation or a city's need for electrical power indefinitely.

To a much lesser extent, a pressure cooker enables the cook to more rapidly prepare a meal for eating. Yet in precisely the same ways, pressure brought to bear through a variety of unrighteous purposes, whether brought on suddenly or through gradual process, inevitably manifests as some level of persecution leading inexorably toward maximum pressure with explosive and therefore annihilating force. This is true both as to persecution of Christians and antisemitism toward Jews.

How Envy Drives Persecution

The driving force of persecution is ever-increasing pressure. That pressure carries many labels and masquerades under many alleged motivations, but the fuel that keeps the engines of persecution running is called ENVY. That is true both as to Christian persecution and Jewish antisemitism.

Envy is the underlying spiritual force of all spiritual persecution, including antisemitism. The persecutorial power of envy is tantamount to a spiritual nuclear bomb or a virally-induced poison calculated, with deadly precision, to destroy all within the proximity of its influential power. For this reason, we are warned:

> Wrath is cruel, and anger is outrageous; but **who is able to stand before envy** (Prov. 27:4; emphasis added)?

> We are also warned that envy is as "rottenness of the bones" (Prov. 14:30). James, the brother of Jesus, knew well the deadly effect of envy, warning the followers of Yeshua:

> If ye have bitter envying and strife in your hearts, glory not… This wisdom descendeth not from above, but is earthly, sensual, devilish.

> For where envying and strife is, there is confusion and every evil work (Jam. 3:14-16).

Precisely what kind and degree of "evil works" does envy produce when unleashed for maximum demonic purpose? The devilish object is first the Jews, the chosen people, who brought forth of the patriarchs the Son of promise prophesied to rule the world as the Prince of Peace, Lord of lords and King of kings (Isa. 9:6-7; Rev. 19:16). The "beast" governing Satan's ultimate beast empire is dedicated to "destroy the mighty and the holy people (Dan. 8:24) and to "wear out the saints of the most High" (Dan. 7:25), which would include both Jewish and Christian believers in Jesus as Messiah, who conduct their lives accordingly (Matt. 7:21-27).

Yet unbelieving Jews, gripped by the demonic spirit of envy in unwitting service to the Destroyer, engaged in envy as a virtual art form. Their misplaced trust, coupled with the intense corruption of the flesh, drove them to horrific acts of violence against the righteous, including the very Hope of Israel, the Son of David, Son of Abraham and Son of God, who had come with long-sought salvation to His own people… yet they "received him not" (Jn. 1:11-12).

We must briefly reiterate the pattern of envy's persecutorial force over perhaps 15 centuries of Israel's promising, yet perverted, history bringing the world to our current cataclysmic moment of unprecedented persecution of both Jew and Gentile Christians. It is a history of vitriolic envy neither Jew nor Gentile desires to see or admit as having been driven by Satan's envious devices. But we must see it for what it is and for its persecutorial power to destroy. And so, we reluctantly look back over the shoulder of history.

JOSEPH—It was Joseph, the son of Abraham's grandson, Jacob, to whom God revealed a destiny and purpose to serve as God's agent to bring deliverance to Israel in a time of intense and deadly famine. But his 10 brothers, the Children of Israel envied him and sold him ultimately into Egyptian slavery for 20 pieces of silver (Gen. 37). His brothers hated him and envied him (Gen. 37: 4, 11). Yet God, despite their deadly envy, fulfilled His promised purposes through Joseph, who has thereafter been seen as a type of Christ himself (Acts 7:8-18).

JESUS—He came unto His own, but "His own received him not" (Jn. 1:11-12). And so, the Jewish leaders, revered among the people, accused Him of "perverting the nation" and that "He stirreth up the people"—an accusation of insurrection against both the religious leaders and of Rome (Lk. 23:1-5).

The religious leaders brought Him to trial before secular Rome, but upon examination by Pilate, he declared "I...have found no fault in this man" (Lk. 23:14). Yet the religious leaders stirred up the people to demand Jesus' ultimate persecution... crucifixion.

But here is the hidden key to the entire persecutorial charade. They despised Caesar, yet declared, "We have no king but Caesar" (Jn. 19:14-15), choosing to place the ultimate pressure upon both Jesus and those who would follow Him. But a crusty Roman governor saw through their persecutorial duplicity. As it is written "For **he knew that for envy** they had delivered him" (Matt. 27:17-23; emphasis added).

STEPHEN—Stephen became the first martyr of the Church. A Martyr is one who gives testimony to his allegiance to Christ through death. At his arrest, again by the religious leaders, he gave his defense of the gospel, tracing God's effort through history to get the attention and affection of His Chosen People.

As it was with Jesus, so it was with Stephen. The religious leaders stirred up the people through perjurious accusations and false witnesses (Acts 6:7-15). To this riotous, yet "religious" assembly, Stephen spoke truth to power, declaring their envious heritage of resisting God, saying: "The patriarchs, **moved with envy**, sold Joseph into Egypt" (Acts 7:9; emphasis added). And that same persecutorial envy brought the stones of ultimate pressure upon the man "full of faith and power, [who] did wonders and miracles among the people" (Acts 6:8). Thus, the ultimate Satanic power of envious pressure was brought upon the pate of Stephen, yet intended to terrify through the power of pressure any who would be so persuaded to publicly follow Jesus as Lord and Messiah.

PAUL—Paul was a Pharisee of distinction among the Jewish elders. Known among them as Saul, he was commissioned to carry out their envy-driven crusade against Followers of the Way (Christians), both near and far. On one of those persecutorial journeys, he was shockingly confronted by Christ himself, who, through a brilliant light and convicting voice, asked "Saul, Saul, why persecutest thou me? (Acts 9:4).

Confronted by the true nature of his persecutorial motivation, Saul of Tarsus' passions were radically changed, accepting the dramatic call, as one who had celebrated Stephen's death, to one who would thereafter proclaim the gospel of Jesus the Messiah—to the Jew first and then to the Gentile world, as a chosen vessel who, as Jesus declared, "must suffer for my name's sake" (Acts 9:15-16).

What then would be the driving force producing the promised suffering? Having preached and reasoned first with his Jewish brethren, Gentiles begged him to preach also to them. "But when the Jews saw the multitudes, they were **filled with envy**...." They "stirred up the devout and honourable women, and the chief men of the city, and raised persecution against Paul and Barnabas" (Acts 13:45-52; emphasis added).

Again, at Thessalonica, Paul preached Christ, "But the Jews which believed not, **moved with envy**, took unto them certain lewd fellows of the baser sort, and gathered a company, and set all the city on an uproar" crying "These that have turned the world upside down are come hither also" (Acts 17:1-6; emphasis added).

Indeed, envy has immense power and still is, and has always been, the underlying driving motivational force of persecution, whether by Jew or Gentile, causing both other religions and rabid disbelievers to rise up against the name of Jesus and those who, with integrity and faith, likewise bear that name. We must clearly understand!

IT IS NOT THE WORD "GOD" THAT UNDERLIES PERESCUTION: IT IS THE NAME OF JESUS, TRULY BELIEVED AND EMBRACED AS THE WORLD'S ONLY HOPE OF SALVATION, BOTH FOR JEW AND GENTILE, THAT THROUGH VITRIOLIC ENVY DRIVES THE WORLD MAD, RESULTING INEVITABLY IN THE PERILOUS TIMES WE NOW FACE, THUS TESTING OUR FAITH.

Envy is Insidious!

Envy has no bounds. Envy is insidious because it proceeds in what appears to be a subtle and gradual way, but in the end has devastating power to place deadly pressure on its objects. While envy must grip individual minds and hearts, the collectivization of envy driven by a perverted sense of godless democracy is one of the most dangerous motivational forces among spiritual beings. And if envy could invade the heavenlies, what might its devastating consequences bring to earth among the children of men?

Lucifer, day star of the morning, the worship leader of heaven, the "anointed cherub that covereth" was "perfect in [his] ways…, till iniquity was found in [him]." He was a glorious leader "upon the holy mountain of God" but that did not suffice the lust of his heart to be equal to God. So "[his] heart [was] lifted up" was "corrupted" because of his greatness and beauty. He was the summation of created beauty and wisdom and was also in Eden the garden of God (Ezekiel 28). He was, by the prophet Ezekiel, euphemistically referred to as the "King of Tyrus."

But envious iniquity was found in him. He was not the eternal Creator God but lusted for God's influential power, corrupting through collective envy a large rebellious enclave of the angelic host, determined to insinuate among humankind the same envious spirit. For he said in his heart…

I will ascend into heaven, I will exalt my throne above the stars of God: I will sit also upon the mount of the congregation [the Temple Mount]… I will be like the most High (Isa. 14:13-14).

The prophet Isaiah lamented the ultimate end of such envy, declaring, "Yet thou shalt be brought down to hell, to the sides of the pit." The peoples of the planet will ultimately see the dramatic devastation caused by such demonic envy saying:

Is this the man that made the earth to tremble, that did shake kingdoms; That made the world as a wilderness… (Isa. 14:16-17)? Which didst weaken the nations (Isa. 14:12)?

Envy comes in subtly, but in the end it bites like a serpent. Like a fog, it comes in gradually "on little cat feet" as observed the poet Robert Frost, but it eventually envelopes the entire spiritual environment so densely that true wisdom, understanding and godly vision is distorted and becomes a violent engine of persecution.

Envy Persecutes the Faithful

Envy has demonic power to place immense pressure through those caught up in its widening web, poisoning all true reason, lending inevitably to persecution of all others not so trapped in its tyrannical grasp.

The trajectory of this tyranny began with Lucifer in the heavenlies, on "the holy mountain of God" (Ezek. 28:14). Lucifer, aka Satan, then choreographed a vast number of the angelic host (the sons of God) into his envious congregation. He was cast to the earth and manifested his presence to the sons of men—to Adam and Eve in Eden, and to kings and all under their authority on the planet (Ezek. 28: 13, 17). His purpose was to engage the sons of men on earth in the same envious web in which he had entrapped the sons of God with the counterfeit spiritual goal of collectively becoming as "God," thus defying or rejecting the Creator's authority. The devious vision was to cause worshippers of God, under God's authority, to the dominion of Satan, aka, the Devil.

Consider soberly our current spiritual situation. Envy, as a premier engine of persecution, now places unprecedented pressure upon all who would otherwise claim allegiance to Jesus Christ as the only way, the only truth and the only life… that "no man cometh to the Father, but by me" (Jn. 14:6). Such a claim of exclusivity is a veritable declaration of war against Lucifer's (aka Satan's, the Devil's) envious and historic agenda to be equal with God. What then is Satan's (your arch enemy's) modus operandi?

Satan is engineering an unprecedented pressure system culminating with imposition of the infamous Mark of the Beast to compel all persons on the planet to accept and submit to his authority, including all who currently profess allegiance to and salvation through Yeshua (Jesus) the Messiah.

Because of the immense pressure brought to bear to effectuate Lucifer's/Satan's supreme envious system, many will fall away from their faith in Yeshua and shift their allegiance to Satan's counterfeit or imposter "christ," the son of perdition (II Thess. 2:3). This earthly "incarnation" of Satan will "exalt himself above all that is called God, or that is worshipped; so that he as God sitteth in the temple of God, showing himself that he is God" (II Thess. 2:2-4).

The echoing consequences of this supreme and ultimate manifestation of Satan's unsatiated envy will precipitate a very painful, yet prophesied, persecution of true and faithful followers of Jesus. This final and accelerated persecution will come as former professing Christians, who have succumbed to the pressure created by presentation of the "Mark," join forces with a frenzied godless world to enforce a counterfeit "peace on earth" through a godless and God-defying world government.

Just as Jesus was betrayed by those closest to him, and just as David was betrayed by Ahithophel his trusted friend, so many professed followers of Jesus will betray to the Antichrist's kingdom their friends and relatives who have not capitulated to the envy-driven pressure. It will be profoundly painful as those who, through spiritual weakness, have refused to stand against the envious wiles of the Devil, decide that, in a perverse sort of envy, all those who remain faithful must be reported and compelled to suffer because their very willingness to stand brings unbearable conviction on those who have fallen away.

Jesus and the Power of Pressure

It is painfully, yet precisely, this very ultimate expression of the power of pressure of which Jesus lamentably warned His disciples. Because His message is not marketable, it is seldom given focus in any of America's ministries, yet it is Jesus' untempered warning to protect and preserve our faith amid the final assault of envy-induced pressure and persecution. Hear… and let us with patient endurance… heed our Lord's words.

The disciple is not above his master, nor the servant above his lord.

It is enough for the disciple that he be as his master, and the servant as his lord. If they have called the master of the house Beelzebub, how much more shall they call them of his household?

Fear them not therefore: for there is nothing covered, that shall not be revealed; and hid, that shall not be known.

What I tell you in darkness, that speak ye in light: and what ye hear in the ear, that preach ye upon the housetops.

And fear not them which kill the body, but are not able to kill the soul: but rather fear him which is able to destroy both soul and body in hell.

Are not two sparrows sold for a farthing? and one of them shall not fall on the ground without your Father.

But the very hairs of your head are all numbered.

Fear ye not therefore, ye are of more value than many sparrows.

Whosoever therefore shall confess me before men, him will I confess also before my Father which is in heaven.

But whosoever shall deny me before men, him will I also deny before my Father which is in heaven.

Think not that I am come to send peace on earth: I came not to send peace, but a sword.

For I am come to set a man at variance against his father, and the daughter against her mother, and the daughter in law against her mother in law.

And a man's foes shall be they of his own household.

He that loveth father or mother more than me is not worthy of me: and he that loveth son or daughter more than me is not worthy of me.

And he that taketh not his cross, and followeth after me, is not worthy of me.

He that findeth his life shall lose it: and he that loseth his life for my sake shall find it (Matt. 10:24-39).

And ye shall be hated of all men for my name's sake: but he that endureth to the end shall be saved (Matt. 10:22).

Identifying Envy's Expressions

The power and pressure of envy has many expressions, the root of which is not overtly apparent. It is these expressions that, both individually and collectively, create the intense pressure that the saints have and will experience, testing our faith beyond levels now comprehended. Each of these expressions are calculated, through the power of envy, to bring the entire world into conformity to the spirit of a promised peace through the coming Antichrist. The not-so-hidden message is: either yield and conform, rejecting your allegiance to Jesus as Savior, or be "selected out" of civil society either by complete ostracization or by death.

Here, then, is a significant, though not exhaustive, list of the many expressions of envy that, through the power of pressure, inure to the persecution of the saints.

Peer Pressure.
Secular and Cultural Intolerance.
Suppression of Speech as to Biblical Morality.
Removal or Prohibition of Christian Symbols.
Intolerance of Christians While Tolerating Other Religions.
Labeling Christians with False Characterizations.
Claiming Christians as a Threat to Democracy.
Criminalization of Christianity or Biblical Morality.
Suppression of Religious Freedom.
Utilizing Laws to Limit Worship and Bible Studies.

Government Sanctions, Bribery and Threats, Including Imposing Fines.
Coercion for Control under Cover and Color of Political Correctness, Multiculturalism and Religious Pluralism.
Usurpation of Parental Authority.
Medical Mandate Rejecting all Moral and Religious Exemptions.
Imposition of Anti-Biblical Authority under Color of Law, Including Environmentalism.
Cultural Mandate to Conform or be Ostracized from Civil Society.
Governmental Mandate to Conform to Global Digitization and Its Accompanying "Mark."
Inquisition and Increasing Intimidation.

Any or all of these expressions owe their life-force to increasing hatred driven by envy. The motivations may be overt, open and obvious; or may be covert, hidden or camouflaged. To be aware and forewarned is to be forearmed in faith to persevere, without compromise or capitulation, yet in a continuing spirit of humility, for as our Master declared:

But he that endureth to the end shall be saved (Matt. 10:22).

Deliver me from mine enemies, O my God: defend me from them that rise up against me (Ps. 59:1).

Chapter 21
PROBING THOUGHTS FOR PROPHETIC TIMES

1. Why do you think envy is so powerful?
2. Were you surprised to see how envy, as a premier motivation of the heart, is woven throughout the Scriptures as the driving force even to the crucifixion of Christ and the multiplied persecutions of His apostles and of Paul?
3. Why is envy insidious?
4. Was not Satan driven by envy to be equal with God? Why then would Satan not employ the demonic power of envy to use persecution against you to do his will rather than to truly trust Christ?
5. Can you see how the immense pressure is increasingly being brought to bear by Lucifer's/Satan's envious system to cause many to fall away from their faith in Yeshua so as to embrace a counterfeit christ?
6. Was Jesus correct when he warned, "And ye shall be hated of all men for my name's sake: but he that endureth [remains steadfast] to the end shall be saved"? How is that understanding connecting in your own mind and heart… even now?

PART 8

PREPARING FOR "THE BLESSED HOPE"

Earth-based hope defrauds us of genuine and eternal hope, leaving us ashamed and devoid of sustaining biblical hope."

WITHOUT THE PROMISE OF HOPE, we will not prepare. That is the unfortunate reality that pervades the fleshly nature of all people, including professing Christians. We must therefore not lose sight of hope, the light at the end of life's tunnel.

Hope That Prevails and Protects

Our persistent problem is that we are largely circumscribed by our earthly viewpoints to rest our hope on our prevailing circumstances. Pursuing our "Best Life Now"—a theme that has hovered over American life both secularly and spiritually since the turn of the 7th millennium—has become a metaphor for the locus and focus of our hope. Reality, unfortunately, is striking at such confidence, raising the head of horror to smash much of our earthly-based hope. Such "hope" defrauds us of genuine and eternal hope, ultimately leaving us ashamed and devoid of biblical hope that enables us to persevere in times of peril and persecution.

We Persevere in Hope

As the apostle Paul so poignantly said… "If in this life only we have hope in Christ, we are of all men most miserable" (I Cor. 15:19). Perhaps much of the increasing misery, anxiety and even despair not only throughout the secular world but also defining much of the life of professing followers of Christ is that we have, in significant measure, a misplaced hope, leaving us weak, disillusioned and unable to truly stand by faith amid rising fear that torments.

In this Part 8, we must confront the lordship of circumstances that is surreptitiously eating away our sustaining hope. Join with us! Hope lies ahead.

I wait for the LORD, my soul doth wait, and in his word do I hope (Ps. 130:5).

Chapter 22

HOPE THROUGH HISTORY

"The early church enables us to both see the sobering challenge that persecution presents and to respond with corresponding courage."

"THE ONLY THING WE LEARN from history," we are often told, "is that we don't learn from history." And as if that were not a sufficient warning, we are further advised that "Those who do not learn from history are doomed to repeat it."

That may be the prevailing record throughout most of human history, but it need not be so for the followers of Jesus, Yeshua the Messiah, in our generation on the near edge of His Second Coming. Whether that historical record prevails for you, for me and for all who profess Jesus as Savior will depend upon the genuineness of our alleged faith, our true love for the Lord and the preparation of our hearts and minds to "endure to the end" so as to be partakers of the eternal hope that lies beyond temporal suffering in this world.

What, then, is the current level of your spiritual preparation? Are you just entering Boot Camp, or have you truly progressed to being a fully equipped saint for the battles that lie ahead? Will you go AWOL, or will you continue amid persecution to "press toward the mark…of the high calling of God in Christ Jesus (Phil. 3:14)?

Encouraged By the Early Church

It is rather difficult—virtually impossible—for a man or woman to purport to be a true coach for a team when that coach has had no significant personal preparation playing the game or participating meaningfully in the sport. Such a purported coach has no legitimacy of convincing authority, since the team recognizes that his best efforts fall far short of the insight and wisdom, coupled with toughened preparation, to enable the team to face the tough challenges ahead.

This, unfortunately, is the plight of the American and western church. There has been no significant assault upon Christians and their faith prior to the past decade, nor have pastors, priests and parachurch leaders themselves faced serious persecution. Therefore, despite best efforts by some to at least discuss the persecution believers are facing or will soon face, they are at a serious loss as to how to prepare those who trust them to courageously lead. They reveal their own lack of preparedness, by their fear and intimidation by the very subject of persecution, to convince any significant number to take heed and seriously prepare. Who then can help us over this hurdle?

The early church provides the needed coaching examples, enabling us to both see the sobering challenge that persecution presents and to respond with corresponding courage.

A History to Encourage Courage

Christopher P. David has provided a wonderful exposé of the early church in dealing with developing persecution, so that by their example of yesteryear we might be better prepared in this consummate moment of history to face these increasingly perilous times.[132] We would all do well to acquaint ourselves with his historical outline for the preparation of our own hearts and minds. And we therefore share here excerpts of his both enlightening and encouraging piece.

Setting the stage for reference to the past, we are reminded that more than 5,600 Christians were killed for their faith in 2022, not to mention the hundreds of thousands who were arrested and imprisoned, tortured and beaten. And those numbers do not include the over 300 million who have had their religious liberties denied, have been governmentally and socially ostracized and have been shunned or disowned by both family and friends. And it could soon include you, whether pastor or priest or all who truly profess Jesus as both Savior and Lord.

And so, we begin our historical tour from which the end-time church can learn and be strengthened by reflecting on the fierce trials of the first century church. The early church was born as an outcome of the persecution of Christ and grew through the onslaught of constant persecution thereafter. It was only a few decades until the 120 spilling out of the upper room at Pentecost became thousands in the midst of fierce opposition.

THE JEWISH PERSECUTIONS

First came growing and intense persecution from Jewish leaders who, through envy, had called for Jesus' crucifixion and who, by the same envious motivation, likewise persecuted the apostles (Mk. 15:10; Matt. 27:18; Jn. 11:47-48; 12:10-11). The Jewish leaders wanted, therefore, to silence the gospel (cancel and censor) because they considered the gospel blasphemous, just as do Muslims today. Eusebius, the early church historian, wrote, "the church of Jerusalem suffered the first and greatest persecution at the hands of the Jews." And yes, today, Orthodox and Chasidic Jews continue that pattern, particularly through their growing anti-missionary efforts to prevent Christian proselytizing under color of law.

Saul of Tarsus, a Jewish Rabbi, carried on a vicious era of persecution, tracking down Followers of the Way (Christians) beyond Jerusalem even to Damascus, Syria, consenting even to the first martyr of the church as he was being stoned. Saul was miraculously converted, took the name of Paul, and became one of the most influential apostles to the gentile world, yet he likewise suffered immense persecution due to Jewish envy and gentile opposition (Acts 17:1-13).

THE ROMAN PERECUTIONS

While the Jewish persecution was severe, it was nothing compared to the Roman persecutions which began in 64 A.D. under Nero. The apostles Paul and Peter were executed and John was banished to the isle of Patmos from which he penned the *Apocalypse* (Book of Revelation).

The Christians dwelt in catacombs for worship yet involved themselves in ministering to the sick and poor for which the Romans had no sympathy. The simple, yet stalwart, believers were nevertheless hunted, tracked and tortured. Some were crucified, sewn into animal skins to be torn apart in gladiatorial events for public pleasure, and burned as torches along public thoroughfares.

Christianity, after largely severed from Judaism, became public enemy number one, and was therefore outlawed in Rome as it was deemed to be a threat to Roman authority. Since the emperor was deemed deity and Christians would not bow to do mandatory obeisance to his image, they were deemed rebels and traitors to be eradicated from Roman society.

While some of the professing Christians abandoned their faith in the face of such trials and persecutions, it seems a majority joyfully endured suffering. Christians regarded martyrdom as a crown to win—the highest honor for a Christian. The calmness and serenity of the martyrs was glaringly obvious to those who witnessed. And many martyrs sang hymns in the face of impending death, praising God until their last breath, realizing that their temporary pain brought eternal gain.

LET HISTORY BE YOUR FRIEND

If we learn from history and are truly inspired by the victorious faith of those who have endured suffering for the name of the Savior from the earliest days and centuries of the church, we also may one day give testimony as they did, and the glory of God will rest upon us. We seek not martyrdom but faithful allegiance to our Master.

Jesus builds and sustains His church "through many dangers, toils and snares" as we so gladly sing Amazing Grace. He provides enduring grace (favor and enabling power) even through fire, sword and alienation from godless society.

Just as the early church stood and even flourished under the onslaught of the mighty Roman Empire, even so we can and will persevere because of the prize set before us (Phil. 3:14), always "Looking unto Jesus the author and finisher of our faith," always "consider[ing] him… lest ye be wearied and faint in your minds" (Heb. 12:2-4).

The Resurrection of Rome

The great, and now late, Roman Empire is rising again, just as the prophet Daniel foretold in his vision of the great colossus, describing very dramatically a fourth and final beast arising to rule the earth in these last days (Dan. 7). This great "beast" is, and always has been, "diverse from all others, exceeding dreadful." Just as ancient Rome warred against the early saints, so also will the now resurrecting "Rome" war with even greater animosity against Christ's followers, making war against the saints and even prevailing against them (Dan. 7:21).

Rome never fully died but became dispersed throughout the western world. Its "resurrection" began with the European Common Market in 1950, just two years after the nation of Israel was reborn in 1948, notwithstanding the resistance of the United Nations born in 1945. The process of Rome's rebirth was then launched with intense vision. Consider the fascinating timeline.

April 4, 1949 - NATO is created.

May 5, 1949 - The Council of Europe is establishing.

May 9, 1950 - Plan presented for European cooperation.

April 18, 1951 - European Coal and Steel Community established.

March 25, 1957 - Treaties of Rome create European
Economic Community.

March 19, 1958 - Birth of European Parliament.

1993   European Union [EU] formed.

January 1, 1999 - The Euro was launched.

January 1, 2002 - Euro coins and currency were
launched—the "biggest cash change-
over in history."

The European Union would then serve as a model for the foundation of many other global unions including the Mediterranean Union conceived by Nicholas Sarkozy, the French president who conceived the concept in his Roman mind as he began his presidency of the European Union. The Mediterranean Union was formed July 13, 2008, for "peace, stability and security," thus revitalizing the historic *Pax Romana* (Roman Peace) for these later days of history. "*The Guardian* from Britain noted: 'Sarkozy's big idea is to use imperial Rome's centre of the world as a unifying factor linking 44 countries that are home to 800 million people'."[133]

History and Prophecy Are Converging

A review of the march of history is hopefully meaningful, yet the clear converging of both history and prophecy should be profoundly moving in both our hearts and minds. And the full story has not yet been told.

The spirit of Rome and of Babylon are now merging with the spirit of Egypt to form mankind's final effort to combine the global powers of Pharaoh, Nebuchadnezzar, and Caesar into their ultimate biblical expression of a one world government or New World Order emerging out of Europe, amplified through America sometimes referred to as the *Pax Americana*, and consolidated now by the full expansion of NATO, all with the papal blessing of three popes in series culminating with the global intensification vision of Pope Francis.

The woman of Revelation 17 is now prepared to prophetically "ride the back" of Daniel's colossus vision, again described as "diverse from all other" before it, and "exceeding dreadful," producing a "horn" or singular leader that will make "war with the saints and prevail against them." He will "speak great words against the most High, and shall wear out the saints" (Dan. 7:19-25).

We must be prepared for this culminating season of biblical prophecy of which both our Lord and His disciples warned. History of our forebearers in the early years of the church must provide hope for each of us as these promised "perilous times" explode before a largely unsuspecting American and westernized church. In order for each of us in our respective roles and relationships to be able to endure to the end as Jesus adjured, we must be confident that His "strength is made perfect in our weakness" (II Cor. 12:9), just as it was for those who endured suffering for the name of Jesus in the first two centuries, for history is repeating itself... this time "on steroids" and globally.

Remember, the "blessed hope" of Jesus' return lies ahead (Tit. 2:13). Keep your eyes fixed on the horizon! We must "lay hold upon the hope set before us" (Heb. 6:18). "And every man that hath this hope in him purifieth himself, even as he [Jesus] is pure" (I Jn. 3:3).

Keep me, O LORD, from the hands of the wicked;
preserve me from the violent man; who have pur-
posed to overthrow my goings (Ps. 140:4).

Chapter 22

PROBING THOUGHTS for PROPHETIC TIMES

1. Why do you think we have such a hard time learning from history?
2. What do you think is your current level of spiritual preparation for serious persecution ahead?
3. Within the Christian community or contacts that you have, do you sense any real awareness or discussion concerning persecution for the name of Christ?
4. Do the leaders you listen to or respect give you the impression you will likely not have to face persecution as did the early church?
5. Why do you think both Jesus and His apostles solemnly warned of end-time persecution?
6. Do you not find it fascinating that "Rome" is rising again even as Israel was reborn as a nation?
7. Can you see how history and prophecy are converging rather dramatically? What does that say to you?

Chapter 23

THE LURE OF FALSE HOPE

*"Our true trust is tested as our choices for how
and where to place our hope are always
before us.... And each of us will make our choices."*

"HOPE SPRINGS ETERNAL in the human breast," we were told by the famed Alexander Pope in *An Essay on Man*. Human beings need hope, but hope, in general, bears no truly measurable definition or destination. Hope is some rather ill-defined state of expectation of something better than current circumstances, feelings or general perceived state of mind and heart. And not surprisingly, hope always seems to be illusive... out there... somewhere... like the proverbial pot at the end of the rainbow.

Yet the soul of man yearns for an anchor. We desperately cry, either with internal tears or with passionate voice, for that in which we can truly trust to provide hope amid the usual, or seemingly surpassing, trials and tribulations that assault our deep desire for peace and security. Many—increasingly—in desperation for that hope that perpetually eludes, are forsaking biblical hope as an eternal illusion, resulting in self-martyrdom to the hope that has so long betrayed.

Welcome to the New World of Perilous Times of which all humanity has been forewarned by the Creator—through both Jesus and His apostles. The catalogue of hope-breakers given by the apostle Paul is both profoundly descriptive, but also prescriptive, of these extraordinary times with which we are now confronted for the glory of God and for those who are truly walking in the "hope of the Gospel" of Yeshua the Messiah, the "hope of Israel" (I Tim. 3:1-8; Col. 1:23; Jer. 14:8, 17:13; Ps. 137:7). Indeed, as Thomas Paine lamented during America's birth-time testing: "These are the times that try men's souls."

The Security of False Hope

Since the genuine felt fulfillment of persistent hope always seems elusive, our human nature naturally gravitates to grasping on to those things seemingly most easily accessible so as to at least somehow self-convince ourselves that the hope we seek still exists… somewhere… somehow. While this natural tendency may not, in and of itself, be evil or malignant, it opens the door to the horror of false hope.

We are oft reminded that "nature abhors a vacuum." And it is true! Something, however desirable or undesirable, will always press into the vacuum or spot left empty, seeking inevitably to fill it or replace that which once occupied the space. Weeds will replace an uncared-for lawn or garden. Anger will replace a peaceful home ruled by drugs and alcohol. Betrayal threatens betrothal when the vacuum of care and affection wanes in a marriage. Poverty replaces prosperity when homes are emptied of loving married partners, and children, once secure, are left virtual orphans in the wake. When an evil spirit is cast out and not replaced with the Holy Spirit of Truth, seven other spirits, more wicked, enter in so that "the last state of that man is worse than the first" (Lk. 11:24-26).

In truth, our natural desire for fulfilled hope and security renders us prone or susceptible to the temptation to open the door of our hearts and homes… and even our churches… to false hopes and promises of security that offer a temporary sense of relief, yet unsuspectingly promise not hope but rather horror lurking in the darkness. Thus, our true Kingdom trust is tested, even on a daily basis, as our choices for how and where we place our hope are always before us to be made. And each of us will make our choices.

False Hope Lies Ahead

As American Christians we have often sung in eras past a hymn called "My Hope is Built…" sometimes called by the title "Solid Rock." It was composed by an English pastor, Edward Mote, in 1836, and was set to the music by William Bradbury. So great was the hymn's impact on the broader Christian church throughout the English-speaking world that it remains prominent in most hymnals and in the minds of many today, almost 200 years later. Throughout this chapter we will remind ourselves of the hope of which this hymn speaks so as to cause us to shrink from the alternative "hope" presented through pressure and promise by the Serpent who once asked "Hath God said" (Gen. 3:1-3)?

> **MY HOPE IS BUILT** on nothing less than Jesus' blood and righteousness; I dare not trust the sweetest frame, but wholly lean on Jesus' name.

Here we understand and must be ever-passionately convinced in soul and spirit of these 5 truths as an anchor in perilous times:

1. There is a genuine HOPE.
2. Our hope must be BUILT.
3. The FOUNDATION of that hope is Jesus' blood, that when received, gives us righteousness by which we must thereafter live.
4. We cannot allow our TRUST to be swayed to promising alternatives.
5. We must wholly and entirely, without reservation, LEAN on the name of Jesus and no other name, however popular or powerful.

A false hope lies directly ahead and is being both announced and pronounced throughout our world by presidents, prime ministers, corporate presidents, and even priests, pastors and popes. While historically mocked as the mantra of conspiracy theorists and political pseudo-prophets, the global media now beats the drums announcing the glorious emergence of a New World Order, a utopian fulfillment of the eternal hopes of humankind from the God-defying Tower of Babel of Genesis 11 to the resurrecting Roman Empire or Pax Romana to precede the Second Coming of the Prince of Peace.

We should therefore expect that this unique moment of prophetic history will present an alternative hope, an alternative security, an alternative faith and alternative promises of prosperity and purpose, all to be, as it were, incarnated in the Serpent's chosen human emissary—a counterfeit Christ... a non-god yet gloriously human "prince of peace"... the very definition by Orthodox Jews of their anticipated "Messiah." Therefore, if and when a third Temple should suddenly emerge from prophesied political negotiations as Israel's foretold "covenant with death" (Dan. 9:27; Isa. 28:14-18), hold on to your trust in "The Solid Rock." The best, and worse, is yet to come.

As Paul once enjoined the Thessalonians of their hope:

> Be not soon shaken in mind, or be troubled, neither by spirit, nor by word... as that the day of Christ is at hand.

> Let no man deceive you by any means: for that day shall not come, except there come a falling away [apostasy] first, and that man of sin be revealed, the son of perdition;

> Who opposeth and exalteth himself above all that is called God, or that is worshipped; so that he as God sitteth in the temple of God, shewing himself that he is God (II Thess. 2:2-4).

Birth Pangs of False Hope

TIKVAT ISRAEL means "the hope of Israel." That hope resides in the expectation of a coming Messiah who will restore Israel and the Jewish people to the fulness of biblically-defined, prophetic promises and purposes, thereby to restore the world for HaShem's (God's) glory—Tikkun Olam, restoration/repair of the world. The Jewish anticipation is that this messianic moment in history will then bring global SHALOM—world justice, security and prosperity.

This Messiah factor is an embedded article of Orthodox Jewish faith. And over the years since the 1970s, messianic expectation has exploded to almost fever pitch. It is of such intensity now in Israel as to be almost palpable. There is a deep-seated certainty that the world is now in the messianic age, however that may be defined.

Interestingly, a campaign began in the late 1970s in Israel bearing the slogan "We Want Moshiach Now." This phenomenon was echoed by Hal Lindsay's *The Late Great Planet Earth* within the greater gentile Christian world, coupled with the release of the soul-gripping, heart-stirring film *A Thief in the Night*. By 1992, as both the western world began to unravel at the seams with Israel and Islam emerging with increasing prominence, the Messiah movement among Jews also picked up steam, declaring, "Prepare for the Coming of the Messiah."[134]

The Messiah Factor then mushroomed amazingly across the planet. By 2005, Russian Chief Rabbi Berel Lazar publicly announced his conviction that the earth will soon see the coming of a Messiah to judge all mankind. "We know that he is very near at hand," he said. And in explaining, Rabbi Lazar noted: "The world today is in the state described by our sages as 'hevley mashiah,' that is labor that precedes the coming of Messiah." "We are living on the verge of history," he said. "It can be felt everywhere."[135]

Rabbi Lazar calls this season "labor that precedes the coming of Messiah." Yeshua the Messiah referred to this season as "the beginning of sorrows" as of a woman experiencing birth pangs as she prepares to be delivered (Matt. 24:8). And perhaps it was no mistake that Jesus followed the description of preliminary birth pangs with a serious warning concerning the persecution to accompany the increasing intensity of those pangs, concluding: "But he that shall endure to the end, the same shall be saved" (Matt. 24:9-13).

Since we are told a false messiah, a satanically inspired counterfeit, will precede the actual return of Christ, it should become immediately apparent to any true follower of Yeshua HaMashiach (Jesus) that a massive and persuasive false hope will be presented to all peoples on the planet. It will force a choice of faith in either Christ as the Savior sent from God or in the Antichrist sent by the Deceiver to draw the inhabitants of the earth to eternal perdition.

The Muslim world has also joined the fray of messianic anticipation. "The COMING is NEAR" declared a video produced by the Iranian government. Muslims anticipate their "messiah," called the Mahdi, who will lead them in the final conquest of earth… an Islamic "apocalypse" or unveiling soon to be revealed.[136] Let the world be wary, for every man, woman and child soon faces the final choice of a "messiah."

Heralding the False Hope

The pressure for and toward world unity, at every level, is unprecedented. This pressure has reached a fever pitch. The flames of global fever are fanned by fear of global conflagration and by a utopian vision for a global peace and prosperity that has heretofore escaped man's grasp. The pressure now coincides with the messianic fervor growing worldwide.

The great and growing river of unity gradually becoming a global sea is fed by the confluence of many streams and tributaries, both religious and secular. We must now bring into focus the emerging sculpture of a global order being forged as man's ultimate achievement and salvation.

This emerging global-ism is being forged out of the multitude of prevalent isms in our world, the most significant of which we can broadly distill as the "science isms," "social-isms," "political-isms" and "religious-isms," with the ultimate goal of unprecedented materi-al-ism. While seemingly separate in their respective disciplines, upon closer inspection one cannot escape the merging and synergetic inter-action of these various broad categories of isms, each reinforcing the other and developing a kind of "magnetic" attraction, chasing each other ever closer into an uncanny bond now universally defined as *global-ism*. It is the religious isms that globalists increasingly, although often reluctantly, acknowledge as the ultimate catalyst to bind the world in the final thrust for global unity.

It is fascinating to watch the threads of the emerging global tap-estry being woven into a discernible pattern through the unprece-dented pursuit of unity. One can easily be trapped in its seductive web of deception, especially because of the sheer weight of the supposed "authorities" and their massing majorities embracing global-ism as a veritable new "gospel."

The Anti-Gospel

Global governance is not a conspiracy theory but a confrontive truth. The "gospel" of global government and the unification of the world is secularly described as ***global-ism***. Its spiritual roots draw life not from trusting God's wisdom, grace and power but rather from man's desire to sever dependence on his Creator and to depend upon mankind's "good nature" to do the right thing for the "common good," and hence save himself. It is the "anti-gospel" precisely because it denies man's fundamental sinful condition necessitating a savior other than himself, shifting ultimate trust to the "arm of flesh," which brings a curse. (Jer. 17:5).

Israel, continuing her search to be like all the other nations (I Sam. 8:5-7), and to be included among them despite God's declaration they "shall not be reckoned among the nations" (Numb. 23:9), now seeks inclusion in the European Union and has been received into the Mediterranean Union. Having rejected her Messiah, she continues to proclaim, "We have no king but Caesar" (Jn. 19:15), trusting the proffered *shalom* (security and prosperity) of man's systems rather than her Savior's sacrifice. And so, a European Commissioner wrote in one of Israel's key daily newspapers, "We will also work with Israel to promote and uphold the values we share and which we believe hold the key to prosperity in Europe and everywhere else in the world."[137]

America, as a Gentile "New Canaan," has followed the path of Israel. Having progressively abandoned the God of her fathers and the fear of the Lord, she now fears man. Having lost actual trust in the Creator, she desperately clings to a motto, *In God We Trust*, that has become little more than a faded symbol and an empty mantra. The God who "made and preserved her a nation" had set her apart from all other nations, yet now, in growing fear, she seeks to wed herself to their pagan global enterprise for *shalom* (security and prosperity).

The Unbelief of False Hope

Nature abhors a vacuum. When our genuine trust in God and His Word wanes, Satan is quick to interject an alternative, inevitably shifting our focus from authentic faith to a fleshly counterfeit. Israel, as with the West and the western Gentile church, suffers from acute spiritual anemia. We are wide open for Satan's final spiritual deception. It has been well designed to entrap both Jew and Gentile, and its final manifestation is soon to be revealed for those who have an eye to see.

For the Jew, a rebuilt Temple may well be the perfect trap, diverting trust from God's "Anointed One" to Satan's appointed one, the "Son of Perdition" who makes ingratiating promises as "the little horn" emerging from the "ten horns" of the resurrecting Roman Empire (Dan. 7:7-8). He will "speak great words against the most High, and shall even wear out the saints...," both Jew and Gentile (Dan. 7:19-25), once he gains power. The mere flattering promise of security and prosperity will be sufficient bait to ensnare and co-opt the trust of most Gentiles, for by the pursuit of peace this imposter will destroy many (Dan. 8:23-25).

Yet, for this latter-time trader in trust to gain global dominion so as to invite men to sacrifice their eternal souls for the promise of temporal peace and prosperity, Satan's global governmental "gospel" must become nearly universally embraced. Shockingly, even now, "Anyone Who Resists the EU Is A Terrorist" according to Italian President Giorgio Napolitano at a news conference.[138] But those broadly labeled "terrorist" today will be deemed "traitor" tomorrow. Just as with ancient Rome, the resurrecting end-time "Rome" will brook no opposition once enthroned.

How will such universal acceptance be achieved? What will win the mind and heart of the world to passionately embrace global-ism as the ultimate "gospel" for "peace on earth, goodwill toward man" (Lk. 2:14)?

Perhaps the fact that the Roman Catholic Popes John Paul II, Benedict XVI and Francis have all vigorously called for global government and a New World Order are definitive confirmation of the world's direction and destination.

Will you recognize Satan's duplicity in the hour of deception? Or will you dance with the Deceiver, seduced by his offer of counterfeit *shalom,* packaged alluringly in religious robes calculated to convince all but those who "keep the commandments of God, and the faith of Jesus" (Rev. 14:12)? Is it not time to "prepare the way of the Lord" in your life and in the life of those in your sphere of influence so that you "may be able to withstand in the evil day" (Eph. 6:13)? The Lord Jesus Christ alone must be our "hope and stay."

The Lure of False Hope

Massive spiritual deception is mounting as the final bridge, bidding politicians, pastors, priests, parishioners and parachurch leaders to cross over a worldly Jordan into a counterfeit Promised Land of global *security* and *prosperity* (Shalom). The rivers and rivulets of the world's religious isms are now combining to propel even professing Christians and Jews in the powerful currents of global "oneness" into the counterfeit Christ's new global order of false hope. As Jesus well warned, "if it were possible, they shall deceive the very elect" (Matt. 24:24). Globalism is, in reality, the "Anti-Gospel,"[139] choreographing an increasingly faithless, feeling-driven world in a final collective rebellion against God in the battle for lordship over your soul.

We will pull back the curtain from what may be the final acts of this deceptive drama in the next chapter. Please prepare your mind and heart in an attitude of profound humility and prayer, for of necessity we must hereafter increasingly delve into delicate issues of doctrine and tradition that potentially impact destiny.

Until then, we conclude with the final stanza of "My Hope is Built…"

> When He shall come with trumpet sound,
> O may I then in Him be found;
> dressed in His righteousness alone,
> faultless to stand before the throne.
>
> On Christ, the solid Rock, I stand:
> all other ground is sinking sand;
> all other ground is sinking sand.

It is better to trust in the LORD than to put confidence in man. It is better to trust in the LORD than to put confidence in princes (Ps. 118:8-9).

Chapter 23
PROBING THOUGHTS for PROPHETIC TIMES

1. Why is hope so necessary… and so powerful?
2. How does hope provide a sense of security, whether or not based upon true or legitimate facts?
3. Why are even Christians susceptible to embracing false hope?
4. As you probe your past thoughts, have you been tempted to, or actually subscribed to, a false hope, however seemingly small?
5. Do you believe, and are you confident, that your hope for the future is securely placed?
6. Can you imagine any lure, any pressure brought to bear, that might seriously test you to embrace a false hope?
7. Can you see how even a rising global desire or expectation for a "messiah" might lure the unwary or weak to embrace a counterfeit promising wonderful things?
8. Can you see how ignorance of the whole of God's Word renders you susceptible to being seduced to embrace a false hope?

Chapter 24

THE HOPE AHEAD

*"It is amid suffering and persecution that the true hope
of our calling is confirmed, not in anxiety but in rejoicing."*

HOPE IS ON THE HORIZON! Yet true hope in Jesus as Savior and Lord must reside presently, with utmost conviction and unswerving expectation, in the very depths of our hearts and be woven deeply through the membranes of our minds. This hope is the anchor that keeps our soul steadfast and sure while the billows of persecution threaten to swamp our spirits.

Faith Secures Hope

"Faith is the substance of things hoped for," we are reminded, but it is also "the evidence of things not seen" (Heb. 11:1). Faith secures our hope both in eternal salvation and in the Second Coming of Yeshua in power and great glory to rule as KING of Kings and as LORD of Lords.

True hope is secured by faith, and we should not be ashamed of such ultimate hope. Yet faith in Christ Jesus is not merely a religious belief system referred to as Christianity. Rather, true faith is defined biblically as active belief such that it defines and governs every aspect of our being including the breadth of our very thoughts and behaviors. Such faith breeds and sustains unwavering hope in the promises given by the Potentate of our souls both to us and to the patriarchs of the faith who have gone before us. For this reason we are told, first in the Tanach and then in the New Covenant that "The just shall live by his faith" (Hab. 2:4; Rom. 1:17). We are not only *justified* by faith but must *live* by faith, a reality that is often overlooked or brushed aside, thus compromising the fulness of our hope.

When we truly LIVE by faith as a state of both mind and heart daily-directing our will, we become securely convinced that "If in this life only we have hope in Christ, we are of all men most miserable" (I Cor. 15:19). Faith then becomes both the root and realization of "the victory that overcometh the world" (I Jn. 5:4)—not only the spirit of the world and its perpetual enticement but also the pressure that it increasingly exerts upon our lives, compelling us to conform to its will.

We must both individually and collectively be absolutely convinced that it is not a mere confession **OF** faith but rather the living **BY** faith that secures our souls and the hope that reigns victoriously over the persecutorial horrors soon pressing upon us to compel every man, woman and child to embrace a false hope. As Jesus' brother so succinctly said, "Be ye doers of the word, and not hearers only, deceiving your own selves" (Jam. 1:22).

Hope Through Patience

Our flesh always wars against patience. The persistent demand of our flesh to demand immediate satisfaction wars against our spirit, compelling us to capitulate to its incessant demands. And yielding to the pressure of impatience renders us a likely casualty of the rising pressure of persecution.

The apostle Paul certainly understood the spiritual necessity of patience so that we might endure the pressure of persecution. None of the original twelve apostles faced such intense and unrelenting persecution as did Paul. And so, he reminded us of those who, through patient endurance, persisted in faith throughout the ages.

For whatsoever things were written aforetime were written for our learning, **that we through patience** and comfort of the scriptures **might have hope** (Rom. 15:4; emphasis added).

The writer of Hebrews reinforced the absolute necessity of patient faith that waits in hope without seeking other alternatives and temporal hopes. Let us take heed, lest we become hearers only, deceiving our own selves in a SELFY world.

Be not slothful, but followers of them who **through faith and patience** inherit the promises (Heb. 6:12; emphasis added).

Cast not away therefore your confidence, which hath great recompence of reward.

For **ye have need of patience**, that, after ye have done the will of God, ye might receive the promise.
Now **the just shall live by faith**: but if any man draw back [fail to press forward by patient faith], my soul shall have no pleasure in him (Heb. 10:35-38; emphasis added).

James was likewise convinced of the call to patience if we would truly live by faith amid times of trial and tribulation (pressure). We would do well to both consider and embrace his words of exhortation.

My brethren, count it all joy when ye fall in divers temptations [many trials]:

Knowing this, that **the trying of your faith worketh patience**.

But **let patience have her perfect work**, that ye may be perfect and entire, wanting [lacking] nothing (Jam. 1:2-4; emphasis added).

A Gospel of Hope

Hope is at the heart of the Gospel. Jesus came as a sinless savior that he, through His sacrifice, might deliver us from eternal perdition to eternal hope with joy unspeakable and full of glory (I Pet. 1:8). Yet that hope demands the "trial of your faith" that it "might be found unto praise and honour and glory at the appearing of Jesus Christ" (I Pet. 1:7). For this reason we, in hope, are…

> Looking for that blessed hope, and the glorious appearing of the great God and our Savior Jesus Christ (Tit. 2:13).

The gospel of Jesus Christ is "good news" precisely because it is a message of ultimate hope amid ever-increasing godless horror. We press on patiently and joyfully, notwithstanding trials and tribulations, for the promised hope that lies ahead, for in God's presence is "fulness of joy" and at His right hand "there are pleasures for evermore" (Ps. 16:11). This genuine gospel of hope is woven throughout Scripture through prophecy, from Genesis 3 through the Psalms and Prophets, with clear-cut revelations found in Isaiah 9:6-7; Isaiah 52 and 53, and then, after 400 years of prophetic silence, to the coming of Yeshua as Emmanuel—God with us, who would "save his people from their sins" (Matt. 1:20-23).

Thirty years later, Yeshua began delivering the good news for the final 2000 years of man's sojourn on the planet, to prepare all who would follow his call to repentance and a life of righteousness to the culminating event of our hope, the great "wedding supper" in the presence of the Lord for all who have, through hope, prepared themselves through patient endurance (Rev. 19:9; 21:1-6).

But until then, the gospel of hope has been preached to the Jew first and then to the Gentiles, just as the ancient prophets foretold. That message of hope for all who profess genuine faith in Christ as both Savior and Lord and who conduct their lives accordingly is made abundantly clear throughout the New Covenant as expressed here as a mere sampling.

Col. 1:14-23—"It pleased the Father… to present you holy and unblameable and unreproveable in his sight: If ye continue in the faith grounded and settled, and be not moved away from the hope of the gospel…" (Quote from vs. 19, 22-23).

Eph. 4:4—"There is one body, and one Spirit, even as ye are called in one hope…."

Col. 1:3-5—"We give thanks to God… since we heard of your faith… for the hope which is laid up for you in heaven…."

I Tim. 1:1—"Lord Jesus Christ, which is our hope."

Tit. 1:2-3—"In hope of eternal life, which God, that cannot lie, promised before the world began; But hath in due times manifested…."

Tit. 2:13—"Looking for that blessed hope, and the glorious appearing of the great God and our Savior Jesus Christ."

I Pet. 1:3—"Blessed be the God and Father of our Lord Jesus Christ, which according to his abundant mercy hath begotten us again unto a lively hope by the resurrection of Jesus Christ from the dead."

Eph. 2:12—Before receiving Christ, we were "strangers from the covenants of promise, having no hope without God in the world."

Col. 1:26-27—"The mystery which hath been hid from ages… is Christ in you, the hope of glory."

Rejoicing in Hope

"Rejoice in the Lord always," declared the apostle Paul, "and again I say, Rejoice" (Phil. 4:4). The word *rejoice* or words with similar meaning appear sixteen times in this short epistle. Yet Philippians was one of four epistles written from prison. In the same letter, scribed from prison, Paul also reveals the context in which our true rejoicing is confirmed as hope-filled reality.

> For unto you it is given in the behalf of Christ, not only to believe on him, but also to suffer for his sake (Phil. 1:29).

It is amid suffering and persecution that the true hope of our calling is confirmed, not in murmuring, complaining and terror-stricken anxiety but in rejoicing. Such hope-driven rejoicing is humanly impossible without a depth of faith and trust revealed in and through the joy that is set before us as demonstrated by Jesus' obedience to the Father's purposes. American and western professing Christians find such a view of Christ's victory over death and the grave to be virtually impossible to grasp because it is not marketable in a feel-good culture calculated to "grow churches" in a spirit of self-driven entitlement in which, lamentably, pastor, people and para-church ministries have become complicit.

The "coin" of the gospel has two sides… on the one side ***salvation,*** but on the other side, ***suffering*** for the Savior's name. Together they compromise the fulness of the good news that necessitates a willingness to joyfully endure persecution for His name's sake through righteous living. This is perhaps best expressed, in summary, by the writer of Hebrews in a very familiar passage, the gravamen of which mysteriously escapes the grasp of American minds. Read… and re-read these verses slowly, giving space to contemplate their implication if we are on the near edge of Christ's Second Coming, well understanding that the same Jesus promised persecution for all His true followers.

> Let us lay aside every weight, and the sin which doth so easily beset us, and let us run with patience [patient endurance] the race that is set before us,

> Looking unto Jesus the author and finisher of our faith; **who for the joy that was set before him endured the cross**, despising the shame....

> For **consider him** that endured such contradiction [hostile opposition] of sinners against himself, **lest ye be wearied and faint in your minds** (Heb. 12:1-3; emphasis added).

The apostle Peter, declaring that "the end of all things is at hand" (I Pet. 4:7), refused to deliver a feel-good message for our times but rather to strengthen us for times of increasing trials and persecution. He called us to "be sober" or serious-minded (I Pet. 4:7). He wanted us to be truly prepared for intensifying persecution:

> Beloved, think it not strange concerning the fiery trial which is to try you, as though some strange thing happened unto you:

> But rejoice, inasmuch as ye are partakers of Christ's sufferings; that, when his glory shall be revealed, ye may be glad also with exceeding joy (I Pet. 4:12-13).

> For even hereunto were ye called: because Christ also suffered for us, leaving us an example, that ye should follow his steps (I Pet. 2:21).

Forasmuch then as Christ hath suffered for us in the flesh, arm yourselves likewise with the same mind (I Pet. 4:1).

A Heritage of Hope

If indeed "faith is the substance of things hoped for" (Heb. 11:1), what shall we make of those who persevered in faithful hope, having obtained a "good report through faith, [yet] received not the [ultimate] promise (Heb. 11:39).

We like to recite the great heroes of faith, lifting up their courage and perseverance against great and seemingly insurmountable odds in order to please God who had called them. Yet many, not so historically recorded, "had trial of cruel mockings and scourgings… bonds and imprisonment." "They were stoned, they were sawn asunder… tempted… slain with the sword: they wandered about in sheepskins and goatskins; being destitute, afflicted, tormented… (Heb. 11:36-38).

How should we respond to this recital of our heritage—of those who for centuries past endured that which precious few of any western professing Christians have ever imagined, even after reading our heritage, could possibly invade our prosperous and insulated lives? Consider… "that they without us should not be made perfect" (Heb. 11:40). They established the pattern, enduring as seeing Him who was invisible (Heb. 11:27). "These all died in faith, not having received the promises, but having seen them afar off, and were persuaded of them, and embraced them, and confessed that they were strangers and pilgrims on the earth" (Heb. 11:13).

What then should we do with such a heritage of hope? It is we who our Lord expects to complete the race that our faithful predecessors began. We are to be the anchor in the divine relay of history, crossing the finish line by faith in the face of end-time persecution.

Jesus' brother, James, exhorts us in no uncertain terms, which we would do well to heed without wavering.

Be patient therefore, brethren, unto the coming of the Lord.

Be ye also patient; stablish your hearts: for the coming of the Lord draweth nigh (Jam. 5:7-8).

A Purifying Hope

Songs of hope have heralded our Lord's soon return. Out of the 1970s came Andraé Crouch's prophetic musical declaration: "Soon and very soon, we're going to see the King." That was reinforced by the Gaither's "The King is Coming." We well know that no man knows either the day or the hour of that grand moment, but of the season preceding it we are well advised by both Jesus and His apostles to prepare.

What, then, does such preparation in the face of prophesied and promised persecution require? While wearing the "helmet of salvation" as part of our spiritual armour, we are told that without holiness "no man shall see the Lord" and to look "diligently lest any man fail of the grace of God" (Heb. 12:14-15).

The grace of God is not merely His "unmerited favor" but even the more so His "enabling power" to obey Him and to walk in righteousness. If the Lord is our righteousness (Jer. 23:6; 33:16), then we who claim His name, must live holy lives in righteousness, for righteousness is the habitation of His throne (Ps. 97:2).

Profession of faith alone will not sustain us in this evil day as persecution rears its defying and commanding head. The just shall… and MUST… live by faith revealed in righteousness, or the alleged profession will collapse in the terrifying onslaught of persecution. We must soberly and sincerely assess our lives, allowing the Holy Spirit of truth to search our hearts to see if there be any evil or wicked way to weaken our ability or will to stand, notwithstanding the cost.

John, the beloved disciple, surely understood both our nature and the Lord's expectation of our lives. Here is what John said.

Every man that hath this hope in him purifieth
himself, even as he [Christ] is pure (I Jn. 3:3).

Paul reiterated the theme of righteous purification for these times.
For the grace of God that bringeth salvation hath appeared to all men,

Teaching us that, denying ungodliness and worldly
lusts, we should live soberly, righteously, and godly, in
this present world;

Looking for that blessed hope, and the glorious
appearing of the great God and our Savior Jesus
Christ (Tit. 2:12-13).

And so, brethren, we close this epistle of hope, preparing ourselves
for our Lord's soon return, with the hope-filled words of a song of yesteryear penned and sung first in 1958 by Stuart Hamblen known as
a Country Western Gospel singer. He was known as radio broadcasting's first "singing cowboy." In 1949 he, with his wife, as unbelievers,
attended a prayer meeting of the Hollywood Christian Group at the
home of Henrietta Mears, where he met a young man named Billy
Graham. Soon after attending Graham's meetings, Stuart fell under
great conviction, ultimately dedicating his life to Christ.

Hamblen's music then changed significantly. Of the over 230
songs he penned and sang, several stand out, having gained great
popularity across America, then perceived as a God-fearing country.
They include: "Teach Me, Lord, To Wait," "His Hands" and "How
Big is God." But it was "Until Then" that deeply captured the hearts
of Christians, making its way into many hymnals. And so, we conclude with those heart and mind directing lyrics. Perhaps you can even
hum the tune, driving the eternal, hope-filled message deeper into the
membranes of your mind.

UNTIL THEN

MY HEART CAN SING when I pause to remember,
A heartache here is but a stepping stone,
Along a trail that's winding always upward,
This troubled world is not my final home.

BUT UNTIL THEN my heart will go on singing,
Until then with joy I'll carry on,
Until the day my eyes behold the city,
Until the day God calls me home.

Until then, our hearts must go on singing and with joy, amid suffering, we must carry on with hope in our hearts that we will never truly walk alone... until the day God calls us to His presence in a home prepared for us, just as Jesus promised. So let not your heart be troubled. Neither let it be afraid (Jn. 14:1-2). Even so, come Lord Jesus! Amen!

He that dwelleth in the secret place of the most
High shall abide under the shadow of the Almighty
(Ps. 91:1).

Chapter 24
PROBING THOUGHTS for PROPHETIC TIMES

1. Does worry and anxiety predominate over hope in your life? Why do you think that is?
2. How does faith secure hope? But, if your faith is securing your hope, why then does fear loom large?
3. Why is patience so important if we would truly live by faith?
4. How is patience an essential spiritual ingredient of faith in the face of persecution? What is your patience quotient today?
5. What enables us to rejoice even when experiencing undeserved persecution and suffering by the ungodly?
6. Was there anything about this chapter that struck a chord of conviction with you?
7. What struck you as the most important aspect of this chapter if we are to live in hope amid growing persecution?

TOP 50 COUNTRIES

Leading Global Persecution as of 2023-2024

The following is a distilled summary of "The 50 Countries Where It's Hardest to Follow Jesus in 2023" as published by the editors of *Christianity Today* at https://www.christianitytoday.com/news/2023/ january/christian-persecution-2023-countries-open-doors-watch-list. html. These excerpts are taken from the report of Open Doors as published by *Christianity Today*, and are said by Open Doors to be very conservative.

Of the Top 50 Nations:

- "11 have 'extreme' levels of persecution and 39 have 'very high' levels. Another five nations outside the top 50 also qualify as 'very high': Kenya, Kuwait, Tanzania, United Arab Emirates, and Nepal."
- "19 are in Africa, 17 are in Asia, and 4 are in Latin America."
- "34 have Islam as a main religion, 4 have Buddhism, 1 has Hinduism, 1 has atheism, 1 has agnosticism—and 10 have Christianity."

"Open Doors tallied 5,621 Christians killed for their faith during the [1-year] reporting period." "The toll remains the second highest since the 2016 record of 7,106 deaths. Nigeria accounted for 89 percent of the total."

Note: "Other advocacy groups…often tally martyrdoms at 100,000 a year."

Other than martyrdoms, "by far the largest [persecutorial] category was displacement:"

- 124,310 Christians were forced to leave their homes or go into hiding because of their faith.
- An additional 14,997 Christians were forced to leave their countries.
- An estimated 4,547 Christian homes and properties were attacked, along with 2,210 shops and businesses.

The Conclusion

"Open Doors believes it is reasonable to call Christianity the world's most severely persecuted religion."

"Most of the nations on Open Door's list also appear on the US State Department's annual list that names and shames governments that have 'engaged in or tolerated systematic, ongoing, and egregious violations of religious freedom'."

HERE ARE THE TOP 50*

Country	Score
1. North Korea	97.77/100
2. Somalia	91.62/100
3. Libya	88.46/100
4. Eritrea	88.78/100
5. Yemen	89.26/100

*As reported by Open Doors: https://www.opendoorscanada.org/worldwatchlist/country-profiles/.

6. Nigeria	87.93/100
7. Pakistan	86.42/100
8. Sudan	82.99/100
9. Iran	85.91/100
10. Afghanistan	83.81/100
11. India	82.13/100
12. Syria	80.49/100
13. Saudia Arabia	80.28/100
14. Mali	76.30/100
15. Algeria	73.18/100
16. Iraq	75.99/100
17. Myanmar	80.21/100
18. Maldives	77.08/100
19. China	76.81/100
20. Burkina Faso	70.61/100
21. Lao People's Democratic Republic	68.29/100
22. Cuba	69.66/100
23. Mauritania	71.54/100
24. Morocco	69.37/100
25. Uzbekistan	71.29/100
26. Bangladesh	68.85/100
27. Niger	69.54/100
28. Central African Republic	70.16/100
29. Turkmenistan	69.74/100
30. Nicaragua	64.53/100
31. Oman	65.10/100
32. Ethiopia	66.48/100
33. Tunisia	67.14/100
34. Colombia	70.92/100
35. Vietnam	70.08/100
36. Bhutan	66.31/100
37. Mexico	66.50/100
38. Egypt	67.79/100

39. Mozambique   68.12/100
40. Qatar   67.88/100
41. Democratic Republic of Congo   66.67/100
42. Indonesia   67.95/100
43. Cameroon   65.18/100
44. Brunei Darussalam   65.14/100
45. Comoros   65.98/100
46. Tajikistan   65.51/100
47. Kazakhstan   64.76/100
48. Jordan   64.59/100
49. Malaysia   65.74/100
50. Türkiye   66.26/100

RESOURCES for FURTHER RESEARCH

THE PERSECUTION CHRONICLES

This is a resource available through SAVE AMERICA Ministries at the website saveus.org. The Persecution Chronicles provide periodically updated articles not only from around the world but especially identifying the rapidly increasing manifestations of both persecution and antisemitism in North America and the USA.

VOICE of the MARTYRS

This is a missionary organization serving persecuted Christians around the world. It was founded by Richard and Sabrina Wurmbrand after being imprisoned for their Christian faith in communist Romania. They have served the Church worldwide for more than 50 years and publish the magazine *Voice of the Martyrs*.

> 1815 SE Bison RD
> Bartlesville OK 74006
> 800-747-0085
> Persecution.com

PERSECUTION.ORG
INTERNATIONAL CHRISTIAN CONCERN

Founded in 1995 to bring relief to persecuted Christians in need worldwide. ICC seeks to awaken the Church to the very real sufferings of God's people through news updates, investigative reporting and a monthly magazine *Persecution.* Jeff King, one of the world's top experts on religious persecution, has served as ICC President since 2003.

2020 Pennsylvania Ave NW #941
Washington DC 2006-1846
800-422-5441
Persecution.org

OPEN DOORS

Founded by Brother Andrew in 1955, known not only by Open Doors but by his autobiography, *God's Smuggler,* which details his dangerous border crossings in getting the Bible into forbidden places. Their work is primarily in non-English speaking countries when extensive connections have been made with local churches, better facilitating aid and distribution of Bibles, also conducting secret seminars such as "Standing Strong Through the Storm," teaching Christians in high-risk areas how to thrive under severe persecution and suffering.

Open Doors US
PO Box 685
Bridgeville PA 15017
800-896-5285
Opendoors.org

BOOKS

- *FOXES BOOK OF MARTYRS* by John Foxe
  This is the classic book regarding persecution of Christians historically. It is impossible to read it without your mind and heart being gripped. It has been republished many times, revealing its provocative significance for all who claim the title "Christians," even in our times on the near edge of Christ's Second Coming.

- *FOXE VOICES OF THE MARTYRS: A.D. 33-TODAY* by
  John Foxe, Voice of the Martyrs
  > First published in 2021, this edition of Foxe's Book of Martyrs includes the stories of more than 100 Christian martyrs not included in John Foxe's original work first published in 1570. It includes not only heroes of the Early Church to the Reformation, but also those in the Enlightenment, the Industrial Revolution, and the 21st Century.

- *PILGRIM'S PROGRESS* by John Bunyan
  > The English preacher John Bunyan penned this all-time classic while in prison in 1678, for preaching outside a church building. It portrays the journey of a Christian through the various challenges and temptations of life that would divert him from reading the Celestial City and salvation, a *Progress from This World to That Which is to Come*.

Endnotes

Chapter 3

1. Ray Stults, *Voice of the Martyrs*, "Start seeing persecution" as reported by Christianhistoryinstitute.org, report printed Aug. 21, 2023.

2. Ibid.

3. "Start seeing persecution," *Christian History Magazine,* Issue 109, https://christianhistoryinstitute.org/magazine/article/start-seeing-persecution/, printed Aug. 21, 2023.

4. Jim Denison, "10 Types of Persecution You Could Face for Your Faith," https://www.charismanews.com/world/68097-10-types-of-persecution-you-could-face-for-your-faith, printed Aug. 21, 2023.

5. Msgr Charles Pope, "The Five Stages of Religious Persecution," September 1, 2014, https://blog.adw.org/2014/09/the-five-stages-of-religious-persecution/, printed on August 23, 2023.

6. Saul O. Alinsky, *Rules For Radicals*, Vintage Books, Jan, 1m 1972, republished Oct. 23, 1989.

Chapter 4

7. "Start seeing persecution," *Christian History Magazine*, Issue 109, https://christianhistoryinstitute.org/magazine/article/start-seeing-persecution/, printed Aug. 21, 2023.

8. Ibid.

9. Ibid.

10. "Christian persecution complex," *Wikipedia,"* https://en.wikipedia.org/wiki/Christian_persecution_complex, printed August 23, 2023.

11. Rob Boston, "The Great 'Persecution of Christians' Myth," April 18, 2017, TheHumanist.com, https://thehumanist.com/magazine/may-june-2017/church-state/great-persecution-christians-myth, printed on August 23, 2023.

12. Lisa Zengarini, "Over 360 million Christians suffering persecution in the world," *Vatican News*, https://www.vaticannews.va/en/church/news/2023-01/over-360-million-christians-suffering-persecution-in-the-world.html, printed August 23, 2023.

13. Richard D. Hunt, "Open Doors 2023 World Watch List: What Persecution Christians Face", January 18, 2023, https://www.air1.com/news/faith/open-doors-2023-world-watch-list-what-persecution-christians-face-sobering-content-39564, printed July 17, 2023.

14. "Christian Persecution—Religious Freedom," 16th edition of *Aid to the Church in Need's Religious Freedom in the World Report*, published every 2 years, June 22, 2023, https://www.churchinneed.org/christian-persecution-religious-freedom/.

15. Bob Unruh, "UN Scheme to Make Christians Criminals," World Net Daily, https://eclj.org/un-scheme-to-make-christians-criminals. Printed July 16, 2023.

16. Bob Unruh, "Modern-day inquisition," wnd.com, July 16, 2023, https://www.wndnewscenter.org/modern-day-inquisition-government-pouncing-on-christian-again-for-belief/. Printed July 16, 2023.

17. "Details of report on Christian church crackdown in Ukraine revealed", July 27, 2023, rt.com, https://www.rt.com/russia/580381-church-crackdown-ukraine-report/. Printed on July 27, 2023.

18. "West 'afraid' of truth about Ukraine's treatment of Christians – Russian Diplomat," July 27, 2023, https://www.theinteldrop.org/2023/07/27/west-afraid-of-truth-about-ukraines-treatment-of-christians-russian-diplomat/. Printed on July 27, 2023.

19. Marisa Herman, "Biden Targets Hungary With New Visa Requirements," *Newsmax*, August 8, 2023, https://www.newsmax.com/politics/joe-biden-hungary-migration/2023/08/08/id/1130028/. Printed on August 8, 2023.

20. Fran Beyer, "Miklos Szantho to Newsmax: Hungary Rejects 'Liberal Values' to Protect 'National Identity,'" *Newsmax*, August 8, 2023, https://www.newsmax.com/newsmax-tv/miklos-szantho-hungary-conservative/2023/08/08/id/1130026/. Printed on August 8, 2023.

21. Raymond Ibrahim, "The Islamic 'Reformation' Is Here, and You Won't Like It," July 26, 2023, https://vachristian.org/the-islamic-reformation-is-here-and-you-wont-like-it/. Printed on July 26, 2023.

22. Raymond Ibrahim, "Muslim Hate for the Cross Is Muslim Hate for the Gospel," August 15, 2023, https://www.raymondibrahim.com/2023/08/15/muslim-hate-for-the-cross-is-muslim-hate-for-the-gospel/. Printed August 21, 2023.

23. Raymond Ibrahim, "An Evil from the Pits of Hell: The Muslim Persecution of Christians, June 2023," July 18, 2023, https://vachristian.org/an-evil-from-the-pits-of-hell-the-muslim-persecution-of-christians-june-2023/. Printed July 18, 2023.

24. Raymond Ibrahim, "Killing Christians Takes Us to Paradise: The Persecution of Christians, July 2023," August 20, 2023, https://www.gatestoneinstitute.org/19909/killing-christians-paradise. Printed August 30, 2023.

25. Bob Unruh, "We wanted to shoot all Christians in the class," August 20, 2023, https://www.wndnewscenter.org/we-wanted-to-shoot-all-christians-in-the-class/. Printed on August 20, 2023

26. "Persecution of Christians is Approaching Genocide Levels, Report Finds: Christianity 'Is at Risk of Disappearing,' by Shane Crowder, May 3, 2019, https://www.newsweek.com/persecution-christians-genocide-christianity-disappearing-report-1414038. Printed on July 17, 2023

Chapter 5

27. Sharon Dierberger and Elizabeth Russell, "Problem parents?", *WORLD* Magazine, September 9, 2023, pp. 12-15.

28. Kate Anderson, " 'Shocked': Christian mom fights to adopt after refusing to affirm kids' gender transitions," *World Net Daily*, August 27, 2023, https://www.wnd.com/2023/08/shocked-christian-mom-fights-adopt-refusing-affirm-kids-gender-transitions/, printed August 30, 2023.

29. "Warning to California parents: You could lose your child under new gender affirmation bill, AB 957," *World Tribune*, September 11, 2023, https://trib247.com/articles/warning-to-california-parents-you-could-lose-your-child-under-new-gender-affirmation-bill-ab-957.

30. Lillian Tweten, "'Burned At The Stake': College Coach Breaks Silence On Fallout rom Sharing Post Critical of Trans Athletes," August 29, 2023, https://yournews.com/2023/08/29/2633822/burned-at-the-stake-college-coach-breaks-silence-on-fallout/.

31. Joe Saunders, "Pro athlete shares her Christian beliefs with sports reporter, left totally shocked by what happened to article," *The Western Journal*, August 20, 2023, https://www.wnd.com/2023/08/pro-golfer-shared-christian-beliefs-sports-reporter-left-totally-shocked-happened-article/.

32. Kate Anderson, "University's Medical Center Claims 'Religious Oppression' Is Just A Christian Thing," August 31, 2023, *Daily Caller*, https://dailycaller.com/2023/08/31/university-religious-oppression-christianity/.

33. Bob Unruh, "God despisers target faith 'release time' for students," September 5, 2023, https://www.wnd.com/2023/09/god-despisers-target-faith-release-time-students/

34. WND Staff, "Senators to FBI: Quit hiding details about anti-Catholic ideology," August 28, 2023, https://www.wndnewscenter.org/senators-to-fbi-quit-hiding-details-about-anti-catholic-ideology/.

35. Bob Unruh, "State demands professors teach government-approved wokeness," *The Liberty Loft*, August 27, 2023, https://thelibertyloft.com/2023/08/27/state-demands-professors-teach-government-approved-wokeness/.

36. Bob Unruh, "Christian student group must be treated like other campus organizations," September 14, 2023, https://www.wnd.com/2023/09/christian-student-group-must-treated-like-campus-organizations/.

37. Fran Beyer, "Activist Seeks Removal of Christian Bookstore rom Military Mini-Mall," *Newsmax*, September 12, 2023, https://www.newsmax.com/newsfront/military-religious-freedom-foundation-activist-christian/2023/09/12/id/1134120/.

38. CP Staff, "Best Buy fires whistleblower after leaks of manager saying Christian displays not OK, but LGBT training is," *The Christian Post*, September 14, 2023, https://www.christianpost.com/news/best-buy-fires-whistleblower-after-audio-leaks-of-manager.html.

39. Bob Unruh, "Bank's attack on renowned vaccine skeptic includes closing accounts," July 26, 2023, https://www.wnd.com/2023/07/banks-attack-vaccine-skeptic-includes-closing-accounts/.

40. World Tribune Staff, "Famed attorney Lin Wood retires after being targeted by 'lawfare' over his contesting 2020 election," July 9, 2023, https://trib247.com/articles/famed-attorney-lin-wood-retires-after-being-targeted-by-lawfare-over-his-contesting-2020-election.

41. Analysis by John Blake, CNN, "An 'imposter Christianity' is threatening American democracy," July 24, 2022, https://www.cnn.com/2022/07/24/us/white-christian-nationalism-blake-cec/index.html.

42. Andrew Whitehead, "The Growing Anti-Democratic Threat of Christian Nationalism in the U.S.," *Time* Magazine, May 27, 2021, https://time.com/6052051/anti-democratic-threat-christian-nationalism/.

43. Alan Goforth and Dwight Widaman, "Seminary leader under fire for exposing woke critical race theory in churches," *Metro Voice*, August 3, 2021, https://metrovoicenews.com/seminary-leader-under-fire-for-exposing-woke-critical-race-theory-in-churches/.

44. Kevin McNeese, "What The Bleep Is Happening To Christian Music?", *NRT*, July 29, 2023, https://www.newreleasetoday.com/article.php?article_id=3892, Printed on August 12, 2023.

45. Bruce Schlesman, "Radical Leftist Candidate Spits on Christianity," email from The Family Foundation Action, August 18, 2023.

46. John and Nisha Whitehead, "A nation of snitches: DHS is grooming Americans to report on each other," *WND*, https://www.wnd.com/2023/09/nation-snitches-dhs-grooming-americans-report/, September 20, 2023.

47. William Wolfe, "Yes, Christians are being persecuted in America. Here's how we can respond," *The Christian Post,* July 18, 2022, https://www.christianpost.com/voices/yes-christians-are-being-persecuted-in-america.html. Printed August 21, 2023.

48. Wesley J. Smith, "The Fear of Suffering is Driving Us Crazy," *The Epoch Times*, December 28, 2022, p. A14, and online, https://m.theepochtimes.com/opinion/the-fear-of-suffering-is-driving-us-crazy-4933555.

Chapter 9

49. Charles Crismier, *Renewing the Soul of America* (Elijah Books, Richmond, VA), 2002, pp. 147-148.

50. A.A. Montaport, ed., *Distilled Wisdom* (Englewood Cliffs, NJ. Prentice Hall Inc, 1964) p. 80.

51. Ibid.

52. Ibid.

Chapter 10

53. William Penn, *No Cross, No Crown*, (8th Edition) 1743, p. 8.

54. William Penn, *Pennsylvania Charter of Privileges*, 28 October 1701.

55. William Penn, *No Cross, No Crown*, 1743, pg. 59.

Chapter 13

56. John Pollock, *Wilberforce* (Lion Publishing, 1986), pp. 276-277.

Chapter 16

57. Dicastery For the Doctrine of the Faith. https://www.vatican.va/roman_curia/congregations/cfaith/documents/rc_con_cfaith_pro_14071997_en.html.

58. Chuck Mason, *How Do I Talk To My Kids About Social Justice?*, Xulon Press Elite, Maitland FL 32757, 2023, pp. 2-3, 5.

59. Grayson Gilbert, "A Sign of the Times: When Persecution Comes from Within the Church," July 9, 2020. https://www.patheos.com/blogs/chorusinthechaos/sign-times-persecution-church/

Chapter 17

60. Greg Garrison, Religion News Service, *USA TODAY*, "Many Americans don't believe in hell, but what about pastors?" posted August 1, 2009. https://virtueonline.org/many-americans-dont-believe-hell-what-about-pastors.

61. Mike Anton and William Lobdell, *Los Angeles Times*, "Hold the Fire and Brimstone," June 19, 2002. https://www.latimes.com/archives/la-xpm-2002-jun-19-me-hell19-story.html.

62. Robert H. Schuller, *Self-Esteem: The New Reformation*. Hardcover, Word Book Publishers, January 1, 1983. (Sold 4,211,658 copies, after thousands were sent to pastor throughout America to get them on board with his

"New Reformation" message of downplaying sin and instead building a new salvation message of "self esteem."

63. Meredith Flynn, *The Baptist Paper*, "In the face of persecution, 'you are blessed,' Charles tells pastors." June 13, 2023. https://thebaptistpaper.org/take-your-burden-to-the-lord-charles-says-in-light-of-reality-of-persecution/.

64. Does persecution truly bring church growth?" December 2012. https://www.sat7uk.org/does-persecution-truly-bring-church-growth/?cn-reloaded=1.

65. Zane Pratt, "Christianity Promises Suffering and Persecution: Here's How to Prepare," International Mission Board, March 28, 2017, (Zane Pratt serves as the VP of Training for the IMB). https://www.imb.org/2017/03/28/suffering-persecution-prepare/.

Chapter 18

66. Brent L. Kipfer, "Overlooked Mentors: What Can Persecuted Christians Teach Us About Leadership?" *Training Leaders International*, https://trainingleadersinternational.org/jgc/104/overlooked-mentors-what-can-persecuted-christians-teach-us-about-leadership, printed December 9, 2023.

67. Ibid.

68. Ibid.

69. Ibid. Kipfer quotes Robert E. Quinn, *Change the World: How Ordinary People Can Accomplish Extraordinary Results* (San Francisco: Jossey-Bass, 2000), 179.

70. David Curry, "Are American Christians on the path to severe persecution for their faith?" Religion News Service, September 19, 2022. https://religionnews.com/2022/09/19/are-american-christians-on-the-path-to-severe-persecution-for-their-faith/.

71. JoAnn L. Fuir, "Growing animosity toward evangelicals" Letter to the Editor, *Lancaster Online,* December 28, 2022. https://lancasteronline.com/opinion/letters_to_editor/growing-animosity-toward-evangelicals-letter/article_3103a4b4-861b-11ed-95cb-2fa6a7def3a8.html.

72. JoAnn L. Fuir, ""Christian persecution increasing in US," Letter to the Editor, *Lancaster Online,* January 31, 2023, https://lancasteronline.com/opinion/letters_to_editor/christian-persecution-increasing-in-us-letter/article_52d2c66c-a0c7-11ed-b5c9-f7f71732a977.html.

73. Brent L. Kipfer, "What Can Persecuted Christians Teach Us About Leadership?", *Training Leaders International.* https://trainingleadersinternational.org/jgc/104/overlooked-mentors-what-can-persecuted-christians-teach-us-about-leadership. Printed December 9, 2023.

74. Ibid.

Chapter 19

75. George Bush Sr., Speech on September 11, 1990, in National Archives.

76. Jerome Rifkin, "New Europe Shapes Its Version of Dream," *Richmond Times Dispatch,* November 7, 2004, p. E-1, from *The Washington Post.*

77. Jeremy Rifkin, "The New Europe Shapes Its Version of Dream," *Richmond Times Dispatch,* November 7, 2004, p. E-1, from *The Washington Post.*

Chapter 20

78. Gary H. Kah, *The New World Religion* (Noblesville, Indiana: Hope International Publishing, Inc., 1998), p. 199.

79. Ibid, p. 202.

80. Ibid, p. 209.

81. Ibid, p. 203.

82. Ibid, p. 204.

83. Ibid, p. 63.

84. Ibid, p. 65.

85. Ibid, p. 65.

86. Ibid, p. 65.

87. Ibid, p. 206

88. Ibid, p. 206

89. Ibid, p. 216.

90. James A. Beverly, "Smorgasborg Spirituality," *Christianity Today*, January 10, 2000, p. 30.

91. "One-world religion on its way?, *World Net Daily*, June 14, 2005, https://www.wnd.com/2005/06/30808/.

92. Ibid.

93. John Dart, "Ecumenism's new basis: testimony," *Christian Century*, August 21, 2007, p. 12.

94. Ibid.

95. Ibid, p. 13.

96. Julian Borger, "Moscow signals place in new world order," *Guardian Unlimited,* April 11, 2007, https://www.theguardian.com/world/2007/apr/11/russia.usa.

97. "Putin Calls Russia Defender of Islamic World," *Mos News, mosnews.com*, December 12, 2005.

98. "Timing not right for papal visit to Russia," *totalcatholic.com*, July 9, 2008.

99. Malachi Martin, *The Keys of This Blood*, "Forces of the 'New Order'." (New York, New York; Touchstone, 1990), p. 370-371.

100. Ibid, p. 489-490.

101. "Pope Calls for a new world order," *CNN News* release from VATICAN CITY, January 1, 2004.

102. Encyclical Letter *Caritas In Veritate* of the Supreme Pontiff Benedict XVI. 29 June 2009. https://www.vatican.va/content/benedict-xvi/en/encyclicals/documents/hf_ben-xvi_enc_20090629_caritas-in-veritate.html.

103. Deb Richmann, "Bush says US wants partnership with Europe," *BRIET-BART.COM*, released from Associated Press, June 12, 2008.

104. Fareed Zakania, "The Post-American World," cover story, *NEWSWEEK.COM*, May 12, 2008, p. 24-31.

105. Will Durant, *Caesar and Christ, The Story of Civilization Part III*, (New York, Simon and Schuster, 1944), p. 618-619.

106. Ibid.

107. Nigel Rogers, *Roman Empire* (New York; Metro Books, Anness Publicity Ltd., 2008), p. 415.

108. Will Durant, *Caesar and Christ*, p. 656.

109. Ibid.

110. John Julius Norwich, *Absolute Monarchs: A History of the Papacy* (New York; Random House, 2011), p. 57.

111. Ibid, p. 58.

112. Ibid, p. 61.

113. Nigel Rogers, *Roman Empire*, p. 13.

114. Alan Franklin, *EU-Final World Empire*, (Oklahoma City, OK; Hearthstone Publishing, 2002), p. 44.

115. "Chief Rabbi Asks Dalai Lama to Help Set Up Religious UN in Jerusalem," *Arutz Sheva, israelnationalnews.com*, February 19, 2006.

116. Alan Franklin, *EU-Final World Empire*, pp. 48-50.

117. "Rome," *The Catholic Encyclopedia*, Thomas Nelson, 1976.

118. Ibid.

119. R.W. Southern, "Western Society and the Church of the Middle Ages," Vol. 2, *Pelican History of the Church Series*, (Penguin Books, 1970), pp.24-25.

120. John Julius Norwich, *Absolute Monarchy: A History of the Papacy* (New York; Random House, 2011).

121. Alan Franklin, *EU-Final World Empire*, pp. 37-38.

122. Ibid, p. 39.

123. "Blair: I'll dedicate the rest of my life to uniting the world's religions," *dailymail.co.uk*, May 29, 2008.

124. James Macintyre, "Religion is the new politics…," *The Independent*, May 31, 2008.

125. Michael Elliott, "Tony Blair's Leap of Faith," *TIME*, June 9, 2008.

126. David Van Brima, "The Global Ambition of Rick Warren," *TIME*, August 18, 2008, cover story pp. 37-42.

127. Ruth Gledhill, "Churches back plan to unite under Pope," *timesonline.co.uk*, February 19, 2007, https://www.thetimes.co.uk/article/churches-back-plan-to-unite-under-pope-fg3p7gfv0zz.

128. Ibid.

129. Robert Broderich, ed, *The Catholic Encyclopedia*, Thomas Nelson, 1976, pp. 103-104.

130. John A. Hardon, S.J., *Pocket Catholic Dictionary*, Image Books – Doubleday, 1985, p. 99.

131. Dave Hunt, *A Woman Rides the Beast* (Eugene, Oregon; Harvest House, 1994), chapter 6.

Chapter 22

132. Christopher Poshin David, "How Can the Early Church Encourage Christians Facing Persecution Today?" *The Gospel Coalition*, June 8, 2023, https://in.thegospelcoalition.org/article/how-can-the-early-church-encourage-christians-facing-persecution-today/.

133. Charles Crismier, *King of the Mountain: The Eternal, Epic, End-Time Battle*, Elijah Books, Richmond, Virginia, 2013, p. 143. Quoting Ian Traynor, "Love tops agenda as Sarkozy launches Mediterranean Union," *The Guardian*, 13 Jul 2008, https://www.theguardian.com/world/2008/jul/14/france.eu.

Chapter 23

134. Herb Keinon, "Messiah Where?" *The Jerusalem Post International Edition*, August 10, 1997, pp. 20-22.

135. "Chief Rabbi Sees Imminent Coming of Messiah," *World Net Daily*, August 12, 2005. https://www.wnd.com/2005/08/31765/.

136. "Iranian Video Says Mahdi is 'Near'," Erick Stackelbeck, CBN News, March 28, 2011, (no longer available). This is referenced https://www.ipcprayer.org/en/pa-pray/regions/worldwide/item/3402-iran-iranian-video-says-mahdi-is-near.html.

See also: *King of the Mountain: The Eternal, Epic, End-Time Battle* by Charles Crismier. Elijah Books, Richmond, VA, 2013, pp. 251-259, chapter titled, "The Mahdi vs. The Messiah."

137. Benita Ferrero-Waldner, "The Secret of Europe's Success," *Haaretz Israel News, haaretz.com*, May 9, 2007.

138. Steve Watson, "Euro Globalists: Anyone Who Resists EU Is A Terrorist," (originally read on prisonplanet.com), June 18, 2007. https://politicalhot-wire.com/t/euro-globalists-anyone-who-resists-eu-is-a-terrorist.15562/.

139. Charles Crismier, *King of the Mountain: The Eternal, Epic, End-Time Battle*, Elijah Books, Richmond, Virginia, 2013, p, 121.

About the Author

FOR A VETERAN TRIAL ATTORNEY to be referred to as "a prophet for our time" is indeed unusual, but many who have heard Charles Crismier's daily radio broadcast, *VIEWPOINT*, believe just that. Now, in *WHEN PERSECUTION COMES*, his words, full of "passion and conviction," provide clear direction to professing believers, both Jew and Gentile, increasingly drawn into the deceptive ways of the rapidly-developing new global order that leads to prophetically promised persecution.

Crismier speaks from an unusual breadth of experience. After nine years as a public schoolteacher, he spent twenty years as a trial attorney, pleading causes before judge and jury. As a pastor's son, also serving in pastoral roles for 36 years, Crismier has been involved with ten distinct Protestant denominations – both mainline and otherwise, together with other independent and charismatic groups from coast to coast and from North to South – providing an enviable insider's view of American Christianity and life. Interestingly, his oldest daughter and lifelong assistant both reads and speaks Hebrew.

Deeply troubled by the direction of the nation, the world and Church he loves, this attorney left his lucrative Southern California law practice in 1992 to form SAVE AMERICA Ministries and was awarded the Valley Forge Freedom Foundation award for his contribution to the cause of "Rebuilding the Foundations of Faith and Freedom." "Chuck probes the heart and conscience with both a rare combination of insight, directness, urgency and compassion, and a message that desperately needs to be heard and heeded before it is too late."

From the birthplace of America – Richmond, Virginia – this former attorney speaks provocatively and prophetically on daily national radio as "a Voice to the Church," declaring "Vision for the Nation" in our world's greatest crisis hour, preparing the way of the Lord for history's final hour.
Charles Crismier can be contacted by writing or calling:

P.O. Box 70879
Richmond, VA 23255
(804) 754-1822 or 1(800) SAVEUSA
crismier@saveus.org
or through his website at
www.saveus.org

Other Life-Changing Books
by Charles Crismier

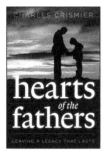

Hearts of the Fathers

Leaving a Legacy That Lasts! There is a fatherhood crisis in America. A serious "father problem" is at the core of nearly all social ills facing America today. Because fatherhood lies at the very root of a righteous relationship with the Creator Himself, the enemy of our souls desperately seeks to destroy that relationship. This book provides a "binocular" view of God's Word, exposing the deception all around us and illuminating the Heavenly Father's perfect prescription for both a temporal and eternal legacy.

$23

Lasting Love

Happily Ever After is the hope for most couples who proclaim their undying love by sacred vow. But is it a reasonable and attainable hope, or merely an illusion rooted in eros and emotion when we declare, "I DO?" The statistics of our time reveal a society tragically torn between the sacredness of a holy vow and the sorry state of marital bliss. In this small book, husband and wife will find marriage-transforming nuggets of truth passionately presented by Chuck and Kathie Crismier, whose 50 years of marriage are transparently translated so as to touch the life of every married couple.

$14

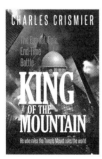

KING of the MOUNTAIN
The Eternal, Epic, End-Time Battle

All other issues and pursuits that consume the passions and purposes of mankind ultimately turn on the eternal question: "who will be king of the mountain?" This is the ultimate question of history which the power brokers and peoples of this planet must answer. Join this amazing journey from the Tower of Babel to the Temple Mount and from Creation to the Coming of Messiah.

$20

The SECRET of the LORD

God has a secret. It is a life-changing, destiny-determining secret. Yet it is a secret God desires to disclose to all who will seek it, unlocking all of the covenantal blessings and promises of God, both on earth and for eternity. Secrets are like mysteries. It remains a mystery until the right connections of fact are discerned, unveiling truth that sweeps away the shroud of "mystery." So it is with secrets. Once uncovered, the secret is no longer "secret" but becomes available for decision-making regarding life direction and eternal destiny.

$20

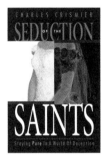

SEDUCTION of the SAINTS
Staying Pure in a World of Deception

"Take heed that no man deceive you," declared Jesus just before his crucifixion. His words were chilling! They cast a frame around life and eternity. In the final moments of his life on earth, Jesus chose to leave the disciples, with whom he had invested his life and ministry, a penetrating and haunting warning they would never forget... a warning that echoes through the centuries to all his disciples preparing for the end of the age.

$18

RENEWING the SOUL of AMERICA
(Endorsed by 38 National Christian Leaders)

"As a country and as individuals, we stand at a crossroads – to continue on the path to godlessness or to return to the way of righteousness." "Renewing the Soul of America is America's ONLY hope." But it must begin with you... one person at a time. Powerful inspiration for these difficult times.

$18

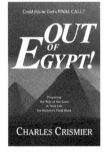

OUT of EGYPT
Building End-time Trust for End-time Trials.

Liberating... yet sobering. If Abraham, Moses, Israel, and... yes, Jesus had to "come out Egypt," how about us? The words "out of Egypt" or similar words appear over 400 times from Genesis to Revelation. Why has this theme been mentioned perhaps more than any other in the entire Bible? You will read... re-read this book!

$17

The POWER of HOSPITALITY
An Open Heart, Open Hand and Open Home Will Change Your World

The Apostle Paul reminds that ALL who claim Christ as savior must, as a demonstration of their faith, be "given to hospitality." Pastors and leaders are to be "lovers of hospitality" as a condition of leadership. And Peter said, "The end of all things is at hand,... therefore use hospitality." Here is life-changing inspiration... PRACTICAL, PERSONAL and PROPHETIC.

$16

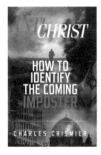

ANTICHRIST
How to Identify the Coming Imposter

As a New World Order is rapidly being formed through "The Great Reset," messianic expectations for a charismatic deliverer or leader are exploding world wide. But the Bible warns the true Messiah will be preceded by a terrifying counterfeit— an imposter. How, then, can we identify this soon-coming Antichrist? Here are fascintating and life-changing answers.

$22

MESSIAH
Unveiling the Mystery of the Ages

Messianic fervor is exploding worldwide, yet many alternative "messiahs" are being promoted, creating for many a "mystery" as to identifying the true Messiah who can be trusted for salvation.

$22

**Find them ALL at saveus.org
or call SAVE AMERICA Ministries 1 (800) SAVEUSA**